BULFINCH'S MYTHOLOGY

LEGENDS OF CHARLEMAGNE

BY THOMAS BULFINCH

PUBLISHERS' PREFACE

No new edition of Bulfinch's classic work can be considered complete without some notice of the American scholar to whose wide erudition and painstaking care it stands as a perpetual monument. "The Age of Fable" has come to be ranked with older books like "Pilgrim's Progress," "Gulliver's Travels," "The Arabian Nights," "Robinson Crusoe," and five or six other productions of world-wide renown as a work with which every one must claim some acquaintance before his education can be called really complete. Many readers of the present edition will probably recall coming in contact with the work as children, and, it may be added, will no doubt discover from a fresh perusal the source of numerous bits of knowledge that have remained stored in their minds since those early years. Yet to the majority of this great circle of readers and students the name Bulfinch in itself has no significance.

Thomas Bulfinch was a native of Boston, Mass., where he was born in 1796. His boyhood was spent in that city, and he prepared for college in the Boston schools. He finished his scholastic training at Harvard College, and after taking his degree was for a period a teacher in his home city. For a long time later in life he was employed as an accountant in the Boston Merchants' Bank. His leisure time he used for further pursuit of the classical studies which he had begun at Harvard, and his chief pleasure in life lay in writing out the results of his reading, in simple, condensed form for young or busy readers. The plan he followed in this work, to give it the greatest possible usefulness, is set forth in the Author's Preface.

"Age of Fable," First Edition, 1855; "The Age of Chivalry," 1858; "The Boy Inventor," 1860; "Legends of Charlemagne, or

Romance of the Middle Ages," 1863; "Poetry of the Age of Fable," 1863; "Oregon and Eldorado, or Romance of the Rivers," 1860.

In this complete edition of his mythological and legendary lore "The Age of Fable," "The Age of Chivalry," and "Legends of Charlemagne" are included. Scrupulous care has been taken to follow the original text of Bulfinch, but attention should be called to some additional sections which have been inserted to add to the rounded completeness of the work, and which the publishers believe would meet with the sanction of the author himself, as in no way intruding upon his original plan but simply carrying it out in more complete detail. The section on Northern Mythology has been enlarged by a retelling of the epic of the "Nibelungen Lied," together with a summary of Wagner's version of the legend in his series of music-dramas. Under the head of "Hero Myths of the British Race" have been included outlines of the stories of Beowulf, Cuchulain, Hereward the Wake, and Robin Hood. Of the verse extracts which occur throughout the text, thirty or more have been added from literature which has appeared since Bulfinch's time, extracts that he would have been likely to quote had he personally supervised the new edition.

Finally, the index has been thoroughly overhauled and, indeed, remade. All the proper names in the work have been entered, with references to the pages where they occur, and a concise explanation or definition of each has been given. Thus what was a mere list of names in the original has been enlarged into a small classical and mythological dictionary, which it is hoped will prove valuable for reference purposes not necessarily connected with "The Age of Fable."

Acknowledgments are due the writings of Dr. Oliver Huckel for information on the point of Wagner's rendering of the Nibelungen legend, and M. I. Ebbutt's authoritative volume on "Hero Myths and Legends of the British Race," from which much of the information concerning the British heroes has been obtained.

AUTHOR'S PREFACE

If no other knowledge deserves to be called useful but that which helps to enlarge our possessions or to raise our station in society, then Mythology has no claim to the appellation. But if that which tends to make us happier and better can be called useful, then we claim that epithet for our subject. For Mythology is the handmaid of literature; and literature is one of the best allies of virtue and promoters of happiness.

Without a knowledge of mythology much of the elegant literature of our own language cannot be understood and appreciated. When Byron calls Rome "the Niobe of nations," or says of Venice, "She looks a Sea-Cybele fresh from ocean," he calls up to the mind of one familiar with our subject, illustrations more vivid and striking than the pencil could furnish, but which are lost to the reader ignorant of mythology. Milton abounds in similar allusions. The short poem "Comus" contains more than thirty such, and the ode "On the Morning of the Nativity" half as many. Through "Paradise Lost" they are scattered profusely. This is one reason why we often hear persons by no means illiterate say that they cannot enjoy Milton. But were these persons to add to their more solid acquirements the easy learning of this little volume, much of the poetry of Milton which has appeared to them "harsh and crabbed" would be found "musical as is Apollo's lute." Our citations, taken from more than twenty-five poets, from Spenser to Longfellow, will show how general has been the practice of borrowing illustrations from mythology.

The prose writers also avail themselves of the same source of elegant and suggestive illustration. One can hardly take up a number of the "Edinburgh" or "Quarterly Review" without meeting with instances. In Macaulay's article on Milton there are twenty such.

But how is mythology to be taught to one who does not learn it through the medium of the languages of Greece and Rome? To devote study to a species of learning which relates wholly to false marvels and obsolete faiths is not to be expected of the general reader in a practical age like this. The time even of the young is claimed by so many sciences of facts and things that little can be spared for set treatises on a science of mere fancy.

But may not the requisite knowledge of the subject be acquired by reading the ancient poets in translations? We reply, the field is too extensive for a preparatory course; and these very translations require some previous knowledge of the subject to make them intelligible. Let any one who doubts it read the first page of the "Aeneid," and see what he can make of "the hatred of Juno," the "decree of the Parcae," the "judgment of Paris," and the "honors of Ganymede," without this knowledge.

Shall we be told that answers to such queries may be found in notes, or by a reference to the Classical Dictionary? We reply, the interruption of one's reading by either process is so annoying that most readers prefer to let an allusion pass unapprehended rather than submit to it. Moreover, such sources give us only the dry facts without any of the charm of the original narrative; and what is a poetical myth when stripped of its poetry? The story of Ceyx and Halcyone, which fills a chapter in our book, occupies but eight lines in the best (Smith's) Classical Dictionary; and so of others.

Our work is an attempt to solve this problem, by telling the stories of mythology in such a manner as to make them a source of amusement. We have endeavored to tell them correctly, according to the ancient authorities, so that when the reader finds them referred to he may not be at a loss to recognize the reference. Thus we hope to teach mythology not as a study, but as a relaxation from study; to give our work the charm of a story-book, yet by means of it to impart a knowledge of an important branch of education. The index at the end will adapt it to the purposes of reference, and make it a Classical Dictionary for the parlor.

Most of the classical legends in "Stories of Gods and Heroes" are derived from Ovid and Virgil. They are not literally translated, for, in the author's opinion, poetry translated into literal prose is very unattractive reading. Neither are they in verse, as well for other reasons as from a conviction that to translate faithfully under all the embarrassments of rhyme and measure is impossible. The attempt has been made to tell the stories in prose, preserving so much of the poetry as resides in the thoughts and is separable from the language itself, and omitting those amplifications which are not suited to the altered form.

The Northern mythological stories are copied with some abridgment from Mallet's "Northern Antiquities." These chapters, with those on Oriental and Egyptian mythology, seemed necessary to complete the subject, though it is believed these topics have not usually been presented in the same volume with the classical fables.

The poetical citations so freely introduced are expected to answer several valuable purposes. They will tend to fix in memory the leading fact of each story, they will help to the attainment of a correct pronunciation of the proper names, and they will enrich the memory with many gems of poetry, some of them such as are most frequently quoted or alluded to in reading and conversation.

Having chosen mythology as connected with literature for our province, we have endeavored to omit nothing which the reader of elegant literature is likely to find occasion for. Such stories and parts of stories as are offensive to pure taste and good morals are not given. But such stories are not often referred to, and if they occasionally should be, the English reader need feel no mortification in confessing his ignorance of them.

Our work is not for the learned, nor for the theologian, nor for the philosopher, but for the reader of English literature, of either sex, who wishes to comprehend the allusions so frequently made by public speakers, lecturers, essayists, and poets, and those which occur in polite conversation.

In the "Stories of Gods and Heroes" the compiler has endeavored to impart the pleasures of classical learning to the English reader, by presenting the stories of Pagan mythology in a form adapted to modern taste. In "King Arthur and His Knights" and "The Mabinogeon" the attempt has been made to treat in the same way the stories of the second "age of fable," the age which witnessed the dawn of the several states of Modern Europe.

It is believed that this presentation of a literature which held unrivalled sway over the imaginations of our ancestors, for many centuries, will not be without benefit to the reader, in addition to the amusement it may afford. The tales, though not to be trusted for their facts, are worthy of all credit as pictures of manners; and it is beginning to be held that the manners and modes of thinking of an age are a more important part of its history than the conflicts of its peoples, generally leading to no result. Besides this, the literature of romance is a treasure-house of poetical material, to which modern poets frequently resort. The Italian poets, Dante and Ariosto, the English, Spenser, Scott, and Tennyson, and our own Longfellow and Lowell, are examples of this.

These legends are so connected with each other, so consistently adapted to a group of characters strongly individualized in Arthur, Launcelot, and their compeers, and so lighted up by the fires of imagination and invention, that they seem as well adapted to the poet's purpose as the legends of the Greek and Roman mythology. And if every well-educated young person is expected to know the story of the Golden Fleece, why is the quest of the Sangreal less worthy of his acquaintance? Or if an allusion to the shield of Achilles ought not to pass unapprehended, why should one to Excalibar, the famous sword of Arthur?--

"Of Arthur, who, to upper light restored,
With that terrific sword,
Which yet he brandishes for future war,
Shall lift his country's fame above the polar star."[1]

It is an additional recommendation of our subject, that it tends to cherish in our minds the idea of the source from which we sprung. We are entitled to our full share in the glories and recollections of the land of our forefathers, down to the time of colonization thence. The associations which spring from this source must be fruitful of good influences; among which not the least valuable is the increased enjoyment which such associations afford to the American traveller when he visits England, and sets his foot upon any of her renowned localities.

The legends of Charlemagne and his peers are necessary to complete the subject.

In an age when intellectual darkness enveloped Western Europe, a constellation of brilliant writers arose in Italy. Of these, Pulci (born in 1432), Boiardo (1434), and Ariosto (1474) took for their subjects the romantic fables which had for many ages been transmitted in the lays of bards and the legends of monkish chroniclers. These fables they arranged in order, adorned with the embellishments of fancy, amplified from their own invention, and stamped with immortality. It may safely be asserted that as long as civilization shall endure these productions will retain their place among the most cherished creations of human genius.

In "Stories of Gods and Heroes," "King Arthur and His Knights" and "The Mabinogeon" the aim has been to supply to

---

[1] Wordsworth

the modern reader such knowledge of the fables of classical and mediaeval literature as is needed to render intelligible the allusions which occur in reading and conversation. The "Legends of Charlemagne" is intended to carry out the same design. Like the earlier portions of the work, it aspires to a higher character than that of a piece of mere amusement. It claims to be useful, in acquainting its readers with the subjects of the productions of the great poets of Italy. Some knowledge of these is expected of every well-educated young person.

In reading these romances, we cannot fail to observe how the primitive inventions have been used, again and again, by successive generations of fabulists. The Siren of Ulysses is the prototype of the Siren of Orlando, and the character of Circe reappears in Alcina. The fountains of Love and Hatred may be traced to the story of Cupid and Psyche; and similar effects produced by a magic draught appear in the tale of Tristram and Isoude, and, substituting a flower for the draught, in Shakspeare's "Midsummer Night's Dream." There are many other instances of the same kind which the reader will recognize without our assistance.

The sources whence we derive these stories are, first, the Italian poets named above; next, the "Romans de Chevalerie" of the Comte de Tressan; lastly, certain German collections of popular tales. Some chapters have been borrowed from Leigh Hunt's Translations from the Italian Poets. It seemed unnecessary to do over again what he had already done so well; yet, on the other hand, those stories could not be omitted from the series without leaving it incomplete.

THOMAS BULFINCH.

LEGENDS OF CHARLEMAGNE

INTRODUCTION

Those who have investigated the origin of the romantic fables relating to Charlemagne and his peers are of opinion that the deeds of Charles Martel, and perhaps of other Charleses, have been blended in popular tradition with those properly belonging to Charlemagne. It was indeed a most momentous era; and if our readers will have patience, before entering on the perusal of the fabulous annals which we are about to lay before them, to take a rapid survey of the real history of the times, they will find it hardly less romantic than the tales of the poets.

In the century beginning from the year 600, the countries bordering upon the native land of our Saviour, to the east and south, had not yet received his religion. Arabia was the seat of an idolatrous religion resembling that of the ancient Persians, who worshipped the sun, moon, and stars. In Mecca, in the year 571, Mahomet was born, and here, at the age of forty, he proclaimed himself the prophet of God, in dignity as superior to Christ as Christ had been to Moses. Having obtained by slow degrees a considerable number of disciples, he resorted to arms to diffuse his religion. The energy and zeal of his followers, aided by the weakness of the neighboring nations, enabled him and his successors to spread the sway of Arabia and the religion of Mahomet over the countries to the east as far as the Indus, northward over Persia and Asia Minor, westward over Egypt and the southern shores of the Mediterranean, and thence over the principal portion of Spain. All this was done within one hundred years from the Hegira, or flight of Mahomet from Mecca to

Medina, which happened in the year 622, and is the era from which Mahometans reckon time, as we do from the birth of Christ.

From Spain the way was open for the Saracens (so the followers of Mahomet were called) into France, the conquest of which, if achieved, would have been followed very probably by that of all the rest of Europe, and would have resulted in the banishment of Christianity from the earth. For Christianity was not at that day universally professed, even by those nations which we now regard as foremost in civilization. Great part of Germany, Britain, Denmark, and Russia were still pagan or barbarous.

At that time there ruled in France, though without the title of king, the first of those illustrious Charleses of whom we have spoken, Charles Martel, the grandfather of Charlemagne. The Saracens of Spain had made incursions into France in 712 and 718, and had retired, carrying with them a vast booty. In 725, Anbessa, who was then the Saracen governor of Spain, crossed the Pyrenees with a numerous army, and took by storm the strong town of Carcassone. So great was the terror excited by this invasion, that the country for a wide extent submitted to the conqueror, and a Mahometan governor for the province was appointed and installed at Narbonne. Anbessa, however, received a fatal wound in one of his engagements, and the Saracens, being thus checked from further advance, retired to Narbonne.

In 732 the Saracens again invaded France under Abdalrahman, advanced rapidly to the banks of the Garonne, and laid siege to Bordeaux. The city was taken by assault and delivered up to the soldiery. The invaders still pressed forward, and spread over the territories of Orleans, Auxerre and Sens. Their advanced parties were suddenly called in by their chief, who had received information of the rich abbey of St. Martin of Tours, and resolved to plunder and destroy it.

Charles during all this time had done nothing to oppose the Saracens, for the reason that the portion of France over which their incursions had been made was not at that time under his dominion, but constituted an independent kingdom, under the name of Aquitaine, of which Eude was king. But now Charles became convinced of the danger, and prepared to encounter it. Abdalrahman was advancing toward Tours, when intelligence of the approach of Charles, at the head of an army of Franks, compelled him to fall back upon Poitiers, in order to seize an advantageous field of battle.

Charles Martel had called together his warriors from every part of his dominions, and, at the head of such an army as had hardly ever been seen in France, crossed the Loire, probably at Orleans, and, being joined by the remains of the army of Aquitaine, came in sight of the Arabs in the month of October, 732. The Saracens seem to have been aware of the terrible enemy they were now to encounter, and for the first time these formidable conquerors hesitated. The two armies remained in presence during seven days before either ventured to begin the attack; but at length the signal for battle was given by Abdalrahman, and the immense mass of the Saracen army rushed with fury on the Franks. But the heavy line of the Northern warriors remained like a rock, and the Saracens, during nearly the whole day, expended their strength in vain attempts to make any impression upon them. At length, about four o'clock in the afternoon, when Abdalrahman was preparing for a new and desperate attempt to break the line of the Franks, a terrible clamor was heard in the rear of the Saracens. It was King Eude, who, with his Aquitanians, had attacked their camp, and a great part of the Saracen army rushed tumultuously from the field to protect their plunder. In this moment of confusion the line of the Franks advanced, and, sweeping the field before it, carried fearful slaughter amongst the enemy. Abdalrahman made desperate efforts to rally his troops, but when he himself, with the bravest of his officers, fell beneath the swords of the Christians, all order disappeared, and the remains of his army sought refuge in their immense camp, from which Eude and his Aquitanians had been repulsed. It was now late, and Charles, unwilling to risk an attack on the camp in the dark, withdrew his army, and passed the night in the plain, expecting to renew the battle in the morning.

Accordingly, when daylight came, the Franks drew up in order of battle, but no enemy appeared; and when at last they ventured to approach the Saracen camp they found it empty. The invaders had taken advantage of the night to begin their retreat, and were already on their way back to Spain, leaving their immense plunder behind to fall into the hands of the Franks.

This was the celebrated battle of Tours, in which vast numbers of the Saracens were slain, and only fifteen hundred of the Franks. Charles received the surname of Martel (the Hammer) in consequence of this victory.

The Saracens, notwithstanding this severe blow, continued to hold their ground in the south of France; but Pepin, the son of Charles Martel, who succeeded to his father's power, and assumed the title of king, successively took from them the strong places they held; and in 759, by the capture of Narbonne, their capital, extinguished the remains of their power in France.

Charlemagne, or Charles the Great, succeeded his father, Pepin, on the throne in the year 768. This prince, though the hero of numerous romantic legends, appears greater in history than in fiction. Whether we regard him as a warrior or as a legislator, as a patron of learning or as the civilizer of a barbarous nation, he is entitled to our warmest admiration. Such he is in history; but the romancers represent him as often weak and passionate, the victim of treacherous counsellors, and at the mercy of turbulent barons, on whose prowess he depends for the maintenance of his throne. The historical representation is doubtless the true one, for it is handed down in trustworthy records, and is confirmed by the events of the age. At the height of his power, the French empire extended over what we now call France, Germany, Switzerland, Holland, Belgium, and great part of Italy.

In the year 800 Charlemagne, being in Rome, whither he had gone with a numerous army to protect the Pope, was crowned by the Pontiff Emperor of the West. On Christmas day Charles entered the Church of St. Peter, as if merely to take his part in the celebration of the mass with the rest of the congregation. When he approached the altar and stooped in the act of prayer the Pope stepped forward and placed a crown of gold upon his head; and immediately the Roman people shouted, "Life and victory to Charles the August, crowned by God the great and pacific Emperor of the Romans." The Pope then prostrated himself before him, and paid him reverence, according to the custom established in the times of the ancient Emperors, and concluded the ceremony by anointing him with consecrated oil.

Charlemagne's wars were chiefly against the pagan and barbarous people, who, under the name of Saxons, inhabited the countries now called Hanover and Holland. He also led expeditions against the Saracens of Spain; but his wars with the Saracens were not carried on, as the romances assert, in France, but on the soil of Spain. He entered Spain by the Eastern Pyrenees, and made an easy conquest of Barcelona and Pampeluna. But Saragossa refused to open her gates to him, and Charles ended by negotiating and accepting a vast sum of gold as the price of his return over the Pyrenees.

On his way back, he marched with his whole army through the gorges of the mountains by way of the valleys of Engui, Eno, and Roncesvalles. The chief of this region had waited upon Charlemagne, on his advance, as a faithful vassal of the monarchy; but now, on the return of the Franks, he had called together all the wild mountaineers who acknowledged him as their chief, and they occupied the heights of the mountains under which the army had to pass. The main body of the troops met with no obstruction, and received no intimation of danger; but the rearguard, which was considerably behind, and encumbered with its plunder, was overwhelmed by the mountaineers in the pass of Roncesvalles, and slain to a man. Some of the bravest of the Frankish chiefs perished on this occasion, among whom is mentioned Roland or Orlando, governor of the marches or frontier of Brittany. His name became famous in after times, and the disaster of Roncesvalles and death of Roland became eventually the most celebrated episode in the vast cycle of romance.

Though after this there were hostile encounters between the armies of Charlemagne and the Saracens, they were of small account, and generally on the soil of Spain. Thus the historical foundation for the stories of the romancers is but scanty, unless we suppose the events of an earlier and of a later age to be incorporated with those of Charlemagne's own time.

There is, however, a pretended history, which for a long time was admitted as authentic, and attributed to Turpin, Archbishop of Rheims, a real personage of the time of Charlemagne. Its title is "History of Charles the Great and Orlando." It is now unhesitatingly considered as a collection of popular traditions, produced by some credulous and unscrupulous monk, who thought to give dignity to his romance by ascribing its authorship to a well-known and eminent individual. It introduces its pretended author, Bishop Turpin, in this manner:

"Turpin, Archbishop of Rheims, the friend and secretary of Charles the Great, excellently skilled in sacred and profane literature, of a genius equally adapted to prose and verse, the advocate of the poor, beloved of God in his life and conversation, who often fought the Saracens, hand to hand, by the Emperor's side, he relates the acts of Charles the Great in one book, and flourished under Charles and his son Louis, to the year of our Lord eight hundred and thirty."

The titles of some of Archbishop Turpin's chapters will show the nature of his history. They are these: "Of the Walls of Pampeluna, that fell of themselves." "Of the War of the holy Facundus, where the Spears grew." (Certain of the Christians fixed their spears in the evening, erect in the ground, before the castle; and found them, in the morning, covered with bark and branches.) "How the Sun stood still for Three Days, and of the Slaughter of Four Thousand Saracens."

Turpin's history has perhaps been the source of the marvellous adventures which succeeding poets and romancers have accumulated around the names of Charlemagne and his Paladins, or Peers. But Ariosto and the other Italian poets have drawn from different sources, and doubtless often from their own invention, numberless other stories which they attribute to the same heroes, not hesitating to quote as their authority "the good Turpin," though his history contains no trace of them; and the more outrageous the improbability, or rather the impossibility, of their narrations, the more attentive are they to cite "the Archbishop," generally adding their testimonial to his unquestionable veracity.

The principal Italian poets who have sung the adventures of the peers of Charlemagne are Pulci, Boiardo, and Ariosto. The characters of Orlando, Rinaldo, Astolpho, Gano, and others, are the same in all, though the adventures attributed to them are different. Boiardo tells us of the loves of Orlando, Ariosto of his disappointment and consequent madness, Pulci of his death.

Ogier, the Dane, is a real personage. History agrees with romance in representing him as a powerful lord who, originally from Denmark and a Pagan, embraced Christianity, and took service under Charlemagne. He revolted from the Emperor, and was driven into exile. He afterwards led one of those bands of piratical Northmen which ravaged France under the reigns of Charlemagne's degenerate successors. The description which an ancient chronicler gives of Charlemagne, as described by Ogier, is so picturesque, that we are tempted to transcribe it. Charlemagne was advancing to the siege of Pavia. Didier, King of the Lombards, was in the city with Ogier, to whom he had given refuge. When they learned that the king was approaching they mounted a high tower, whence they could see far and wide over the country. "They first saw advancing the engines of war, fit for the armies of Darius or Julius Caesar. 'There is Charlemagne,' said Didier. 'No,' said Ogier. The Lombard next saw a vast body of soldiers, who filled all the plain. 'Certainly Charles advanced with that host,' said the king. 'Not yet,' replied Ogier. 'What hope for us,' resumed the king, 'if he brings with him a greater host than that?' At last Charles appeared, his head covered with an iron helmet, his hands with iron gloves, his breast and shoulders with a cuirass of iron, his left hand holding an iron lance, while his right hand grasped his sword. Those who went before the monarch, those who marched at his side, and those who followed him, all had similar arms. Iron covered the fields and the roads; iron points reflected the rays of the sun. This iron, so hard, was borne by a people whose hearts were harder still. The blaze of the weapons flashed terror into the streets of the city."

This picture of Charlemagne in his military aspect would be incomplete without a corresponding one of his "mood of peace." One of the greatest of modern historians, M. Guizot, has compared the glory of Charlemagne to a brilliant meteor, rising suddenly out of the darkness of barbarism to disappear no less suddenly in the darkness of feudalism. But the light of this meteor was not extinguished, and reviving civilization owed much that was permanently beneficial to the great Emperor of the Franks. His ruling hand is seen in the legislation of his time, as well as in the administration of the laws. He encouraged learning; he upheld the clergy, who were the only peaceful and intellectual class, against the encroaching and turbulent barons; he was an affectionate father, and watched carefully over the education of his children, both sons and daughters. Of his encouragement of learning we will give some particulars.

He caused learned men to be brought from Italy and from other foreign countries to revive the public schools of France, which had been prostrated by the disorders of preceding times. He recompensed these learned men liberally, and kept some of them near himself, honoring them with his friendship. Of these the most celebrated is Alcuin, an Englishman, whose writings still remain, and prove him to have been both a learned and a wise man. With the assistance of Alcuin, and others like him, he founded an academy or royal school, which should have the direction of the studies of all the schools of the kingdom. Charlemagne himself was a member of this academy on equal terms with the rest. He attended its meetings, and fulfilled all the duties of an academician. Each member took the name of some famous man of antiquity. Alcuin called himself Horace, another took the name of Augustin, a third of Pindar. Charlemagne, who knew the Psalms by heart, and who had an ambition to be, according to his conception, A KING AFTER GOD'S OWN HEART, received from his brother academicians the name of David.

Of the respect entertained for him by foreign nations an interesting proof is afforded in the embassy sent to him by the Caliph of the Arabians, the celebrated Haroun al Raschid, a prince in character and conduct not unlike to Charlemagne. The ambassadors brought with them, besides other rich presents, a clock, the first that was seen in Europe, which excited universal admiration. It had the form of a twelve-sided edifice with twelve doors. These doors formed niches, in each of which was a little statue representing one of the hours. At the striking of the hour the doors, one for each stroke, was seen to open, and from the doors to issue as many of the little statues, which, following one another, marched gravely round the tower. The motion of the clock was caused by water, and the striking was effected by balls of brass equal to the number of the hours, which fell upon a cymbal of the same metal, the number falling being determined by the discharge of the water, which, as it sunk in the vessel, allowed their escape.

Charlemagne was succeeded by his son Louis, a well-intentioned but feeble prince, in whose reign the fabric reared by Charles began rapidly to crumble. Louis was followed successively by two Charleses, incapable princes, whose weak and often tyrannical conduct is no doubt the source of incidents of that character ascribed in the romances to Charlemagne.

The lawless and disobedient deportment of Charles's paladins, instances of which are so frequent in the romantic legends, was also a trait of the declining empire, but not of that of Charlemagne.

THE PEERS, OR PALADINS

The twelve most illustrious knights of Charlemagne were called Peers, for the equality that reigned among them; while the name of Paladins, also conferred on them, implies that they were inmates of the palace and companions of the king. Their names are always given alike by the romancers, yet we may enumerate the most distinguished of them as follows: Orlando or Roland (the former the Italian, the latter the French form of the name), favorite nephew of Charlemagne; Rinaldo of Montalban, cousin of Orlando; Namo, Duke of Bavaria; Salomon, king of Brittany; Turpin, the Archbishop; Astolpho, of England; Ogier, the Dane; Malagigi, the Enchanter; and Florismart, the friend of Orlando. There were others who are sometimes named as paladins, and the number cannot be strictly limited to twelve. Charlemagne himself must be counted one, and Ganelon, or Gano, of Mayence, the treacherous enemy of all the rest, was rated high on the list by his deluded sovereign, who was completely the victim of his arts.

We shall introduce more particularly to our readers a few of the principal peers, leaving the others to make their own introduction as they appear in the course of our narrative. We begin with Orlando.

ORLANDO

Milon, or Milone, a knight of great family, and distantly related to Charlemagne, having secretly married Bertha, the Emperor's sister, was banished from France, and excommunicated by the Pope. After a long and miserable wandering on foot as mendicants Milon and his wife arrived at Sutri, in Italy, where they took refuge in a cave, and in that cave Orlando was born. There his mother continued, deriving a scanty support from the compassion of the neighboring peasants; while Milon, in quest of honor and fortune, went into foreign lands. Orlando grew up among the children of the peasantry, surpassing them all in strength and manly graces. Among his companions in age, though in station far more elevated, was Oliver, son of the governor of the town. Between the two boys a feud arose that led to a fight, in which Orlando thrashed his rival; but this did not prevent a friendship springing up between the two, which lasted through life.

Orlando was so poor that he was sometimes half naked. As he was a favorite of the boys, one day four of them brought some cloth to make him clothes. Two brought white and two red; and from this circumstance Orlando took his coat-of-arms, or quarterings.

When Charlemagne was on his way to Rome to receive the imperial crown he dined in public in Sutri. Orlando and his mother that day had nothing to eat, and Orlando coming suddenly upon the royal party, and seeing abundance of provisions, seized from the attendants as much as he could carry off, and made good his retreat in spite of their resistance. The Emperor, being told of this incident, was reminded of an intimation he had received in a dream, and ordered the boy to be followed. This was done by three of the knights, whom Orlando would have encountered with a cudgel on their entering the grotto, had not his mother restrained him. When they heard from her who she was they threw themselves at her feet, and promised to obtain her pardon from the Emperor. This was easily effected. Orlando was received into favor by the Emperor, returned with him to France, and so distinguished himself that he became the most powerful support of the throne and of Christianity. [2]

ROLAND AND FERRAGUS

Orlando, or Roland, particularly distinguished himself by his combat with Ferragus. Ferragus was a giant, and moreover his skin was of such impenetrable stuff that no sword could make any impression upon it. The giant's mode of fighting was to seize his adversary in his arms and carry him off, in spite of all the struggles he could make. Roland's utmost skill only availed to keep him out of the giant's clutches, but all his efforts to wound him with the sword were useless. After long fighting Ferragus was so weary that he proposed a truce, and when it was agreed upon he lay down and immediately fell asleep. He slept in perfect security, for it was against all the laws of chivalry to take advantage of an adversary under such circumstances. But Ferragus lay so uncomfortably for the want of a pillow that Orlando took pity upon him, and brought a smooth stone and placed it under his head. When the giant woke up, after a refreshing nap, and perceived what Orlando had done, he seemed quite grateful,

---

[2] It is plain that Shakspeare borrowed from this source the similar incident in his "As you Like it." The names of characters in the play, Orlando, Oliver, Rowland indicate the same thing.

became sociable, and talked freely in the usual boastful style of such characters. Among other things he told Orlando that he need not attempt to kill him with a sword, for that every part of his body was invulnerable, except this; and as he spoke, he put his hand to the vital part, just in the middle of his breast. Aided by this information Orlando succeeded, when the fight was renewed, in piercing the giant in the very spot he had pointed out, and giving him a death-wound. Great was the rejoicing in the Christian camp, and many the praises showered upon the victorious paladin by the Emperor and all his host.

On another occasion Orlando encountered a puissant Saracen warrior, and took from him, as the prize of victory, the sword Durindana. This famous weapon had once belonged to the illustrious prince Hector of Troy. It was of the finest workmanship, and of such strength and temper that no armor in the world could stand against it.

A ROLAND FOR AN OLIVER

Guerin de Montglave held the lordship of Vienne, subject to Charlemagne. He had quarrelled with his sovereign, and Charles laid siege to his city, having ravaged the neighboring country. Guerin was an aged warrior, but relied for his defence upon his four sons and two grandsons, who were among the bravest knights of the age. After the siege had continued two months Charlemagne received tidings that Marsilius, king of Spain, had invaded France, and, finding himself unopposed, was advancing rapidly in the Southern provinces. At this intelligence Charles listened to the counsel of his peers, and consented to put the quarrel with Guerin to the decision of Heaven, by single combat between two knights, one of each party, selected by lot. The proposal was acceptable to Guerin and his sons. The names of the four, together with Guerin's own, who would not be excused, and of the two grandsons, who claimed their lot, being put into a helmet, Oliver's was drawn forth, and to him, the youngest of the grandsons, was assigned the honor and the peril of the combat. He accepted the award with delight, exulting in being thought worthy to maintain the cause of his family. On Charlemagne's side Roland was the designated champion, and neither he nor Oliver knew who his antagonist was to be.

They met on an island in the Rhone, and the warriors of both camps were ranged on either shore, spectators of the battle. At the first encounter both lances were shivered, but both riders kept their seats, immovable. They dismounted, and drew their swords. Then ensued a combat which seemed so equal, that the spectators could not form an opinion as to the probable issue. Two hours and more the knights continued to strike and parry, to thrust and ward, neither showing any sign of weariness, nor ever being taken at unawares. At length Orlando struck furiously upon Oliver's shield, burying Durindana in its edge so deeply that he could not draw it back, and Oliver, almost at the same moment, thrust so vigorously upon Orlando's breastplate that his sword snapped off at the handle. Thus were the two warriors left weaponless. Scarcely pausing a moment, they rushed upon one another, each striving to throw his adversary to the ground, and failing in that, each snatched at the other's helmet to tear it away. Both succeeded, and at the same moment they stood bare-headed face to face, and Roland recognized Oliver, and Oliver Roland. For a moment they stood still; and the next, with open arms, rushed into one another's embrace. "I am conquered," said Orlando. "I yield me." said Oliver.

The people on the shore knew not what to make of all this. Presently they saw the two late antagonists standing hand in hand, and it was evident the battle was at an end. The knights crowded round them, and with one voice hailed them as equals in glory. If there were any who felt disposed to murmur that the battle was left undecided they were silenced by the voice of Ogier the Dane, who proclaimed aloud that all had been done that honor required, and declared that he would maintain that award against all gainsayers.

The quarrel with Guerin and his sons being left undecided, a truce was made for four days, and in that time, by the efforts of Duke Namo on the one side, and of Oliver on the other, a reconciliation was effected. Charlemagne, accompanied by Guerin and his valiant family, marched to meet Marsilius, who hastened to retreat across the frontier.

RINALDO

Rinaldo was one of the four sons of Aymon, who married Aya, the sister of Charlemagne. Thus Rinaldo was nephew to Charlemagne and cousin of Orlando.

When Rinaldo had grown old enough to assume arms Orlando had won for himself an illustrious name by his exploits against the Saracens, whom Charlemagne and his brave knights had driven out of France. Orlando's fame excited a noble emulation in Rinaldo. Eager to go in pursuit of glory, he wandered in the country near Paris, and one day saw at the foot of a tree a superb horse, fully equipped and loaded with a complete suit of armor. Rinaldo clothed himself in the armor and mounted the horse, but took not the sword. On the day when, with his brothers, he had received the honor of knighthood from the Emperor he had sworn never to bind a sword to his side till he had wrested one from some famous knight.

Rinaldo took his way to the forest of Arden, celebrated for so many adventures. Hardly had he entered it when he met an old man, bending under the weight of years, and learned from him that the forest was infested with a wild horse, untamable, that broke and overturned everything that opposed his career. To attack him, he said, or even to meet him, was certain death. Rinaldo, far from being alarmed, showed the most eager desire to combat the animal. This was the horse Bayard, afterward so famous. He had formerly belonged to Amadis of Gaul. After the death of that hero he had been held under enchantment by the power of a magician, who predicted that, when the time came to break the spell, he should be subdued by a knight of the lineage of Amadis, and not less brave than he.

To win this wonderful horse it was necessary to conquer him by force or skill; for from the moment when he should be thrown down he would become docile and manageable. His habitual resort was a cave on the borders of the forest; but woe be to any one who should approach him, unless gifted with strength and courage more than mortal. Having told this, the old man departed. He was not, in fact, an old man, but Malagigi, the enchanter, cousin of Rinaldo, who, to favor the enterprises of the young knight, had procured for him the horse and armor which he so opportunely found, and now put him in the way to acquire a horse unequalled in the world.

Rinaldo plunged into the forest, and spent many days in seeking Bayard, but found no traces of him. One day he encountered a Saracen knight, with whom he made acquaintance, as often happened to knights, by first meeting him in combat. This knight, whose name was Isolier, was also in quest of Bayard. Rinaldo succeeded in the encounter, and so severe was the shock that Isolier was a long time insensible. When he revived, and was about to resume the contest, a peasant who passed by (it was Malagigi) interrupted them with the news that the terrible horse was near at hand, advising them to unite their powers to subdue him, for it would require all their ability.

Rinaldo and Isolier, now become friends, proceeded together to the attack of the horse. They found Bayard, and stood a long time, concealed by the wood, admiring his strength and beauty.

A bright bay in color (whence he was called Bayard), with a silver star in his forehead, and his hind feet white, his body slender, his head delicate, his ample chest filled out with swelling muscles, his shoulders broad and full, his legs straight and sinewy, his thick mane falling over his arching neck,--he came rushing through the forest, regardless of rocks, bushes, or trees, rending everything that opposed his way, and neighing defiance.

He first descried Isolier, and rushed upon him. The knight received him with lance in rest, but the fierce animal broke the spear, and his course was not delayed by it for an instant. The Spaniard adroitly stepped aside, and gave way to the rushing tempest. Bayard checked his career, and turned again upon the knight, who had already drawn his sword. He drew his sword, for he had no hope of taming the horse; that, he was satisfied, was impossible.

Bayard rushed upon him; fiercely rearing, now on this side, now on that. The knight struck him with his sword, where the white star adorned his forehead, but struck in vain, and felt ashamed, thinking that he had struck feebly, for he did not know that the skin of that horse was so tough that the keenest sword could make no impression upon it.

Whistling fell the sword once more, and struck with greater force, and the fierce horse felt it, and drooped his head under the blow, but the next moment turned upon his foe with such a buffet that the Pagan fell stunned and lifeless to the earth.

Rinaldo, who saw Isolier fall, and thought that his life was reft, darted towards the horse, and, with his fist gave him such a blow on the jaws that the blood tinged his mouth with vermilion. Quicker than an arrow leaves the bow the horse turned upon him, and tried to seize his arm with his teeth.

The knight stepped back, and then, repeating his blow, struck him on the forehead. Bayard turned, and kicked with both his feet with a force that would have shattered a mountain. Rinaldo was on his guard, and evaded his attacks, whether made with head or heels. He kept at his side avoiding both; but, making a false step, he at last received a terrible blow from the horse's foot, and at the shock almost fainted away. A second such blow would have killed him, but the horse kicked at random, and a second blow did not reach Rinaldo, who in a moment recovered himself. Thus the contest continued until by chance Bayard's foot got caught between the branches of an oak. Rinaldo seized it and putting forth all his strength and address, threw him on the ground.

No sooner had Bayard touched the ground than all his rage subsided. No longer an object of terror, he became gentle and quiet, yet with dignity in his mildness.

The paladin patted his neck, stroked his breast, and smoothed his mane, while the animal neighed and showed delight to be caressed by his master. Rinaldo, seeing him now completely subdued, took the saddle and trappings from the other horse, and adorned Bayard with the spoils.

Rinaldo became one of the most illustrious knights of Charlemagne's court,--indeed, the most illustrious, if we except Orlando. Yet he was not always so obedient to the Emperor's commands as he should have been, and every fault he committed was sure to be aggravated by the malice of Gan, Duke of Maganza, the treacherous enemy of Rinaldo and all his house.

At one time Rinaldo had incurred the severe displeasure of Charlemagne, and been banished from court. Seeing no chance of being ever restored to favor, he went to Spain, and entered into the service of the Saracen king, Ivo. His brothers, Alardo, Ricardo, and Ricciardetto, accompanied him, and all four served the king so faithfully that they rose to high favor with him. The king gave them land in the mountains on the frontiers of France and Spain, and subjected all the country round to Rinaldo's authority. There was plenty of marble in the mountains, the king furnished workmen, and they built a castle for Rinaldo, surrounded with high walls, so as to be almost impregnable. Built of white stone, and placed on the brow of a marble promontory, the castle shone like a star, and Rinaldo gave it the name of Montalban. Here he assembled his friends, many of whom were banished men like himself, and the country people furnished them with provisions in return for the protection the castle afforded. Yet some of Rinaldo's men were lawless, and sometimes the supplies were not furnished in sufficient abundance, so that Rinaldo and his garrison got a bad name for taking by force what they could not obtain by gift; and we sometimes find Montalban spoken of as a nest of freebooters, and its defenders called a beggarly garrison.

Charlemagne's displeasure did not last long, and, at the time our history commences, Rinaldo and his brothers were completely restored to the favor of the Emperor, and none of his cavaliers served him with greater zeal and fidelity than they, throughout all his wars with the Saracens and Pagans.

THE TOURNAMENT

It was the month of May, and the feast of Pentecost. Charlemagne had ordered magnificent festivities, and summoned to them, besides his paladins and vassals of the crown, all strangers, Christian or Saracen, then sojourning at Paris. Among the guests were King Grandonio, from Spain; and Ferrau, the Saracen, with eyes like an eagle; Orlando and Rinaldo, the Emperor's nephews; Duke Namo; Astolpho, of England, the handsomest man living; Malagigi, the Enchanter; and Gano, of Maganza, that wily traitor, who had the art to make the Emperor think he loved him, while he plotted against him.

High sat Charlemagne at the head of his vassals and his paladins, rejoicing in the thought of their number and their might, while all were sitting and hearing music, and feasting, when suddenly there came into the hall four enormous giants, having between them a lady of incomparable beauty, attended by a single knight. There were many ladies present who had seemed beautiful till she made her appearance, but after that they all seemed nothing. Every Christian knight turned his eyes to her, and every Pagan crowded round her, while she, with a sweetness that might have touched a heart of stone, thus addressed the Emperor:

"High-minded lord, the renown of your worthiness, and of the valor of these your knights, which echoes from sea to sea, encourages me to hope that two pilgrims, who have come from the ends of the world to behold you, will not have encountered their fatigue in vain. And, before I show the motive which has brought us hither, learn that this knight is my brother Uberto, and that I am his sister Angelica. Fame has told us of the jousting this day appointed, and so the prince my brother has come to prove his valor, and to say that, if any of the knights here assembled choose to meet him in the joust, he will encounter them, one by one, at the stair of Merlin, by the Fountain of the Pine. And his conditions are these: No knight who chances to be thrown shall be allowed to renew the combat, but shall remain prisoner to my brother; but if my brother be overthrown he shall depart out of the country, leaving me as the prize of the conqueror."

Now it must be stated that this Angelica and her brother, who called himself Uberto, but whose real name was Argalia, were the children of Galafron, king of Cathay, who had sent them to be the destruction of the Christian host; for Argalia was armed with an enchanted lance, which unfailingly overthrew everything it touched, and he was mounted on a horse, a creature of magic, whose swiftness outstripped the wind. Angelica possessed also a ring which was a defence against all enchantments, and when put into the mouth rendered the bearer invisible. Thus Argalia was expected to subdue and take prisoners whatever knights should dare to encounter him; and the charms of Angelica were relied on to entice the paladins to make the fatal venture, while her ring would afford her easy means of escape.

When Angelica ceased sneaking she knelt before the king and awaited his answer, and everybody gazed on her with admiration. Orlando especially felt irresistibly drawn towards her, so that he trembled and changed countenance. Every knight in the hall was infected with the same feeling, not excepting old white-headed Duke Namo and Charlemagne himself.

All stood for a while in silence, lost in the delight of looking at her. The fiery youth Ferrau could hardly restrain himself from seizing her from the giants and carrying her away; Rinaldo turned as red as fire, while Malagigi, who had discovered by his art that the stranger was not speaking truth, muttered softly, as he looked at her, "Exquisite false creature! I will play thee such a trick for this, as will leave thee no cause to boast of thy visit."

Charlemagne, to detain her as long as possible before him, delayed his assent till he had asked her a number of questions, all which she answered discreetly, and then the challenge was accepted.

As soon as she was gone Malagigi consulted his book, and found out the whole plot of the vile, infidel king, Galafron, as we have explained it, so he determined to seek the damsel and frustrate her designs. He hastened to the appointed spot, and there found the prince and his sister in a beautiful pavilion, where they lay asleep, while the four giants kept watch. Malagigi took his book and cast a spell out of it, and immediately the four giants fell into a deep sleep. Drawing his sword (for he was a belted knight), he softly approached the young lady, intending to despatch her at once; but, seeing her look so lovely, he paused for a moment, thinking there was no need of hurry, as he believed his spell was upon her, and she could not wake. But the ring which she wore secured her from the effect of the spell, and some slight noise, or whatever else it was, caused her at that moment to awake. She uttered a great cry, and flew to her brother, and waked him. By the help of her knowledge of enchantment, they took and bound fast the magician, and, seizing his book, turned his arts against himself. Then they summoned a crowd of demons, and bade them seize their prisoner and bear him to King Galafron, at his great city of Albracca, which they did, and, on his arrival, he was locked up in a rock under the sea.

While these things were going on all was uproar at Paris, since Orlando insisted upon being the first to try the adventure at the stair of Merlin. This was resented by the other pretenders to Angelica, and all contested his right to the precedence. The tumult was stilled by the usual expedient of drawing lots, and the first prize was drawn by Astolpho. Ferrau, the Saracen, had the second, and Grandonio the third. Next came Berlinghieri, and Otho; then Charles himself, and, as his ill-fortune would have it, after thirty more, the indignant Orlando.

Astolpho, who drew the first lot, was handsome, brave, and rich. But, whether from heedlessness or want of skill, he was an unlucky jouster, and very apt to be thrown, an accident which he bore with perfect good-humor, always ready to mount again and try to mend his fortune, generally with no better success.

Astolpho went forth upon his adventure with great gayety of dress and manner, encountered Argalia, and was immediately tilted out of the saddle. He railed at fortune, to whom he laid all the fault; but his painful feelings were somewhat relieved by the kindness of Angelica, who, touched by his youth and good looks, granted him the liberty of the pavilion, and caused him to be treated with all kindness and respect.

The violent Ferrau had the next chance in the encounter, and was thrown no less speedily than Astolpho; but he did not so easily put up with his mischance. Crying out, "What are the emperor's engagements to me?" he rushed with his sword against Argalia, who, being forced to defend himself, dismounted and drew his sword, but got so much the worse of the fight that he made a signal of surrender, and, after some words, listened to a proposal of marriage from Ferrau to his sister. The beauty, however, feeling no inclination to match with such a rough and savage-looking person, was so dismayed at the offer, that, hastily bidding her brother to meet her in the forest of Arden, she vanished from the sight of both by means of the enchanted ring. Argalia, seeing this, took to his horse of swiftness, and dashed away in the same direction. Ferrau pursued him, and Astolpho, thus left to himself, took possession of the enchanted lance in place of his own, which was broken, not knowing the treasure he possessed in it, and returned to the tournament. Charlemagne, finding the lady and her brother gone, ordered the jousting to proceed as at first intended, in which Astolpho, by aid of the enchanted lance, unhorsed all comers against him, equally to their astonishment and his own.

The paladin Rinaldo, on learning the issue of the combat of Ferrau and the stranger, galloped after the fair fugitive in an agony of love and impatience. Orlando, perceiving his disappearance, pushed forth in like manner; and, at length, all three are in the forest of Arden, hunting about for her who is invisible.

Now in this forest there were two fountains, the one constructed by the sage Merlin, who designed it for Tristram and the fair Isoude; [Footnote: See their story in "King Arthur and His Knights."] for such was the virtue of this fountain, that a draught of its waters produced on oblivion of the love which the drinker might feel, and even produced aversion for the object formerly beloved. The other fountain was endowed with exactly opposite qualities, and a draught of it inspired love for the first living object that was seen after tasting it. Rinaldo happened to come to the first mentioned fountain, and, being flushed with heat, dismounted, and quenched in one draught both his thirst and his passion. So far from loving Angelica as before he hated her from the bottom of his heart, became disgusted with the search he was upon, and, feeling fatigued with his ride, finding a sheltered and flowery nook, laid himself down and fell asleep.

Shortly after came Angelica, but, approaching in a different direction, she espied the other fountain, and there quenched her thirst. Then resuming her way, she came upon the sleeping Rinaldo. Love instantly seized her, and she stood rooted to the spot.

The meadow round was all full of lilies of the valley and wild roses. Angelica, not knowing what to do, at length plucked a handful of these, and dropped them, one by one, on the face of the sleeper. He woke up, and, seeing who it was, received her salutations with averted countenance, remounted his horse, and galloped away. In vain the beautiful creature followed and called after him, in vain asked him what she had done to be so despised. Rinaldo disappeared, leaving her in despair, and she returned in tears to the spot where she had found him sleeping. There, in her turn, she herself lay down, pressing the spot of earth on which he had lain, and, out of fatigue and sorrow, fell asleep.

As Angelica thus lay, fortune conducted Orlando to the same place. The attitude in which she was sleeping was so lovely that it is not to be conceived, much less expressed. Orlando stood gazing like a man who had been transported to another sphere. "Am I on earth," he exclaimed, "or am I in Paradise? Surely it is I that sleep, and this is my dream."

But his dream was proved to be none in a manner which he little desired. Ferrau, who had slain Argalia, came up, raging with jealousy, and a combat ensued which awoke the sleeper.

Terrified at what she beheld, she rushed to her palfrey, and, while the fighters were occupied with one another, fled away through the forest. The champions continued their fight till they were interrupted by a messenger, who brought word to Ferrau that king Marsilius, his sovereign, was in pressing need of his assistance, and conjured him to return to Spain. Ferrau, upon this, proposed to suspend the combat, to which Orlando, eager to pursue Angelica, agreed. Ferrau, on the other hand, departed with the messenger to Spain.

Orlando's quest for the fair fugitive was all in vain. Aided by the powers of magic, she made a speedy return to her own country.

But the thought of Rinaldo could not be banished from her mind, and she determined to set Malagigi at liberty, and to employ him to win Rinaldo, if possible, to make her a return of affection. She accordingly freed him from his dungeon, unlocking his fetters with her own hands, and restored him his book, promising him ample honors and rewards on condition of his bringing Rinaldo to her feet.

Malagigi accordingly, with the aid of his book, called up a demon, mounted him, and departed. Arrived at his destination, he inveigled Rinaldo into an enchanted bark, which conveyed him, without any visible pilot, to an island where stood an edifice called Joyous Castle. The whole island was a garden. On the western side, close to the sea, was the palace, built of marble, so clear and polished that it reflected the landscape about it. Rinaldo leapt ashore, and soon met a lady, who invited him to enter. The house was as beautiful within as without, full of rooms adorned with azure and gold, and with noble paintings. The lady led the knight into an apartment painted with stories, and opening to the garden, through pillars of crystal, with golden capitals. Here he found a bevy of ladies, three of whom were singing in concert, while another played on an instrument of exquisite accord, and the rest danced round about them. When the ladies beheld him coming they turned the dance into a circuit round him, and then one of them, in the sweetest manner, said, "Sir knight, the tables are set, and the hour for the banquet is come;" and, with these words, still dancing, they drew him across the lawn in front of the apartment, to a table that was spread with cloth of gold and fine linen, under a bower of damask roses by the side of a fountain.

Four ladies were already seated there, who rose, and placed Rinaldo at their head, in a chair set with pearls. And truly indeed was he astonished. A repast ensued, consisting of viands the most delicate, and wines as fragrant as they were fine, drunk out of jewelled cups; and, when it drew towards its conclusion, harps and lutes were heard in the distance, and one of the ladies said in the knight's ear: "This house and all that you see in it are yours; for you alone was it built, and the builder is a queen. Happy indeed must you think yourself, for she loves you, and she is the greatest beauty in the world! Her name is Angelica."

The moment Rinaldo heard the name he so detested he started up, with a changed countenance, and, in spite of all that the lady could say, broke off across the garden, and never ceased hastening till he reached the place where he landed. The bark was still on the shore. He sprang into it, and pushed off, though he saw nobody in it but himself. It was in vain for him to try to control its movements, for it dashed on as if in fury, till it reached a distant shore covered with a gloomy forest. Here Rinaldo, surrounded by enchantments of a very different sort from those which he had lately resisted, was entrapped into a pit.

The pit belonged to a castle called Altaripa, which was hung with human heads, and painted red with blood. As the paladin was viewing the scene with amazement a hideous old woman made her appearance at the edge of the pit, and told him that he was destined to be thrown to a monster, who was only kept from devastating the whole country by being supplied with living human flesh. Rinaldo said, "Be it so; let me but remain armed as I am, and I fear nothing." The old woman laughed in derision. Rinaldo remained in the pit all night, and the next morning was taken to the place where the monster had his den. It was a court surrounded by a high wall. Rinaldo was shut in with the beast, and a terrible combat ensued. Rinaldo was unable to make any impression on the scales of the monster, while he, on the contrary, with his dreadful claws, tore away plate and mail from the paladin. Rinaldo began to think his last hour was come, and cast his eyes around and above to see if there was any means of escape. He perceived a beam projecting from the wall at the height of some ten feet, and, taking a leap almost miraculous, he succeeded in reaching it, and in flinging himself up across it. Here he sat for hours, the hideous brute continually trying to reach him. All at once he heard the sound of something coming through the air like a bird, and suddenly Angelica herself alighted on the end of the beam. She held something in her hand towards him, and spoke to him in a loving voice. But the moment Rinaldo saw her he commanded her to go away, refused all her offers of assistance, and at length declared that, if she did not leave him, he would cast himself down to the monster, and meet his fate.

Angelica, saying she would lose her life rather than displease him, departed; but first she threw to the monster a cake of wax she had prepared, and spread around him a rope knotted with nooses. The beast took the bait, and, finding his teeth glued together by the wax, vented his fury in bounds and leaps, and, soon getting entangled in the nooses, drew them tight by his struggles, so that he could scarcely move a limb.

Rinaldo, watching his chance, leapt down upon his back, seized him round the neck, and throttled him, not relaxing his gripe till the beast fell dead.

Another difficulty remained to be overcome. The walls were of immense height, and the only opening in them was a grated window of such strength that he could not break the bars. In his distress Rinaldo found a file, which Angelica had left on the ground, and, with the help of this, effected his deliverance.

What further adventures he met with will be told in another chapter.

THE SIEGE OF ALBRACCA

At the very time when Charlemagne was holding his plenary court and his great tournament his kingdom was invaded by a mighty monarch, who was moreover so valiant and strong in battle that no one could stand against him. He was named Gradasso, and his kingdom was called Sericane. Now, as it often happens to the greatest and the richest to long for what they cannot have, and thus to lose what they already possess, this king could not rest content without Durindana, the sword of Orlando, and Bayard, the horse of Rinaldo. To obtain these he determined to war upon France, and for this purpose put in array a mighty army.

He took his way through Spain, and, after defeating Marsilius, the king of that country, in several battles, was rapidly advancing on France. Charlemagne, though Marsilius was a Saracen, and had been his enemy, yet felt it needful to succor him in this extremity from a consideration of common danger, and, with the consent of his peers, despatched Rinaldo with a strong body of soldiers against Gradasso.

There was much fighting, with doubtful results, and Gradasso was steadily advancing into France. But, impatient to achieve his objects, he challenged Rinaldo to single combat, to be fought on foot, and upon these conditions: If Rinaldo conquered, Gradasso agreed to give up all his prisoners and return to his own country; but if Gradasso won the day, he was to have Bayard.

The challenge was accepted, and would have been fought had it not been for the arts of Malagigi, who just then returned from Angelica's kingdom with set purpose to win Rinaldo to look with favor upon the fair princess who was dying for love of him. Malagigi drew Rinaldo away from the army by putting on the semblance of Gradasso, and, after a short contest, pretending to fly before him, by which means Rinaldo was induced to follow him into a boat, in which he was borne away, and entangled in various adventures, as we have already related.

The army, left under the command of Ricciardetto, Rinaldo's brother, was soon joined by Charlemagne and all his peerage, but experienced a disastrous rout, and the Emperor and many of his paladins were taken prisoners. Gradasso, however, did not abuse his victory; he took Charles by the hand, seated him by his side, and told him he warred only for honor. He renounced all conquests, on condition that the Emperor should deliver to him Bayard and Durindana, both of them the property of his vassals, the former of which, as he maintained, was already forfeited to him by Rinaldo's failure to meet him as agreed. To these terms Charlemagne readily acceded.

Bayard, after the departure of his master, had been taken in charge by Ricciardetto, and sent back to Paris, where Astolpho was in command, in the absence of Charlemagne. Astolpho received with great indignation the message despatched for Bayard, and replied by a herald that "he would not surrender the horse of his kinsman Rinaldo without a contest. If Gradasso wanted the steed he might come and take him, and that he, Astolpho, was ready to meet him in the field."

Gradasso was only amused at this answer, for Astolpho's fame as a successful warrior was not high, and Gradasso willingly renewed with him the bargain which he had made with Rinaldo. On these conditions the battle was fought. The enchanted lance, in the hands of Astolpho, performed a new wonder; and Gradasso, the terrible Gradasso, was unhorsed.

He kept his word, set free his prisoners, and put his army on the march to return to his own country, renewing his oath, however, not to rest till he had taken from Rinaldo his horse, and from Orlando his sword, or lost his life in the attempt.

Charlemagne, full of gratitude to Astolpho, would have kept him near his person and loaded him with honors, but Astolpho preferred to seek Rinaldo, with the view of restoring to him his horse, and departed from Paris with that design.

Our story now returns to Orlando, whom we left fascinated with the sight of the sleeping beauty, who, however, escaped him while engaged in the combat with Ferrau. Having long sought her in vain through the recesses of the wood, he resolved to follow her to her father's court. Leaving, therefore, the camp of Charlemagne, he travelled long in the direction of the East, making inquiry everywhere, if, perchance, he might get tidings of the fugitive. After many adventures, he arrived one day at a place where many roads crossed, and meeting there a courier, he asked him for news. The courier replied that he had been despatched by Angelica to solicit the aid of Sacripant, king of Circassia, in favor of her father Galafron, who was besieged in his city, Albracca, by Agrican, king of Tartary. This Agrican had been an unsuccessful suitor to the damsel, whom he now pursued with arms. Orlando thus learned that he was within a day's journey of Albracca; and, feeling now secure of Angelica, he proceeded with all speed to her city.

Thus journeying he arrived at a bridge, under which flowed a foaming river. Here a damsel met him with a goblet, and informed him that it was the usage of this bridge to present the traveller with a cup. Orlando accepted the offered cup and drank its contents. He had no sooner done so than his brain reeled, and he became unconscious of the object of his journey, and of everything else. Under the influence of this fascination he followed the damsel into a magnificent and marvellous palace. Here he found himself in company with many knights, unknown to him and to each other, though if it had not been for the Cup of Oblivion of which they all had partaken they would have found themselves brothers in arms.

Astolpho, proceeding on his way to seek Rinaldo, splendidly dressed and equipped, as was his wont, arrived in Circassia, and found there a great army encamped under the command of Sacripant, the king of that country, who was leading it to the defence of Galafron, the father of Angelica. Sacripant, much struck by the appearance of Astolpho and his horse, accosted him courteously, and tried to enlist him in his service; but Astolpho, proud of his late victories, scornfully declined his offers, and pursued his way. King Sacripant was too much attracted by his appearance to part with him so easily, and having laid aside his kingly ornaments, set out in pursuit of him.

Astolpho next day encountered on his way a stranger knight, named Sir Florismart, Lord of the Sylvan Tower, one of the bravest and best of knights, having as his guide a damsel, young, fair, and virtuous, to whom he was tenderly attached, whose name was Flordelis. Astolpho, as he approached, defied the knight, bidding him yield the lady, or prepare to maintain his right by arms. Florismart accepted the contest, and the knights encountered. Florismart was unhorsed and his steed fell dead, while Bayard sustained no injury by the shock.

Florismart was so overwhelmed with despair at his own disgrace and the sight of the damsel's distress, that he drew his sword, and was about to plunge it into his own bosom. But Astolpho held his hand, told him that he contended only for glory, and was contented to leave him the lady.

While Florismart and Flordelis were vowing eternal gratitude King Sacripant arrived, and coveting the damsel of the one champion as much as the horse and arms of the other, defied them to the joust. Astolpho met the challenger, whom he instantly overthrew, and presented his courser to Florismart, leaving the king to return to his army on foot.

The friends pursued their route, and ere long Flordelis discovered, by signs which were known to her, that they were approaching the waters of Oblivion, and advised them to turn back, or to change their course. This the knights would not hear of, and, continuing their march, they soon arrived at the bridge where Orlando had been taken prisoner.

The damsel of the bridge appeared as before with the enchanted cup, but Astolpho, forewarned, rejected it with scorn. She dashed it to the ground, and a fire blazed up which rendered the bridge unapproachable. At the same moment the two knights were assailed by sundry warriors, known and unknown, who, having no recollection of anything, joined blindly in defence of their prison-house. Among these was Orlando, at sight of whom Astolpho, with all his confidence not daring to encounter him, turned and fled, owing his escape to the strength and fleetness of Bayard.

Florismart, meanwhile, overlaid by fearful odds, was compelled to yield to necessity, and comply with the usage of the fairy. He drank of the cup and remained prisoner with the rest. Flordelis, deprived of her two friends, retired from the scene, and devoted herself to untiring efforts to effect her lover's deliverance. Astolpho pursued his way to Albracca, which Agrican was about to besiege. He was kindly welcomed by Angelica, and enrolled among her defenders. Impatient to distinguish himself, he one night sallied forth alone, arrived in Agrican's camp, and unhorsed his warriors right and left by means of the enchanted lance. But he was soon surrounded and overmatched, and made prisoner to Agrican.

Relief was, however, at hand; for as the citizens and soldiers were one day leaning over their walls they descried a cloud of dust, from which horsemen were seen to prick forth, as it rolled on towards the camp of the besiegers. This turned out to be the army of Sacripant, which immediately attacked that of Agrican, with the view of cutting a passage through his camp to the besieged city. But Agrican, mounted upon Bayard, taken from Astolpho, but not armed with the lance of gold, the virtues of which were unknown to him, performed wonders, and rallied his scattered troops, which had given way to the sudden and unexpected assault. Sacripant, on the other hand, encouraged his men by the most desperate acts of valor, having as an additional incentive to his courage the sight of Angelica, who showed herself upon the city walls.

There she witnessed a single combat between the two leaders, Agrican and Sacripant. In this, at length, her defender appeared to be overmatched, when the Circassians broke the ring, and separated the combatants, who were borne asunder in the rush. Sacripant, severely wounded, profited by the confusion, and escaped into Albracca, where he was kindly received and carefully tended by Angelica.

The battle continuing, the Circassians were at last put to flight, and, being intercepted between the enemy's lines and the town, sought for refuge under the walls. Angelica ordered the drawbridge to be let down, and the gates thrown open to the fugitives. With these Agrican, not distinguished in the crowd, entered the place, driving both Circassians and Cathayans before him, and the portcullis being dropped, he was shut in.

For a time the terror which he inspired put to flight all opposers, but when at last it came to be known that few or none of his followers had effected an entrance with him, the fugitives rallied and surrounded him on all sides. While he was thus apparently reduced to the last extremities, he was saved by the very circumstance which threatened him with destruction. The soldiers of Angelica, closing upon him from all sides, deserted their defences; and his own besieging army entered the city in a part where the wall was broken down.

In this way was Agrican rescued, the city taken, and the inhabitants put to the sword. Angelica, however, with some of the knights who were her defenders, among whom was Sacripant, saved herself in the citadel, which was planted upon a rock.

The fortress was impregnable, but it was scantily victualled, and ill provided with other necessaries. Under these circumstances Angelica announced to those blockaded with her in the citadel her intention to go in quest of assistance, and, having plighted her promise of a speedy return, she set out, with the enchanted ring upon her finger. Mounted upon her palfrey, the damsel passed through the enemy's lines, and by sunrise was many miles clear of their encampment.

It so happened that her road led her near the fatal bridge of Oblivion, and as she approached it she met a damsel weeping bitterly. It was Flordelis, whose lover, Florismart, as we have related, had met the fate of Orlando and many more, and fallen a victim to the enchantress of the cup. She related her adventures to Angelica, and conjured her to lend what aid she might to rescue her lord and his companions. Angelica, accordingly, watching her opportunity and aided by her ring, slipped into the castle unseen, when the door was opened to admit a new victim. Here she speedily disenchanted Orlando and the rest by a touch of her talisman. But Florismart was not there. He had been given up to Falerina, a more powerful enchantress, and was still in durance. Angelica conjured the rescued captives to assist her in the recovery of her kingdom, and all departed together for Albracca.

The arrival of Orlando, with his companions, nine in all, and among the bravest knights of France, changed at once the fortunes of the war. Wherever the great paladin came, pennon and standard fell before him. Agrican in vain attempted to rally his troops. Orlando kept constantly in his front, forcing him to attend to nobody else. The Tartar king at length bethought him of a stratagem. He turned his horse, and made a show of flying in despair. Orlando dashed after him as he desired, and Agrican fled till he reached a green place in a wood, where there was a fountain.

The place was beautiful, and the Tartar dismounted to refresh himself at the fountain, but without taking off his helmet, or laying aside any of his armor. Orlando was quickly at his back, crying out, "So bold, and yet a fugitive! How could you fly from a single arm and think to escape?"

The Tartar king had leaped on his saddle the moment he saw his enemy, and when the paladin had done speaking, he said in a mild voice, "Without doubt you are the best knight I ever encountered, and fain would I leave you untouched for your own sake, if you would cease to hinder me from rallying my people. I pretended to fly, in order to bring you out of the field. If you insist upon fighting I must needs fight and slay you, but I call the sun in the heavens to witness I would rather not. I should be very sorry for your death."

The Count Orlando felt pity for so much gallantry, and he said, "The nobler you show yourself the more it grieves me to think that in dying without a knowledge of the true faith you will be lost in the other world. Let me advise you to save body and soul at once. Receive baptism, and go your way in peace."

Agrican replied: "I suspect you to be the paladin Orlando. If you are I would not lose this opportunity of fighting with you to be king of Paradise. Talk to me no more about your things of another world, for you will preach in vain. Each of us for himself, and let the sword be umpire."

The Saracen drew his sword, boldly advancing upon Orlando, and a combat began, so obstinate and so long, each warrior being a miracle of prowess, that the story says it lasted from noon till night. Orlando then seeing the stars come out was the first to propose a respite.

"What are we to do," said he, "now that daylight has left us?"

Agrican answered readily enough, "Let us repose in this meadow, and renew the combat at dawn."

The repose was taken accordingly. Each tied up his horse, and reclined himself on the grass, not far from the other, just as if they had been friends, Orlando by the fountain, Agrican beneath a pine. It was a beautiful clear night, and, as they talked together before addressing themselves to sleep, the champion of Christendom, looking up at the firmament, said, "That is a fine piece of workmanship, that starry spectacle; God made it all, that moon of silver, and those stars of gold, and the light of day, and the sun,--all for the sake of human kind."

"You wish, I see, to talk of matters of faith," said the Tartar. "Now I may as well tell you at once that I have no sort of skill in such matters, nor learning of any kind. I never could learn anything when I was a boy. I hated it so that I broke the man's head who was commissioned to teach me; and it produced such an effect on others that nobody ever afterwards dared so much as show me a book. My boyhood was therefore passed, as it should be, in horsemanship and hunting, and learning to fight. What is the good of a gentleman's poring all day over a book? Prowess to the knight, and preaching to the clergyman, that is my motto."

"I acknowledge," returned Orlando, "that arms are the first consideration of a gentleman; but not at all that he does himself dishonor by knowledge. On the contrary, knowledge is as great an embellishment of the rest of his attainments, as the flowers are to the meadow before us; and as to the knowledge of his Maker, the man that is without it is no better than a stock or a stone or a brute beast. Neither without study can he reach anything of a due sense of the depth and divineness of the contemplation."

"Learned or not learned," said Agrican, "you might show yourself better bred than by endeavoring to make me talk on a subject on which you have me at a disadvantage. If you choose to sleep I wish you good night; but if you prefer talking I recommend you to talk of fighting or of fair ladies. And, by the way, pray tell me, are you not that Orlando who makes such a noise in the world? And what is it, pray, that brings you into these parts? Were you ever in love? I suppose you must have been; for to be a knight, and never to have been in love, would be like being a man without a heart in his breast."

The count replied: "Orlando I am, and in love I am. Love has made me abandon everything, and brought me into these distant regions, and, to tell you all in one word, my heart is in the hands of the daughter of King Galafron. You have come against him with fire and sword, to get possession of his castles and his dominions; and I have come to help him, for no object in the world but to please his daughter and win her beautiful hand. I care for nothing else in existence."

Now when the Tartar king, Agrican, heard his antagonist speak in this manner, and knew him to be indeed Orlando, and to be in love with Angelica, his face changed color for grief and jealousy, though it could not be seen for the darkness. His heart began beating with such violence that he felt as if he should have died. "Well," said he to Orlando, "we are to fight when it is daylight, and one or other is to be left here, dead on the ground. I have a proposal to make to you--nay, an entreaty. My love is so excessive for the same lady that I beg you to leave her to me. I will owe you my thanks, and give up the siege and put an end to the war. I cannot bear that any one should love her, and that I should live to see it. Why, therefore, should either of us perish? Give her up. Not a soul shall know it."

"I never yet," answered Orlando, "made a promise which I did not keep, and nevertheless I own to you that, were I to make a promise like that, and even swear to keep it, I should not. You might as well ask me to tear away the limbs from my body, and the eyes out of my head. I could as well live without breath itself as cease loving Angelica."

Agrican had hardly patience to let him finish speaking, ere he leapt furiously on horseback, though it was midnight. "Quit her," said he, "or die!"

Orlando seeing the infidel getting up, and not being sure that he would not add treachery to fierceness, had been hardly less quick in mounting for the combat. "Never," exclaimed he; "I never could have quitted her if I would, and now I would not if I could. You must seek her by other means than these."

Fiercely dashed their horses together, in the nighttime, on the green mead. Despiteful and terrible were the blows they gave and took by the moonlight. Agrican fought in a rage, Orlando was cooler. And now the struggle had lasted more than five hours, and day began to dawn, when the Tartar king, furious to find so much trouble given him, dealt his enemy a blow sharp and violent beyond conception. It cut the shield in two as if it had been made of wood, and, though blood could not be drawn from Orlando, because he was fated, it shook and bruised him as if it had started every joint in his body.

His body only, however, not a particle of his soul. So dreadful was the blow which the paladin gave in return, that not only shield, but every bit of mail on the body of Agrican was broken in pieces, and three of his ribs cut asunder.

The Tartar, roaring like a lion, raised his sword with still greater vehemence than before, and dealt a blow on the paladin's helmet, such as he had never yet received from mortal man. For a moment it took away his senses. His sight failed, his ears tingled, his frightened horse turned about to fly; and he was falling from the saddle, when the very action of falling threw his head upwards, and thus recalled his recollection.

"What a shame is this!" thought he; "how shall I ever again dare to face Angelica! I have been fighting hour after hour with this man, and he is but one, and I call myself Orlando! If the combat last any longer I will bury myself in a monastery, and never look on sword again."

Orlando muttered with his lips closed and his teeth ground together; and you might have thought that fire instead of breath came out of his nose and mouth. He raised his sword Durindana with both his hands, and sent it down so tremendously on Agrican's shoulder that it cut through breastplate down to the very haunch, nay, crushed the saddle-bow, though it was made of bone and iron, and felled man and horse to the earth. Agrican turned as white as ashes, and felt death upon him. He called Orlando to come close to him, with a gentle voice, and said, as well as he could: "I believe on Him who died on the cross. Baptize me, I pray thee, with the fountain, before my senses are gone. I have lived an evil life, but need not be rebellious to God in death also. May He who came to save all the rest of the world save me!" And he shed tears, that great king, though he had been so lofty and fierce.

Orlando dismounted quickly, with his own face in tears. He gathered the king tenderly in his arms, and took and laid him by the fountain, on a marble rim that it had, and then he wept in concert with him heartily, and asked his pardon, and so baptized him in the water of the fountain, and knelt and prayed to God for him with joined hands.

He then paused and looked at him; and when he perceived his countenance changed, and that his whole person was cold, he left him there on the marble rim of the fountain, all armed as he was, with the sword by his side, and the crown upon his head.

ADVENTURES OF RINALDO AND ORLANDO

We left Rinaldo when, having overcome the monster, he quitted the castle of Altaripa, and pursued his way on foot. He soon met with a weeping damsel, who, being questioned as to the cause of her sorrow, told him she was in search of one to do battle to rescue her lover, who had been made prisoner by a vile enchantress, together with Orlando and many more. The damsel was Flordelis, the lady-love of Florismart, and Rinaldo promised his assistance, trusting to accomplish the adventure either by valor or skill. Flordelis insisted upon Rinaldo's taking her horse, which he consented to do, on condition of her mounting behind him.

As they rode on through a wood, they heard strange noises, and Rinaldo, reassuring the damsel, pressed forward towards the quarter from which they proceeded. He soon perceived a giant standing under a vaulted cavern, with a huge club in his hand, and of an appearance to strike the boldest spirit with dread. By the side of the cavern was chained a griffin, which, together with the giant, was stationed there to guard a wonderful horse, the same which was once Argalia's. This horse was a creature of enchantment, matchless in vigor, speed, and form, which disdained to share the diet of his fellow-steeds,--corn or grass,-- and fed only on air. His name was Rabican.

This marvellous horse, after his master Argalia had been slain by Ferrau, finding himself at liberty, returned to his native cavern, and was here stabled under the protection of the giant and the griffin. As Rinaldo approached, the giant assailed him with his club. Rinaldo defended himself from the giant's blows, and gave him one in return, which, if his skin had not been of the toughest, would have finished the combat. But the giant, though wounded, escaped, and let loose the griffin. This monstrous bird towered in air, and thence pounced down upon Rinaldo, who, watching his opportunity, dealt her a desperate wound. She had, however, strength for another flight, and kept repeating her attacks, which Rinaldo parried as he could, while the damsel stood trembling by, witnessing the contest.

The battle continued, rendered more terrible by the approach of night, when Rinaldo determined upon a desperate expedient to bring it to a conclusion. He fell, as if fainting from his wounds, and, on the close approach of the griffin, dealt her a blow which sheared away one of her wings. The beast, though sinking, griped him fast with her talons, digging through plate and mail; but Rinaldo plied his sword in utter desperation, and at last accomplished her destruction.

Rinaldo then entered the cavern, and found there the wonderful horse, all caparisoned. He was coal-black, except for a star of white on his forehead, and one white foot behind. For speed he was unrivalled, though in strength he yielded to Bayard. Rinaldo mounted upon Rabican, and issued from the cavern.

As he pursued his way he met a fugitive from Agrican's army, who gave such an account of the prowess of a champion who fought on the side of Angelica, that Rinaldo was persuaded this must be Orlando, though at a loss to imagine how he could have been freed from captivity. He determined to repair to the scene of the contest to satisfy his curiosity, and Flordelis, hoping to find Florismart with Orlando, consented to accompany him.

While these things were doing, all was rout and dismay in the Tartarian army, from the death of Agrican. King Galafron, arriving at this juncture with an army for the relief of his capital, Albracca, assaulted the enemy's camp, and carried all before him.

Rinaldo had now reached the scene of action, and was looking on as an unconcerned spectator, when he was espied by Galafron. The king instantly recognized the horse Rabican, which he had given to Argalia when he sent him forth on his ill-omened mission to Paris. Possessed with the idea that the rider of the horse was the murderer of Argalia, Galafron rode at Rinaldo, and smote him with all his force. Rinaldo was not slow to avenge the blow, and it would have gone hard with the king had not his followers instantly closed round him and separated the combatants.

Rinaldo thus found himself, almost without his own choice, enlisted on the side of the enemies of Angelica, which gave him no concern, so completely had his draught from the fountain of hate steeled his mind against her.

For several successive days the struggle continued, without any important results, Rinaldo meeting the bravest knights of Angelica's party, and defeating them one after the other. At length he encountered Orlando, and the two knights bitterly reproached one another for the cause they had each adopted, and engaged in a furious combat. Orlando was mounted upon Bayard, Rinaldo's horse, which Agrican had by chance become possessed of, and Orlando had taken from him as the prize of victory. Bayard would not fight against his master, and Orlando was getting the worse of the encounter, when suddenly Rinaldo, seeing Astolpho, who for love of him had arrayed himself on his side, hard beset by numbers, left Orlando to rush to the defence of his friend. Night prevented the combat from being renewed; but a challenge was given and accepted for their next meeting.

But Angelica, sighing in her heart for Rinaldo, was not willing that he should be again exposed to so terrible a venture. She begged a boon of Orlando, promising she would be his if he would do her bidding. On receiving his promise, she enjoined him to set out without delay to destroy the garden of the enchantress

Falerina, in which many valiant knights had been entrapped, and were imprisoned.

Orlando departed on his horse Brigliadoro, leaving Bayard in disgrace for his bad deportment the day before. Angelica, to conciliate Rinaldo, sent Bayard to him; but Rinaldo remained unmoved by this as by all her former acts of kindness.

When Rinaldo learned Orlando's departure, he yielded to the entreaties of the lady of Florismart, and prepared to fulfil his promise, and rescue her lover from the power of the enchantress. Thus both Rinaldo and Orlando were bound upon the same adventure, but unknown to one another.

The castle of Falerina was protected by a river, which was crossed by a bridge, kept by a ruffian, who challenged all comers to the combat; and such was his strength that he had thus far prevailed in every encounter, as appeared by the arms of various knights which he had taken from them, and piled up as a trophy on the shore. Rinaldo attacked him, but with as bad success as the rest, for the bridge-ward struck him so violent a blow with an iron mace that he fell to the ground. But when the villain approached to strip him of his armor, Rinaldo seized him, and the bridge-ward, being unable to free himself, leapt with Rinaldo into the lake, where they both disappeared.

Orlando, meanwhile, in discharge of his promise to Angelica, pursued his way in quest of the same adventure. In passing through a wood he saw a cavalier armed at all points, and mounted, keeping guard over a lady who was bound to a tree, weeping bitterly. Orlando hastened to her relief, but was exhorted by the knight not to interfere, for she had deserved her fate by her wickedness. In proof of which he made certain charges against her. The lady denied them all, and Orlando believed her, defied the knight, overthrew him, and, releasing the lady, departed with her seated on his horse's croup.

While they rode another damsel approached on a white palfrey, who warned Orlando of impending danger, and informed him that he was near the garden of the enchantress. Orlando was delighted with the intelligence, and entreated her to inform him how he was to gain admittance. She replied that the garden could only be entered at sunrise and gave him such instructions as would enable him to gain admittance. She gave him also a book in which was painted the garden and all that it contained, together with the palace of the false enchantress, where she had secluded herself for the purpose of executing a magic work in which she was engaged. This was the manufacture of a sword capable of cutting even through enchanted substances. The object of this labor, the damsel told him, was the destruction of a knight of the west, by name Orlando, who she had read in the book of Fate was coming to demolish her garden. Having thus instructed him, the damsel departed.

Orlando, finding he must delay his enterprise till the next morning, now lay down and was soon asleep. Seeing this, the base woman whom he had rescued, and who was intent on making her escape to rejoin her paramour, mounted Brigliadoro, and rode off, carrying away Durindana.

When Orlando awoke, his indignation, as may be supposed, was great on the discovery of the theft; but, like a good knight and true, he was not to be diverted from his enterprise. He tore off a huge branch of an elm to supply the place of his sword; and, as the sun rose, took his way towards the gate of the garden, where a dragon was on his watch. This he slew by repeated blows, and entered the garden, the gate of which closed behind him, barring retreat. Looking round him, he saw a fair fountain, which overflowed into a river, and in the centre of the fountain a figure, on whose forehead was written:

"The stream which waters violet and rose,
From hence to the enchanted palace goes."

Following the banks of this flowing stream, and rapt in the delights of the charming garden, Orlando arrived at the palace, and entering it, found the mistress, clad in white, with a crown of gold upon her head, in the act of viewing herself in the surface of the magic sword. Orlando surprised her before she could escape, deprived her of the weapon, and holding her fast by her long hair, which floated behind, threatened her with immediate death if she did not yield up her prisoners, and afford him the means of egress. She, however, was firm of purpose, making no reply, and Orlando, unable to move her either by threats or entreaties, was under the necessity of binding her to a beech, and pursuing his quest as he best might.

He then bethought him of his book, and, consulting it, found that there was an outlet to the south, but that to reach it a lake was to be passed, inhabited by a siren, whose song was so entrancing as to be quite irresistible to whoever heard it; but his book instructed him how to protect himself against this danger. According to its directions, while pursuing his path, he gathered abundance of flowers, which sprung all around, and filled his helmet and his ears with them; then listened if he heard the birds sing. Finding that, though he saw the gaping beak, the swelling throat, and ruffled plumes, he could not catch a note, he felt satisfied with his defence, and advanced toward the lake. It was small but deep, and so clear and tranquil that the eye could penetrate to the bottom.

He had no, sooner arrived upon the banks than the waters were seen to gurgle, and the siren, rising midway out of the pool, sung so sweetly that birds and beasts came trooping to the water-side to listen. Of this Orlando heard nothing, but, feigning to yield to the charm, sank down upon the bank. The siren issued from the water with the intent to accomplish his destruction. Orlando seized her by the hair, and while she sang yet louder (song being her only defence) cut off her head. Then, following the directions of the book, he stained himself all over with her blood.

Guarded by this talisman, he met successively all the monsters set for defence of the enchantress and her garden, and at length found himself again at the spot where he had made captive the enchantress, who still continued fastened to the beech. But the scene was changed. The garden had disappeared, and Falerina, before so haughty, now begged for mercy, assuring him that many lives depended upon the preservation of hers. Orlando promised her life upon her pledging herself for the deliverance of her captives.

This, however, was no easy task. They were not in her possession, but in that of a much more powerful enchantress, Morgana, the Lady of the Lake, the very idea of opposing whom made Falerina turn pale with fear. Representing to him the hazards of the enterprise, she led him towards the dwelling of Morgana. To approach it he had to encounter the same uncourteous bridge-ward who had already defeated and made captive so many knights, and last of all, Rinaldo. He was a churl of the most ferocious character, named Arridano. Morgana had provided him with impenetrable armor, and endowed him in such a manner that his strength always increased in proportion to that of the adversary with whom he was matched. No one had ever yet escaped from the contest, since, such was his power of endurance, he could breathe freely under water. Hence, having grappled with a knight, and sunk with him to the bottom of the lake, he returned, bearing his enemy's arms in triumph to the surface.

While Falerina was repeating her cautions and her counsels Orlando saw Rinaldo's arms erected in form of a trophy, among other spoils made by the villain, and, forgetting their late quarrel, determined upon revenging his friend. Arriving at the pass, the churl presuming to bar the way, a desperate contest ensued, during which Falerina escaped. The churl finding himself overmatched at a contest of arms, resorted to his peculiar art, grappled his antagonist, and plunged with him into the lake. When he reached the bottom Orlando found himself in another world, upon a dry meadow, with the lake overhead, through which shone the beams of our sun, while the water stood on all sides like a crystal wall. Here the battle was renewed, and Orlando had in his magic sword an advantage which none had hitherto possessed. It had been tempered by Falerina so that no spells could avail against it. Thus armed, and countervailing the strength of his adversary by his superior skill and activity, it was not long before he laid him dead upon the field.

Orlando then made all haste to return to the upper air, and, passing through the water, which opened a way before him (such was the power of the magic sword), he soon regained the shore, and found himself in a field as thickly covered with precious stones as the sky is with stars.

Orlando crossed the field, not tempted to delay his enterprise by gathering any of the brilliant gems spread all around him. He next passed into a flowery meadow planted with trees, covered with fruit and flowers, and full of all imaginable delights.

In the middle of this meadow was a fountain, and fast by it lay Morgana asleep; a lady of a lovely aspect, dressed in white and vermilion garments, her forehead well furnished with hair, while she had scarcely any behind.

While Orlando stood in silence contemplating her beauty he heard a voice exclaim: "Seize the fairy by the forelock, if thou hopest fair success." But his attention was arrested by another object, and he heeded not the warning. He saw on a sudden an array of towers, pinnacles and columns, palaces with balconies and windows, extended alleys with trees, in short a scene of architectural magnificence surpassing all he had ever beheld. While he stood gazing in silent astonishment the scene slowly melted away and disappeared. [Footnote: This is a poetical description of a phenomenon which is said to be really exhibited in the strait of Messina, between Sicily and Calabria. It is called Fata Morgana, or Mirage.]

When he had recovered from his amazement he looked again toward the fountain. The fairy had awaked and risen, and was dancing round its border with the lightness of a leaf, timing her footsteps to this song:

"Who in this world would wealth and treasure share,
Honor, delight, and state, and what is best,
Quick let him catch me by the lock of hair
Which flutters from my forehead; and be blest.

"But let him not the proffered good forbear,
Nor till he seize the fleeting blessing rest;
For present loss is sought in vain to-morrow,
And the deluded wretch is left in sorrow."

The fairy, having sung thus, bounded off, and fled from the flowery meadow over a high and inaccessible mountain. Orlando pursued her through thorns and rocks, while the sky gradually became overcast, and at last he was assailed by tempest, lightning, and hail.

While he thus pursued, a pale and meagre woman issued from a cave, armed with a whip, and, treading close upon his steps, scourged him with vigorous strokes. Her name was Repentance, and she told him it was her office to punish those who neglected to obey the voice of Prudence, and seize the fairy Fortune when he might.

Orlando, furious at this chastisement, turned upon his tormentor, but might as well have stricken the wind. Finding it useless to resist, he resumed his chase of the fairy, gained upon her, and made frequent snatches at her white and vermilion garments, which still eluded his grasp. At last, on her turning her head for an instant, he profited by the chance, and seized her by the forelock. In an instant the tempest ceased, the sky became serene, and Repentance retreated to her cave.

Orlando now demanded of Morgana the keys of her prison, and the fairy, feigning a complacent aspect, delivered up a key of silver, bidding him to be cautious in the use of it, since to break the lock would be to involve himself and all in inevitable destruction; a caution which gave the Count room for long meditation, and led him to consider

How few amid the suitors who importune
The dame, know how to turn the keys of Fortune.

Keeping the fairy still fast by the forelock, Orlando proceeded toward the prison, turned the key, without occasioning the mischiefs apprehended, and delivered the prisoners.

Among these were Florismart, Rinaldo, and many others of the bravest knights of France. Morgana had disappeared, and the knights, under the guidance of Orlando, retraced the path by which he had come. They soon reached the field of treasure. Rinaldo, finding himself amidst this mass of wealth, remembered his needy garrison of Montalban, and could not resist the temptation of seizing part of the booty. In particular a golden chain, studded with diamonds, was too much for his self-denial, and he took it and was bearing it off, notwithstanding the remonstrances of Orlando, when a violent wind caught him and whirled him back, as he approached the gate. This happened a second and a third time, and Rinaldo at length yielded to necessity, rather than to the entreaties of his friends, and cast away his prize.

They soon reached the bridge and passed over without hindrance to the other side, where they found the trophy decorated with their arms. Here each knight resumed his own, and all, except the paladins and their friends, separated as their inclinations or duty prompted. Dudon, the Dane, one of the rescued knights, informed the cousins that he had been made prisoner by Morgana while in the discharge of an embassy to them from Charlemagne, who called upon them to return to the defence of Christendom. Orlando was too much fascinated by Angelica to obey this summons, and, followed by the faithful Florismart, who would not leave him, returned towards Albracca. Rinaldo, Dudon, Iroldo, Prasildo, and the others took their way toward the west.

THE INVASION OF FRANCE

Agramant, King of Africa, convoked the kings, his vassals, to deliberate in council. He reminded them of the injuries he had sustained from France, that his father had fallen in battle with Charlemagne, and that his early years had hitherto not allowed him to wipe out the stain of former defeats. He now proposed to them to carry war into France.

Sobrino, his wisest councillor, opposed the project, representing the rashness of it; but Rodomont, the young and fiery king of Algiers, denounced Sobrino's counsel as base and cowardly, declaring himself impatient for the enterprise. The king of the Garamantes, venerable for his age and renowned for his prophetic lore, interposed, and assured the King that such an attempt would be sure to fail, unless he could first get on his side a youth marked out by destiny as the fitting compeer of the most puissant knights of France, the young Rogero, descended in direct line from Hector of Troy. This prince was now a dweller upon the mountain Carena, where Atlantes, his foster-father, a powerful magician, kept him in retirement, having discovered by his art that his pupil would be lost to him if allowed to mingle with the world. To break the spells of Atlantes, and draw Rogero from his retirement, one only means was to be found. It was a ring possessed by Angelica, Princess of Cathay, which was a talisman against all enchantments. If this ring could be procured all would go well; without it the enterprise was desperate.

Rodomont treated this declaration of the old prophet with scorn, and it would probably have been held of little weight by the council, had not the aged king, oppressed by the weight of years, expired in the very act of reaffirming his prediction. This made so deep an impression on the council that it was unanimously resolved to postpone the war until an effort should be made to win Rogero to the camp.

King Agramant thereupon proclaimed that the sovereignty of a kingdom should be the reward of whoever should succeed in obtaining the ring of Angelica. Brunello the dwarf, the subtlest thief in all Africa, undertook to procure it.

In prosecution of this design, he made the best of his way to Angelica's kingdom, and arrived beneath the walls of Albracca while the besieging army was encamped before the fortress. While the attention of the garrison was absorbed by the battle that raged below he scaled the walls, approached the Princess unnoticed, slipped the ring from her finger, and escaped unobserved. He hastened to the seaside, and, finding a vessel ready to sail, embarked, and arrived at Biserta, in Africa. Here he found Agramant impatient for the talisman which was to foil the enchantments of Atlantes and to put Rogero into his hands. The dwarf, kneeling before the king, presented him with the ring, and Agramant, delighted at the success of his mission, crowned him in recompense King of Tingitana.

All were now anxious to go in quest of Rogero. The cavalcade accordingly departed, and in due time arrived at the mountain of Carena.

At the bottom of this was a fruitful and well-wooded plain, watered by a large river, and from this plain was descried a beautiful garden on the mountain-top, which contained the mansion of Atlantes; but the ring, which discovered what was before invisible, could not, though it revealed this paradise, enable Agramant or his followers to enter it. So steep and smooth was the rock by nature, that even Brunello failed in every attempt to scale it. He did not, for this, despair of accomplishing the object; but, having obtained Agramant's consent, caused the assembled courtiers and knights to celebrate a tournament upon the plain below. This was done with the view of seducing Rogero from his fastness, and the stratagem was attended with success.

Rogero joined the tourney, and was presented by Agramant with a splendid horse, Frontino, and a magnificent sword. Having learned from Agramant his intended invasion of France, he gladly consented to join the expedition.

Rodomont, meanwhile, was too impatient to wait for Agramant's arrangements, and embarked with all the forces he could raise, made good his landing on the coast of France, and routed the Christians in several encounters. Previously to this, however, Gano, or Ganelon (as he is sometimes called), the traitor, enemy of Orlando and the other nephews of Charlemagne, had entered into a traitorous correspondence with Marsilius, the Saracen king of Spain, whom he invited into France. Marsilius, thus encouraged, led an army across the frontiers, and joined Rodomont. This was the situation of things when Rinaldo and the other knights who had obeyed the summons of Dudon set forward on their return to France.

When they arrived at Buda in Hungary they found the king of that country about despatching his son, Ottachiero, with an army to the succor of Charlemagne. Delighted with the arrival of Rinaldo, he placed his son and troops under his command. In due time the army arrived on the frontiers of France, and, united with the troops of Desiderius, king of Lombardy, poured down into Provence. The confederate armies had not marched many days through this gay tract before they heard a crash of drums and trumpets behind the hills, which spoke the conflict between the paynims, led by Rodomont, and the Christian forces. Rinaldo, witnessing from a mountain the prowess of Rodomont, left his troops in charge of his friends, and galloped towards him with his lance in rest. The impulse was irresistible, and Rodomont was unhorsed. But Rinaldo, unwilling to avail himself of his advantage, galloped back to the hill, and having secured Bayard among the baggage, returned to finish the combat on foot.

During this interval the battle had become general, the Hungarians were routed, and Rinaldo, on his return, had the mortification to find that Ottachiero was wounded, and Dudon taken prisoner. While he sought Rodomont in order to renew the combat a new sound of drums and trumpets was heard, and Charlemagne, with the main body of his army, was descried advancing in battle array.

Rodomont, seeing this, mounted the horse of Dudon, left Rinaldo, who was on foot, and galloped off to encounter this new enemy.

Agramant, accompanied by Rogero, had by this time made good his landing, and joined Rodomont with all his forces. Rogero eagerly embraced this first opportunity of distinguishing himself, and spread terror wherever he went, encountering in turn and overthrowing many of the bravest knights of France. At length he found himself opposite to Rinaldo, who, being interrupted, as we have said, in his combat with Rodomont, and unable to follow him, being on foot, was shouting to his late foe to return and finish their combat. Rogero also was on foot, and seeing the Christian knight so eager for a contest, proffered himself to supply the place of his late antagonist. Rinaldo saw at a glance that the Moorish prince was a champion worthy of his arm, and gladly accepted the defiance. The combat was stoutly maintained for a time; but now fortune declared decisively in favor of the infidel army, and Charlemagne's forces gave way at all points in irreparable confusion. The two combatants were separated by the crowd of fugitives and pursuers, and Rinaldo hastened to recover possession of his horse. But Bayard, in the confusion, had got loose, and Rinaldo followed him into a thick wood, thus becoming effectually separated from Rogero.

Rogero, also seeking his horse in the medley, came where two warriors were engaged in mortal combat. Though he knew not who they were, he could distinguish that one was a paynim and the other a Christian; and moved by the spirit of courtesy he approached them and exclaimed, "Let him of the two who worships Christ pause, and hear what I have to say. The army of Charles is routed and in flight, so that if he wishes to follow his leader he has no time for delay." The Christian knight, who was none other than Bradamante, a female warrior, in prowess equal to the best of knights, was thunderstruck with the tidings, and would gladly leave the contest undecided, and retire from the field; but Rodomont, her antagonist, would by no means consent. Rogero, indignant at his discourtesy, insisted upon her departure, while he took up her quarrel with Rodomont.

The combat, obstinately maintained on both sides, was interrupted by the return of Bradamante. Finding herself unable to overtake the fugitives, and reluctant to leave to another the burden and risk of a contest which belonged to herself, she had returned to reclaim the combat. She arrived, however, when her champion had dealt his enemy such a blow as obliged him to drop both his sword and bridle. Rogero, disdaining to profit by his adversary's defenceless situation, sat apart upon his horse, while that of Rodomont bore his rider, stunned and stupefied, about the field.

Bradamante approached Rogero, conceiving a yet higher opinion of his valor on beholding such an instance of forbearance. She addressed him, excusing herself for leaving him exposed to an enemy from his interference in her cause; pleading her duty to her sovereign as the motive. While she spoke Rodomont, recovered from his confusion, rode up to them. His bearing was, however, changed; and he disclaimed all thoughts of further contest with one who, he said, "had already conquered him by his courtesy." So saying, he quitted his antagonist, picked up his sword, and spurred out of sight.

Bradamante was now again desirous of retiring from the field, and Rogero insisted on accompanying her, though yet unaware of her sex.

As they pursued their way, she inquired the name and quality of her new associate; and Rogero informed her of his nation and family. He told her that Astyanax, the son of Hector of Troy, established the kingdom of Messina in Sicily. From him were derived two branches, which gave origin to two families of renown. From one sprang the royal race of Pepin and Charlemagne, and from the other, that of Reggio, in Italy. "From that of Reggio am I derived," he continued. "My mother, driven from her home by the chance of war, died in giving me life, and I was taken in charge by a sage enchanter, who trained me to feats of arms amidst the dangers of the desert and the chase."

Having thus ended his tale, Rogero entreated a similar return of courtesy from his companion, who replied, without disguise, that she was of the race of Clermont, and sister to Rinaldo, whose fame was perhaps known to him. Rogero, much moved by this intelligence, entreated her to take off her helmet, and at the discovery of her face remained transported with delight.

While absorbed in this contemplation, an unexpected danger assailed them. A party which was placed in a wood, in order to intercept the retreating Christians, broke from its ambush upon the pair, and Bradamante, who was uncasqued, was wounded in the head. Rogero was in a fury at this attack; and Bradamante, replacing her helmet, joined him in taking speedy vengeance on their enemies. They cleared the field of them, but became separated in the pursuit, and Rogero, quitting the chase, wandered by hill and vale in search of her whom he had no sooner found than lost.

While pursuing this quest he fell in with two knights, whom he joined, and engaged them to assist him in the search of his companion, describing her arms, but concealing, from a certain feeling of jealousy, her quality and sex.

It was evening when they joined company, and having ridden together through the night the morning was beginning to break, when one of the strangers, fixing his eyes upon Rogero's shield, demanded of him by what right he bore the Trojan arms. Rogero declared his origin and race, and then, in his turn, interrogated the inquirer as to his pretensions to the cognizance of Hector, which he bore. The stranger replied, "My name is Mandricardo, son of Agrican, the Tartar king, whom Orlando treacherously slew. I say treacherously, for in fair fight he could not have done it. It is in search of him that I have come to France, to take vengeance for my father, and to wrest from him Durindana, that famous sword, which belongs to me, and not to him." When the knights demanded to know by what right he claimed Durindana, Mandricardo thus related his history:

"I had been, before the death of my father, a wild and reckless youth. That event awakened my energies, and drove me forth to seek for vengeance. Determined to owe success to nothing but my own exertions, I departed without attendants or horse or arms. Travelling thus alone, and on foot, I espied one day a pavilion, pitched near a fountain, and entered it, intent on adventure. I found therein a damsel of gracious aspect, who replied to my inquiries that the fountain was the work of a fairy, whose castle stood beyond a neighboring hill, where she kept watch over a treasure which many knights had tried to win, but fruitlessly, having lost their life or liberty in the attempt. This treasure was the armor of Hector, prince of Troy, whom Achilles treacherously slew. Nothing was wanting but his sword, Durindana, and this had fallen into the possession of a queen named Penthesilea, from whom it passed through her descendants to Almontes, whom Orlando slew, and thus became possessed of the sword. The rest of Hector's arms were saved and carried off by Aeneas, from whom this fairy received them in recompense of service rendered. 'If you have the courage to attempt their acquisition,' said the damsel, 'I will be your guide.'"

Mandricardo went on to say that he eagerly embraced the proposal, and being provided with horse and armor by the damsel, set forth on his enterprise, the lady accompanying him.

As they rode she explained the dangers of the quest. The armor was defended by a champion, one of the numerous unsuccessful adventurers for the prize, all of whom had been made prisoners by the fairy, and compelled to take their turn, day by day, in defending the arms against all comers. Thus speaking they arrived at the castle, which was of alabaster, overlaid with gold. Before it, on a lawn, sat an armed knight on horseback, who was none other than Gradasso, king of Sericane, who, in his return home from his unsuccessful inroad into France, had fallen into the power of the fairy, and was held to do her bidding. Mandricardo, upon seeing him, dropt his visor, and laid his lance in rest. The champion of the castle was equally ready, and each spurred towards his opponent. They met one another with equal force, splintered their spears, and, returning to the charge, encountered with their swords. The contest was long and doubtful, when Mandricardo, determined to bring it to an end, threw his arms about Gradasso, grappled with him, and both fell to the ground. Mandricardo, however, fell uppermost, and, preserving his advantage, compelled Gradasso to yield himself conquered. The damsel now interfered, congratulating the victor, and consoling the vanquished as well as she might.

Mandricardo and the damsel proceeded to the gate of the castle, which they found undefended. As they entered they beheld a shield suspended from a pilaster of gold. The device was a white eagle on an azure field, in memory of the bird of Jove, which bore away Ganymede, the flower of the Phrygian race. Beneath was engraved the following couplet:

"Let none with hand profane my buckler wrong
Unless he be himself as Hector strong."

The damsel, alighting from her palfrey, made obeisance to the arms, bending herself to the ground. The Tartar king bowed his head with equal reverence; then advancing towards the shield, touched it with his sword. Thereupon an earthquake shook the ground, and the way by which he had entered closed. Another and an opposite gate opened, and displayed a field bristling with stalks and grain of gold. The damsel, upon this, told him that he had no means of retreat but by cutting down the harvest which was before him, and by uprooting a tree which grew in the middle of the field. Mandricardo, without replying, began to mow the harvest with his sword, but had scarce smitten thrice when he perceived that every stalk that fell was instantly transformed into some poisonous or ravenous animal, which prepared to assail him. Instructed by the damsel, he snatched up a stone and cast it among the pack. A strange wonder followed; for no sooner had the stone fallen among the beasts, than they turned their rage against one another, and rent each other to pieces. Mandricardo did not stop to marvel at the miracle, but proceeded to fulfil his task, and uproot the tree. He clasped it round the trunk, and made vigorous efforts to tear it up by the roots. At each effort fell a shower of leaves, that were instantly changed into birds of prey, which attacked the knight, flapping their wings in his face, with horrid screeching. But undismayed by this new annoyance, he continued to tug at the trunk till it yielded to his efforts. A burst of wind and thunder followed, and the hawks and vultures flew screaming away.

But these only gave place to a new foe; for from the hole made by tearing up the tree issued a furious serpent, and, darting at Mandricardo, wound herself about his limbs with a strain that almost crushed him. Fortune, however, again stood his friend, for, writhing under the folds of the monster, he fell backwards into the hole, and his enemy was crushed beneath his weight.

Mandricardo, when he was somewhat recovered, and assured himself of the destruction of the serpent, began to contemplate the place into which he had fallen, and saw that he was in a vault, incrusted with costly metals, and illuminated by a live coal. In the middle was a sort of ivory bier, and upon this was extended what appeared to be a knight in armor, but was in truth an empty trophy, composed of the rich and precious arms once Hector's, to which nothing was wanting but the sword. While Mandricardo stood contemplating the prize a door opened behind him, and a bevy of fair damsels entered, dancing, who, taking up the armor piece by piece, led him away to the place where the shield was suspended; where he found the fairy of the castle seated in state. By her he was invested with the arms he had won, first pledging his solemn oath to wear no other blade but Durindana, which he was to wrest from Orlando, and thus complete the conquest of Hector's arms.

THE INVASION OF FRANCE (Continued)

Mandricardo, having completed his story, now turned to Rogero, and proposed that arms should decide which of the two was most worthy to bear the symbol of the Trojan knight.

Rogero felt no other objection to this proposal than the scruple which arose on observing that his antagonist was without a sword. Mandricardo insisted that this need be no impediment, since his oath prevented him from using a sword until he should have achieved the conquest of Durindana.

This was no sooner said than a new antagonist started up in Gradasso, who now accompanied Mandricardo. Gradasso vindicated his prior right to Durindana, to obtain which he had embarked (as was related in the beginning) in that bold inroad upon France. A quarrel was thus kindled between the kings of Tartary and Sericane. While the dispute was raging a knight arrived upon the ground, accompanied by a damsel, to whom Rogero related the cause of the strife. The knight was Florismart, and his companion Flordelis. Florismart succeeded in bringing the two champions to accord, by informing them that he could bring them to the presence of Orlando, the master of Durindana.

Gradasso and Mandricardo readily made truce, in order to accompany Florismart, nor would Rogero be left behind.

As they proceeded on their quest they were met by a dwarf, who entreated their assistance in behalf of his lady, who had been carried off by an enchanter, mounted on a winged horse. However unwilling to leave the question of the sword undecided, it was not possible for the knights to resist this appeal. Two of their number, Gradasso and Rogero, therefore accompanied the dwarf. Mandricardo persisted in his search for Orlando, and Florismart, with Flordelis, pursued their way to the camp of Charlemagne.

Atlantes, the enchanter, who had brought up Rogero, and cherished for him the warmest affection, knew by his art that his pupil was destined to be severed from him, and converted to the Christian faith through the influence of Bradamante, that royal maiden with whom chance had brought him acquainted. Thinking to thwart the will of Heaven in this respect, he now put forth all his arts to entrap Rogero into his power. By the aid of his subservient demons he reared a castle on an inaccessible height, in the Pyrenean mountains, and to make it a pleasant abode to his pupil, contrived to entrap and convey thither knights and damsels many a one, whom chance had brought into the vicinity of his castle. Here, in a sort of sensual paradise, they were but too willing to forget glory and duty, and to pass their time in indolent enjoyment.

It was by the enchanter that the dwarf had now been sent to tempt the knights into his power.

But we must now return to Rinaldo, whom we left interrupted in his combat with Rodomont. In search of his late antagonist and intent on bringing their combat to a decision he entered the forest of Arden, whither he suspected Rodomont had gone. While engaged on this quest he was surprised by the vision of a beautiful child dancing naked, with three damsels as beautiful as himself. While he was lost in admiration at the sight the child approached him, and, throwing at him handfuls of roses and lilies, struck him from his horse. He was no sooner down than he was seized by the dancers, by whom he was dragged about and scourged with flowers till he fell into a swoon. When he began to revive one of the group approached him, and told him that his punishment was the consequence of his rebellion against that power before whom all things bend; that there was but one remedy to heal the wounds that had been inflicted, and that was to drink of the waters of Love. Then they left him.

Rinaldo, sore and faint, dragged himself toward a fountain which flowed near by, and, being parched with thirst, drank greedily and almost unconsciously of the water, which was sweet to the taste, but bitter to the heart. After repeated draughts he recovered his strength and recollection, and found himself in the same place where Angelica had formerly awakened him with a rain of flowers, and whence he had fled in contempt of her courtesy.

This remembrance of the scene was followed by the recognition of his crime; and, repenting bitterly his ingratitude, he leaped upon Bayard, with the intention of hastening to Angelica's country, and soliciting his pardon at her feet.

Let us now retrace our steps, and revert to the time when the paladins having learned from Dudon the summons of Charlemagne to return to France to repel the invaders, had all obeyed the command with the exception of Orlando, whose passion for Angelica still held him in attendance on her. Orlando, arriving before Albracca, found it closely beleaguered. He, however, made his way into the citadel, and related his adventures to Angelica, from the time of his departure up to his separation from Rinaldo and the rest, when they departed to the assistance of Charlemagne. Angelica, in return, described the distresses of the garrison, and the force of the besiegers; and in conclusion prayed Orlando to favor her escape from the pressing danger, and escort her into France. Orlando, who did not suspect that love for Rinaldo was her secret motive, joyfully agreed to the proposal, and the sally was resolved upon.

Leaving lights burning in the fortress, they departed at nightfall, and passed in safety through the enemy's camp. After encountering numerous adventures they reached the sea-side, and embarked on board a pinnace for France. The vessel arrived safely, and the travellers, disembarking in Provence, pursued their way by land. One day, heated and weary, they sought shelter from the sun in the forest of Arden, and chance directed Angelica to the fountain of Disdain, of whose waters she eagerly drank.

Issuing thence, the Count and damsel encountered a stranger-knight. It was no other than Rinaldo, who was just on the point of setting off on a pilgrimage in search of Angelica, to implore her pardon for his insensibility, and urge his new found passion. Surprise and delight at first deprived him of utterance, but soon recovering himself, he joyfully saluted her, claiming her as his, and exhorting her to put herself under his protection. His presumption was repelled by Angelica with disdain, and Orlando, enraged at the invasion of his rights, challenged him to decide their claims by arms.

Terrified at the combat which ensued, Angelica fled amain through the forest, and came out upon a plain covered with tents. This was the camp of Charlemagne, who led the army of reserve destined to support the troops which had advanced to oppose Marsilius. Charles having heard the damsel's tale, with difficulty separated the two cousins, and then consigned Angelica, as the cause of quarrel, to the care of Namo, Duke of Bavaria, promising that she should be his who should best deserve her in the impending battle.

But these plans and hopes were frustrated. The Christian army, beaten at all points, fled from the Saracens; and Angelica, indifferent to both her lovers, mounted a swift palfrey and plunged into the forest, rejoicing, in spite of her terror, at having regained her liberty. She stopped at last in a tufted grove, where a gentle zephyr blew, and whose young trees were watered by two clear runnels, which came and mingled their waters, making a pleasing murmur. Believing herself far from Rinaldo, and overcome by fatigue and the summer heat, she saw with delight a bank covered with flowers so thick that they almost hid the green turf, inviting her to alight and rest. She dismounted from her palfrey, and turned him loose to recruit his strength with the tender grass which bordered the streamlets. Then, in a sheltered nook tapestried with moss and fenced in with roses and hawthorn-flowers, she yielded herself to grateful repose.

She had not slept long when she was awakened by the noise made by the approach of a horse. Starting up, she saw an armed knight who had arrived at the bank of the stream. Not knowing whether he was to be feared or not, her heart beat with anxiety. She pressed aside the leaves to allow her to see who it was, but scarce dared to breathe for fear of betraying herself. Soon the knight threw himself on the flowery bank, and leaning his head on his hand fell into a profound reverie. Then arousing himself from his silence he began to pour forth complaints, mingled with deep sighs. Rivers of tears flowed down his cheeks, and his breast seemed to labor with a hidden flame. "Ah, vain regrets!" he exclaimed; "cruel fortune! others triumph, while I endure hopeless misery! Better a thousand times to lose life, than wear a chain so disgraceful and so oppressive!"

Angelica by this time had recognized the stranger, and perceived that it was Sacripant, king of Circassia, one of the worthiest of her suitors. This prince had followed Angelica from his country, at the very gates of the day, to France, where he heard with dismay that she was under the guardianship of the Paladin Orlando, and that the Emperor had announced his decree to award her as the prize of valor to that one of his nephews who should best deserve her.

As Sacripant continued to lament, Angelica, who had always opposed the hardness of marble to his sighs, thought with herself that nothing forbade her employing his good offices in this unhappy crisis. Though firmly resolved never to accept him as a spouse, she yet felt the necessity of giving him a gleam of hope in reward for the service she required of him. All at once, like Diana, she stepped forth from the arbor. "May the gods preserve thee," she said, "and put far from thee all hard thoughts of me!" Then she told him all that had befallen her since she parted with him at her father's court, and how she had availed herself of Orlando's protection to escape from the beleaguered city. At that moment the noise of horse and armor was heard as of one approaching; and Sacripant, furious at the interruption, resumed his helmet, mounted his horse, and placed his lance in rest. He saw a knight advancing, with scarf and plume of snowy whiteness. Sacripant regarded him with angry eyes, and, while he was yet some distance off, defied him to the combat. The other, not moved by his angry tone to make reply, put himself on his defence. Their horses, struck at the same moment with the spur, rushed upon one another with the impetuosity of a tempest. Their shields were pierced each with the other's lance, and only the temper of their breastplates saved their lives. Both the horses recoiled with the violence of the shock; but the unknown knight's recovered itself at the touch of the spur; the Saracen king's fell dead, and bore down his master with him. The white knight, seeing his enemy in this condition, cared not to renew the combat, but, thinking he had done enough for glory, pursued his way through the forest, and was a mile off before Sacripant had got free from his horse.

As a ploughman, stunned by a thunder-clap which has stricken dead the oxen at his plough, stands motionless, sadly contemplating his loss, so Sacripant stood confounded and overwhelmed with mortification at having Angelica a witness of his defeat. He groaned, he sighed, less from the pain of his bruises than for the shame of being reduced to such a state before her. The princess took pity on him, and consoled him as well as she could. "Banish your regrets, my lord," she said, "this accident has happened solely in consequence of the feebleness of your horse, which had more need of rest and food than of such an encounter as this. Nor can your adversary gain any credit by it, since he has hurried away, not venturing a second trial." While she thus consoled Sacripant they perceived a person approach, who seemed a courier, with bag and horn. As soon as he came up, he accosted Sacripant, and inquired if he had seen a knight pass that way, bearing a white shield and with a white plume to his helmet. "I have, indeed, seen too much of him," said Sacripant, "it is he who has brought me to the ground; but at least I hope to learn from you who that knight is." "That I can easily inform you," said the man; "know then that, if you have been overthrown, you owe your fate to the high prowess of a lady as beautiful as she is brave. It is the fair and illustrious Bradamante who has won from you the honors of victory."

At these words the courier rode on his way, leaving Sacripant more confounded and mortified than ever. In silence he mounted the horse of Angelica, taking the lady behind him on the croup, and rode away in search of a more secure asylum. Hardly had they ridden two miles when a new sound was heard in the forest, and they perceived a gallant and powerful horse, which, leaping the ravines and dashing aside the branches that opposed his passage, appeared before them, accoutred with a rich harness adorned with gold.

"If I may believe my eyes, which penetrate with difficulty the underwood," said Angelica, "that horse that dashes so stoutly through the bushes is Bayard, and I marvel how he seems to know the need we have of him, mounted as we are both on one feeble animal." Sacripant, dismounting from the palfrey, approached the fiery courser, and attempted to seize his bridle, but the disdainful animal, turning from him, launched at him a volley of kicks enough to have shattered a wall of marble. Bayard then approached Angelica with an air as gentle and loving as a faithful dog could his master after a long separation. For he remembered how she had caressed him, and even fed him, in Albracca. She took his bridle in her left hand, while with her right she patted his neck. The beautiful animal, gifted with wonderful intelligence, seemed to submit entirely. Sacripant, seizing the moment to vault upon him, controlled his curvetings, and Angelica, quitting the croup of the palfrey, regained her seat.

But, turning his eyes toward a place where was heard a noise of arms, Sacripant beheld Rinaldo. That hero now loves Angelica more than his life, and she flies him as the timid crane the falcon.

The fountain of which Angelica had drunk produced such an effect on the beautiful queen that, with distressed countenance and trembling voice, she conjured Sacripant not to wait the approach of Rinaldo, but to join her in flight.

"Am I, then," said Sacripant, "of so little esteem with you that you doubt my power to defend you? Do you forget the battle of Albracca, and how, in your defence, I fought single-handed against Agrican and all his knights?"

Angelica made no reply, uncertain what to do; but already Rinaldo was too near to be escaped. He advanced menacingly to the Circassian king, for he recognized his horse.

"Vile thief," he cried, "dismount from that horse, and prevent the punishment that is your due for daring to rob me of my property. Leave, also, the princess in my hands; for it would indeed be a sin to suffer so charming a lady and so gallant a charger to remain in such keeping."

The king of Circassia, furious at being thus insulted, cried out, "Thou liest, villain, in giving me the name of thief, which better belongs to thyself than to me. It is true, the beauty of this lady and the perfection of this horse are unequalled; come on, then, and let us try which of us is most worthy to possess them."

At these words the king of Circassia and Rinaldo attacked one another with all their force, one fighting on foot, the other on horseback. You need not, however, suppose that the Saracen king found any advantage in this; for a young page, unused to horsemanship, could not have failed more completely to manage Bayard than did this accomplished knight. The faithful animal loved his master too well to injure him, and refused his aid as well as his obedience to the hand of Sacripant, who could strike but ineffectual blows, the horse backing when he wished him to go forward, and dropping his head and arching his back, throwing out with his legs, so as almost to shake the knight out of the saddle. Sacripant, seeing that he could not manage him, watched his opportunity, rose on his saddle, and leapt lightly to the earth; then, relieved from the embarrassment of the horse, renewed the combat on more equal terms. Their skill to thrust and parry were equal; one rises, the other stoops; with one foot set firm they turn and wind, to lay on strokes or to dodge them. At last Rinaldo, throwing himself on the Circassian, dealt him a blow so terrible that Fusberta, his good sword, cut in two the buckler of Sacripant, although it was made of bone, and covered with a thick plate of steel well tempered. The arm of the Saracen was deprived of its defence, and almost palsied with the stroke. Angelica, perceiving how victory was likely to incline, and shuddering at the thought of becoming the prize of Rinaldo, hesitated no longer. Turning her horse's head, she fled with the utmost speed; and, in spite of the round pebbles which covered a steep descent, she plunged into a deep valley, trembling with the fear that Rinaldo was in pursuit. At the bottom of this valley she encountered an aged hermit, whose white beard flowed to his middle, and whose venerable appearance seemed to assure his piety.

This hermit, who appeared shrunk by age and fasting, travelled slowly, mounted upon a wretched ass. The princess, overcome with fear, conjured him to save her life; and to conduct her to some port of the sea, whence she might embark and quit France, never more to hear the odious name of Rinaldo.

The old hermit was something of a wizard. He comforted Angelica, and promised to protect her from all peril. Then he opened his scrip, and took from thence a book, and had read but a single page when a goblin, obedient to his incantations, appeared, under the form of a laboring man, and demanded his orders. He received them, transported himself to the place where the knights still maintained their conflict, and boldly stepped between the two.

"Tell me, I pray you," he said, "what benefit will accrue to him who shall get the better in this contest? The object you are contending for is already disposed of; for the Paladin Orlando, without effort and without opposition, is now carrying away the princess Angelica to Paris. You had better pursue them promptly; for if they reach Paris you will never see her again."

At these words you might have seen those rival warriors confounded, stupefied, silently agreeing that they were affording their rival a fair opportunity to triumph over them. Rinaldo, approaching Bayard, breathes a sigh of shame and rage, and swears a terrible oath that, if he overtakes Orlando, he will tear his heart out. Then mounting Bayard and pressing his flanks with his spurs, he leaves the king of Circassia on foot in the forest.

Let it not appear strange that Rinaldo found Bayard obedient at last, after having so long prevented any one from even touching his bridle; for that fine animal had an intelligence almost human; he had fled from his master only to draw him on the track of Angelica, and enable him to recover her. He saw when the princess fled from the battle, and Rinaldo being then engaged in a fight on foot, Bayard found himself free to follow the traces of Angelica. Thus he had drawn his master after him, not permitting him to approach, and had brought him to the sight of the princess. But Bayard now, deceived like his master with the false intelligence of the goblin, submits to be mounted and to serve his master as usual, and Rinaldo, animated with rage, makes him fly toward Paris, more slowly than his wishes, though the speed of Bayard outstripped the winds. Full of impatience to encounter Orlando, he gave but a few hours that night to sleep. Early the next day he saw before him the great city, under the walls of which the Emperor Charles had collected the scattered remains of his army. Foreseeing that he would soon be attacked on all sides, the Emperor had caused the ancient fortifications to be repaired, and new ones to be built, surrounded by wide and deep ditches. The desire to hold the field against the enemy made him seize every means of procuring new allies. He hoped to receive from England aid sufficient to enable him to form a new camp, and as soon as Rinaldo rejoined him he selected him to go as his ambassador into England, to plead for auxiliaries. Rinaldo was far from pleased with his commission, but he obeyed the Emperor's commands, without giving himself time to devote a single day to the object nearest his heart. He hastened to Calais, and lost not a moment in embarking for England, ardently desiring a hasty despatch of his commission, and a speedy return to France.

BRADAMANTE AND ROGERO

Bradamante, the knight of the white plume and shield, whose sudden appearance and encounter with Sacripant we have already told, was in quest of Rogero, from whom chance had separated her, almost at the beginning of their acquaintance. After her encounter with Sacripant Bradamante pursued her way through the forest, in hopes of rejoining Rogero, and arrived at last on the brink of a fair fountain.

This fountain flowed through a broad meadow. Ancient trees overshadowed it, and travellers, attracted by the sweet murmur of its waters, stopped there to cool themselves. Bradamante, casting her eyes on all sides to enjoy the beauties of the spot, perceived, under the shade of a tree, a knight reclining, who seemed to be oppressed with the deepest grief.

Bradamante accosted him, and asked to be informed of the cause of his distress. "Alas! my lord," said he, "I lament a young and charming friend, my affianced wife, who has been torn from me by a villain,--let me rather call him a demon,--who, on a winged horse, descended from the air, seized her, and bore her screaming to his den. I have pursued them over rocks and through ravines till my horse is no longer able to bear me, and I now wait only for death." He added that already a vain attempt on his behalf had been made by two knights, whom chance had brought to the spot. Their names were Gradasso, king of Sericane, and Rogero, the Moor. Both had been overcome by the wiles of the enchanter, and were added to the number of the captives, whom he held in an impregnable castle, situated on the height of the mountain. At the mention of Rogero's name Bradamante started with delight, which was soon changed to an opposite sentiment when she heard that her lover was a prisoner in the toils of the enchanter. "Sir Knight," she said, "do not surrender yourself to despair; this day may be more happy for you than you think, if you will only lead me to the castle which enfolds her whom you deplore."

The knight responded, "After having lost all that made life dear to me I have no motive to avoid the dangers of the enterprise, and I will do as you request; but I forewarn you of the perils you will have to encounter. If you fall impute it not to me."

Having thus spoken, they took their way to the castle, but were overtaken by a messenger from the camp, who had been sent in quest of Bradamante to summon her back to the army, where her presence was needed to reassure her disheartened forces, and withstand the advance of the Moors.

The mournful knight, whose name was Pinabel, thus became aware that Bradamante was a scion of the house of Clermont, between which and his own of Mayence there existed an ancient feud. From this moment the traitor sought only how he might be rid of the company of Bradamante, from whom he feared no good would come to him, but rather mortal injury, if his name and lineage became known to her. For he judged her by his own base model, and, knowing his ill deserts, he feared to receive his due.

Bradamante, in spite of the summons to return to the army, could not resolve to leave her lover in captivity, and determined first to finish the adventure on which she was engaged. Pinabel leading the way, they at length arrived at a wood, in the centre of which rose a steep, rocky mountain. Pinabel, who now thought of nothing else but how he might escape from Bradamante, proposed to ascend the mountain to extend his view, in order to discover a shelter for the night, if any there might be within sight. Under this pretence he left Bradamante, and advanced up the side of the mountain till he came to a cleft in the rock, down which he looked, and perceived that it widened below into a spacious cavern. Meanwhile Bradamante, fearful of losing her guide, had followed close on his footsteps, and rejoined him at the mouth of the cavern. Then the traitor, seeing the impossibility of escaping her, conceived another design. He told her that before her approach he had seen in the cavern a young and beautiful damsel, whose rich dress announced her high birth, who with tears and lamentations implored assistance; that before he could descend to relieve her a ruffian had seized her, and hurried her away into the recesses of the cavern.

Bradamante, full of truth and courage, readily believed this lie of the Mayencian traitor. Eager to succor the damsel, she looked round for the means of facilitating the descent, and seeing a large elm with spreading branches she lopped off with her sword one of the largest, and thrust it into the opening. She told Pinabel to hold fast to the larger end, while, grasping the branches with her hands, she let herself down into the cavern.

The traitor smiled at seeing her thus suspended, and, asking her in mockery, "Are you a good leaper?" he let go the branch with perfidious glee, and saw Bradamante precipitated to the bottom of the cave. "I wish your whole race were there with you," he muttered, "that you might all perish together."

But Pinabel's atrocious design was not accomplished. The twigs and foliage of the branch broke its descent, and Bradamante, not seriously injured, though stunned with her fall, was reserved for other adventures.

As soon as she recovered from the shock Bradamante cast her eyes around and perceived a door, through which she passed into a second cavern, larger and loftier than the first. It had the appearance of a subterranean temple. Columns of the purest alabaster adorned it, and supported the roof; a simple altar rose in the middle; a lamp, whose radiance was reflected by the alabaster walls, cast a mild light around.

Bradamante, inspired by a sense of religious awe, approached the altar, and, falling on her knees, poured forth her prayers and thanks to the Preserver of her life, invoking the protection of his power. At that moment a small door opened, and a female issued from it with naked feet, and flowing robe and hair, who called her by her name, and thus addressed her: "Brave and generous Bradamante, know that it is a power from above that has brought you hither. The spirit of Merlin, whose last earthly abode was in this place, has warned me of your arrival, and of the fate that awaits you. This famous grotto," she continued, "was the work of the enchanter Merlin; here his ashes repose. You have no doubt heard how this sage and virtuous enchanter ceased to be. Victim of the artful fairy of the lake, Merlin, by a fatal compliance with her request, laid himself down living in his tomb, without power to resist the spell laid upon him by that ingrate, who retained him there as long as he lived. His spirit hovers about this spot, and will not leave it, until the last trumpet shall summon the dead to judgment. He answers the questions of those who approach his tomb, where perhaps you may be privileged to hear his voice."

Bradamante, astonished at these words, and the objects which met her view, knew not whether she was awake or asleep. Confused, but modest, she cast down her eyes, and a blush overspread her face. "Ah, what am I," said she, "that so great a prophet should deign to speak to me!" Still, with a secret satisfaction, she followed the priestess, who led her to the tomb of Merlin. This tomb was constructed of a species of stone hard and resplendent like fire. The rays which beamed from the stone sufficed to light up that terrible place, where the sun's rays never penetrated; but I know not whether that light was the effect of a certain phosphorescence of the stone itself, or of the many talismans and charms with which it was wrought over.

Bradamante had hardly passed the threshold of this sacred place when the spirit of the enchanter saluted her with a voice firm and distinct: "May thy designs be prosperous, O chaste and noble maiden, the future mother of heroes, the glory of Italy, and destined to fill the whole world with their fame. Great captains, renowned knights, shall be numbered among your descendants, who shall defend the Church and restore their country to its ancient splendor. Princes, wise as Augustus and the sage Numa, shall bring back the age of gold. [Footnote: This prophecy is introduced by Ariosto in this place to compliment the noble house of Este, the princes of his native state, the dukedom of Ferrara.] To accomplish these grand destinies it is ordained that you shall wed the illustrious Rogero. Fly then to his deliverance, and lay prostrate in the dust the traitor who has snatched him from you, and now holds him in chains!"

Merlin ceased with these words, and left to Melissa, the priestess, the charge of more fully instructing the maiden in her future course. "To-morrow," said she, "I will conduct you to the castle on the rock where Rogero is held captive. I will not leave you till I have guided you through this wild wood, and I will direct you on your way so that you shall be in no danger of mistaking it."

The next morning Melissa conducted Bradamante between rocks and precipices, crossing rapid torrents, and traversing intricate passes, employing the time in imparting to her such information as was necessary to enable her to bring her design to a successful issue.

"Not only would the castle, impenetrable by force, and that winged horse of his baffle your efforts, but know that he possesses also a buckler whence flashes a light so brilliant that the eyes of all who look upon it are blinded. Think not to avoid it by shutting your eyes, for how then will you be able to avoid his blows, and make him feel your own? But I will teach you the proper course to pursue.

"Agramant, the Moorish prince, possesses a ring stolen from a queen of India, which has power to render of no avail all enchantments. Agramant, knowing that Rogero is of more importance to him than any one of his warriors, is desirous of rescuing him from the power of the enchanter, and has sent for that purpose Brunello, the most crafty and sagacious of his servants, provided with his wonderful ring, and he is even now at hand, bent on this enterprise. But, beautiful Bradamante, as I desire that no one but yourself shall have the glory of delivering from thraldom your future spouse, listen while I disclose the means of success. Following this path which leads by the seashore, you will come ere long to a hostelry, where the Saracen Brunello will arrive shortly before you. You will readily know him by his stature, under four feet, his great disproportioned head, his squint eyes, his livid hue, his thick eyebrows joining his tufted beard. His dress, moreover, that of a courier, will point him out to you.

"It will be easy for you to enter into conversation with him, announcing yourself as a knight seeking combat with the enchanter, but let not the knave suspect that you know anything about the ring. I doubt not that he will be your guide to the castle of the enchanter. Accept his offer, but take care to keep behind him till you come in sight of the brilliant dome of the castle. Then hesitate not to strike him dead, for the wretch deserves no pity, and take from him the ring. But let him not suspect your intention, for by putting the ring into his mouth he will instantly become invisible, and disappear from your eyes."

Saying thus, the sage Melissa and the fair Bradamante arrived near the city of Bordeaux, where the rich and wide river Garonne pours the tribute of its waves into the sea. They parted with tender embraces. Bradamante, intent wholly on her purpose, hastened to arrive at the hostelry, where Brunello had preceded her a few moments only. The young heroine knew him without difficulty. She accosted him, and put to him some slight questions, to which he replied with adroit falsehoods. Bradamante, on her part, concealed from him her sex, her religion, her country, and the blood from whence she sprung. While they talk together, sudden cries are heard from all parts of the hostelry. "O queen of heaven!" exclaimed Bradamante, "what can be the cause of this sudden alarm?" She soon learned the cause. Host, children, domestics, all, with upturned eyes, as if they saw a comet or a great eclipse, were gazing on a prodigy which seemed to pass the bounds of possibility. She beheld distinctly a winged horse, mounted with a cavalier in rich armor, cleaving the air with rapid flight. The wings of this strange courser were wide extended, and covered with feathers of various colors. The polished armor of the knight made them shine with rainbow tints. In a short time the horse and rider disappeared behind the summits of the mountains.

"It is an enchanter," said the host, "a magician who often is seen traversing the air in that way. Sometimes he flies aloft as if among the stars, and at others skims along the land. He possesses a wonderful castle on the top of the Pyrenees. Many knights have shown their courage by going to attack him, but none have ever returned, from which it is to be feared they have lost either their life or their liberty."

Bradamante, addressing the host, said, "Could you furnish me a guide to conduct me to the castle of this enchanter?" "By my faith," said Brunello, interrupting, "that you shall not seek in vain; I have it all in writing, and I will myself conduct you." Bradamante, with thanks, accepted him for her guide.

The host had a tolerable horse to dispose of, which Bradamante bargained for, and the next day, at the first dawn of morning, she took her route by a narrow valley, taking care to have the Saracen Brunello lead the way.

They reached the summit of the Pyrenees, whence one may look down on France, Spain, and the two seas. From this height they descended again by a fatiguing road into a deep valley. From the middle of this valley an isolated mountain rose, composed of rough and perpendicular rock, on whose summit was the castle, surrounded with a wall of brass. Brunello said, "Yonder is the stronghold where the enchanter keeps his prisoners; one must have wings to mount thither; it is easy to see that the aid of a flying horse must be necessary for the master of this castle, which he uses for his prison and for his abode."

Bradamante, sufficiently instructed, saw that the time had now come to possess herself of the ring; but she could not resolve to slay a defenceless man. She seized Brunello before he was aware, bound him to a tree, and took from him the ring which he wore on one of his fingers. The cries and entreaties of the perfidious Saracen moved her not. She advanced to the foot of the rock whereon the castle stood, and, to draw the magician to the combat, sounded her horn, adding to it cries of defiance.

The enchanter delayed not to present himself, mounted on his winged horse. Bradamante was struck with surprise mixed with joy when she saw that this person, described as so formidable, bore no lance nor club, nor any other deadly weapon. He had only on his arm a buckler, covered with a cloth, and in his hand an open book. As to the winged horse, there was no enchantment about him. He was a natural animal, of a species which exists in the Riphaean mountains. Like a griffin, he had the head of an eagle, claws armed with talons, and wings covered with feathers, the rest of his body being that of a horse. This strange animal is called a Hippogriff.

The heroine attacked the enchanter on his approach, striking on this side and on that, with all the energy of a violent combat, but wounding only the wind; and after this pretended attack had lasted some time dismounted from her horse, as if hoping to do battle more effectually on foot. The enchanter now prepares to employ his sole weapon, by uncovering the magic buckler which never failed to subdue an enemy by depriving him of his senses. Bradamante, confiding in her ring, observed all the motions of her adversary, and, at the unveiling of the shield, cast herself on the ground, pretending that the splendor of the shield had overcome her, but in reality to induce the enchanter to dismount and approach her.

It happened according to her wish. When the enchanter saw her prostrate he made his horse alight on the ground, and, dismounting, fixed the shield on the pommel of his saddle, and approached in order to secure the fallen warrior. Bradamante, who watched him intently, as soon as she saw him near at hand, sprang up, seized him vigorously, threw him down, and, with the same chain which the enchanter had prepared for herself, bound him fast, without his being able to make any effectual resistance.

The enchanter, with the accents of despair, exclaimed, "Take my life, young man!" but Bradamante was far from complying with such a wish. Desirous of knowing the name of the enchanter, and for what purpose he had formed with so much art this impregnable fortress, she commanded him to inform her.

"Alas!" replied the magician, while tears flowed down his cheeks, "it is not to conceal booty, nor for any culpable design that I have built this castle; it was only to guard the life of a young knight, the object of my tenderest affection, my art having taught me that he is destined to become a Christian, and to perish, shortly after, by the blackest of treasons.

"This youth, named Rogero, is the most beautiful and most accomplished of knights. It is I, the unhappy Atlantes, who have reared him from his childhood. The call of honor and the desire of glory led him from me to follow Agramant, his prince, in his invasion of France, and I, more devoted to Rogero than the tenderest of parents, have sought the means of bringing him back to this abode, in the hope of saving him from the cruel fate that menaces him.

"For this purpose I have got him in my possession by the same means as I attempted to employ against you; and by which I have succeeded in collecting a great many knights and ladies in my castle. My purpose was to render my beloved pupil's captivity light, by affording him society to amuse him, and keep his thoughts from running on subjects of war and glory. Alas! my cares have been in vain! Yet, take, I beseech you, whatever else I have, but spare me my beloved pupil. Take this shield, take this winged courser, deliver such of your friends as you may find among my prisoners, deliver them all if you will, but leave me my beloved Rogero; or if you will snatch him too from me, take also my life, which will cease then to be to me worth preserving."

Bradamante replied: "Old man, hope not to move me by your vain entreaties. It is precisely the liberty of Rogero that I require. You would keep him here in bondage and in slothful pleasure, to save him from a fate which you foresee. Vain old man! how can you foresee his fate when you could not foresee your own? You desire me to take your life. No, my aim and my soul refuse the request." This said, she required the magician to go before, and guide her to the castle. The prisoners were set at liberty, though some, in their secret hearts, regretted the voluptuous life which was thus brought to an end. Bradamante and Rogero met one another with transports of joy.

They descended from the mountain to the spot where the encounter had taken place. There they found the Hippogriff, with the magic buckler in its wrapper, hanging to his saddle-bow. Bradamante advanced to seize the bridle; the Hippogriff seemed to wait her approach, but before she reached him he spread his wings and flew away to a neighboring hill, and in the same manner, a second time, eluded her efforts. Rogero and the other liberated knights dispersed over the plain and hilltops to secure him, and at last the animal allowed Rogero to seize his rein. The fearless Rogero hesitated not to vault upon his back, and let him feel his spurs, which so roused his mettle that, after galloping a short distance, he suddenly spread his wings, and soared into the air. Bradamante had the grief to see her lover snatched away from her at the very moment of reunion. Rogero, who knew not the art of directing the horse, was unable to control his flight. He found himself carried over the tops of the mountains, so far above them that he could hardly distinguish what was land and what water. The Hippogriff directed his flight to the west, and cleaved the air as swiftly as a new-rigged vessel cuts the waves, impelled by the freshest and most favorable gales.

ASTOLPHO AND THE ENCHANTRESS

In the long flight which Rogero took on the back of the Hippogriff he was carried over land and sea, unknowing whither. As soon as he had gained some control over the animal he made him alight on the nearest land. When he came near enough to earth Rogero leapt lightly from his back, and tied the animal to a myrtle-tree. Near the spot flowed the pure waters of a fountain, surrounded by cedars and palm-trees. Rogero laid aside his shield, and, removing his helmet, breathed with delight the fresh air, and cooled his lips with the waters of the fountain. For we cannot wonder that he was excessively fatigued, considering the ride he had taken. He was preparing to taste the sweets of repose when he perceived that the Hippogriff, which he had tied by the bridle to a myrtle-tree, frightened at something, was making violent efforts to disengage himself. His struggle shook the myrtle-tree so that many of its beautiful leaves were torn off, and strewed the ground.

A sound like that which issues from burning wood seemed to come from the myrtle-tree, at first faint and indistinct, but growing stronger by degrees, and at length was audible as a voice which spoke in this manner: "O knight, if the tenderness of your heart corresponds to the beauty of your person, relieve me, I pray you, from this tormenting animal. I suffer enough inwardly without having outward evils added to my lot."

Rogero, at the first accents of this voice, turned his eyes promptly on the myrtle, hastened to it, and stood fixed in astonishment when he perceived that the voice issued from the tree itself. He immediately untied his horse, and, flushed with surprise and regret, exclaimed, "Whoever thou art, whether mortal or the goddess of these woods, forgive me, I beseech you, my involuntary fault. Had I imagined that this hard bark covered a being possessed of feeling, could I have exposed such a beautiful myrtle to the insults of this steed? May the sweet influences of the sky and air speedily repair the injury I have done! For my part, I promise by the sovereign lady of my heart to do everything you wish in order to merit your forgiveness."

At these words the myrtle seemed to tremble from root to stem, and Rogero remarked that a moisture as of tears trickled down its bark, like that which exudes from a log placed on the fire. It then spoke:

"The kindness which inspires your words compels me to disclose to you who I once was, and by what fatality I have been changed into this shape. My name was Astolpho, cousin of Orlando and Rinaldo, whose fame has filled the earth. I was myself reckoned among the bravest paladins of France, and was by birth entitled to reign over England, after Otho, my father. Returning from the distant East, with Rinaldo and many other brave knights, called home to aid with our arms the great Emperor of France, we reached a spot where the powerful enchantress Alcina possessed a castle on the borders of the sea. She had gone to the water-side to amuse herself with fishing, and we paused to see how, by her art, without hook or line, she drew from the water whatever she would.

"Not far from the shore an enormous whale showed a back so broad and motionless that it looked like an island. Alcina had fixed her eyes on me, and planned to get me into her power. Addressing us, she said: 'This is the hour when the prettiest mermaid in the sea comes regularly every day to the shore of yonder island. She sings so sweetly that the very waves flow smoother at the sound. If you wish to hear her come with me to her resort.' So saying, Alcina pointed to the fish, which we all supposed to be an island. I, who was rash, did not hesitate to follow her; but swam my horse over, and mounted on the back of the fish. In vain Rinaldo and Dudon made signs to me to beware; Alcina, smiling, took me in charge, and led the way. No sooner were we mounted upon him than the whale moved off, spreading his great fins, and cleft rapidly the waters. I then saw my folly, but it was too late to repent. Alcina soothed my anger, and professed that what she had done was for love of me. Ere long we arrived at this island, where at first everything was done to reconcile me to my lot, and to make my days pass happily away. But soon Alcina, sated with her conquest, grew indifferent, then weary of me, and at last, to get rid of me, changed me into this form, as she had done to many lovers before me, making some of them olives, some palms, some cedars, changing others into fountains, rocks, or even into wild beasts. And thou, courteous knight, whom accident has brought to this enchanted isle, beware that she get not the power over thee, or thou shalt haply be made like us, a tree, a fountain, or a rock."

Rogero expressed his astonishment at this recital. Astolpho added that the island was in great part subject to the sway of Alcina. By the aid of her sister Morgana, she had succeeded in dispossessing a third sister, Logestilla, of nearly the whole of her patrimony, for the whole isle was hers originally by her father's bequest. But Logestilla was temperate and sage, while the other sisters were false and voluptuous. Her empire was divided from theirs by a gulf and chain of mountains, which alone had thus far prevented her sister from usurping it.

Astolpho here ended his tale, and Rogero, who knew that he was the cousin of Bradamante, would gladly have devised some way for his relief; but, as that was out of his power, he consoled him as well as he could, and then begged to be told the way to the palace of Logestilla, and how to avoid that of Alcina. Astolpho directed him to take the road to the left, though rough and full of rocks. He warned him that this road would present serious obstacles; that troops of monsters would oppose his passage, employed by the art of Alcina to prevent her subjects from escaping from her dominion. Rogero thanked the myrtle, and prepared to set out on his way.

He at first thought he would mount the winged horse, and scale the mountain on his back; but he was too uncertain of his power to control him to wish to encounter the hazard of another flight through the air, besides that he was almost famished for the want of food. So he led the horse after him, and took the road on foot, which for some distance led equally to the dominions of both the sisters.

He had not advanced more than two miles when he saw before him the superb city of Alcina. It was surrounded with a wall of gold, which seemed to reach the skies. I know that some think that this wall was not of real gold, but only the work of alchemy; it matters not; I prefer to think it gold, for it certainly shone like gold.

A broad and level road led to the gates of the city, and from this another branched off, narrow and rough, which led to the mountain region. Rogero took without hesitation the narrow road; but he had no sooner entered upon it than he was assailed by a numerous troop which opposed his passage.

You never have seen anything so ridiculous, so extraordinary, as this host of hobgoblins were. Some of them bore the human form from the neck to the feet, but had the head of a monkey or a cat;

others had the legs and the ears of a horse; old men and women, bald and hideous, ran hither and thither as if out of their senses, half clad in the shaggy skins of beasts; one rode full speed on a horse without a bridle, another jogged along mounted on an ass or a cow; others, full of agility, skipped about, and clung to the tails and manes of the animals which their companions rode. Some blew horns, others brandished drinking-cups; some were armed with spits, and some with pitchforks. One, who appeared to be the captain, had an enormous belly and a gross fat head; he was mounted on a tortoise, that waddled, now this way, now that, without keeping any one direction.

One of these monsters, who had something approaching the human form, though he had the neck, ears, and muzzle of a dog, set himself to bark furiously at Rogero, to make him turn off to the right, and reenter upon the road to the gay city; but the brave chevalier exclaimed, "That will I not, so long as I can use this sword,"--and he thrust the point directly at his face. The monster tried to strike him with a lance, but Rogero was too quick for him, and thrust his sword through his body, so that it appeared a hand's breadth behind his back. The paladin, now giving full vent to his rage, laid about him vigorously among the rabble, cleaving one to the teeth, another to the girdle; but the troop were so numerous, and in spite of his blows pressed around him so close, that, to clear his way, he must have had as many arms as Briareus.

If Rogero had uncovered the shield of the enchanter, which hung at his saddle-bow, he might easily have vanquished this monstrous rout; but perhaps he did not think of it, and perhaps he preferred to seek his defence nowhere but in his good sword. At that moment, when his perplexity was at its height, he saw issue from the city gate two young beauties, whose air and dress proclaimed their rank and gentle nurture. Each of them was mounted on a unicorn, whose whiteness surpassed that of ermine. They advanced to the meadow where Rogero was contending so valiantly against the hobgoblins, who all retired at their approach.

They drew near, they extended their hands to the young warrior, whose cheeks glowed with the flush of exercise and modesty. Grateful for their assistance, he expressed his thanks, and, having no heart to refuse them, followed their guidance to the gate of the city.

This grand and beautiful entrance was adorned by a portico of four vast columns, all of diamond. Whether they were real diamond or artificial I cannot say. What matter is it, so long as they appeared to the eye like diamond, and nothing could be more gay and splendid.

On the threshold, and between the columns, was seen a bevy of charming young women, who played and frolicked together. They all ran to receive Rogero, and conducted him into the palace, which appeared like a paradise.

We might well call by that name this abode, where the hours flew by, without account, in ever-new delights. The bare idea of satiety, want, and, above all, of age, never entered the minds of the inhabitants. They experienced no sensations except those of luxury and gayety; the cup of happiness seemed for them ever-flowing and exhaustless. The two young damsels to whom Rogero owed his deliverance from the hobgoblins conducted him to the apartment of their mistress. The beautiful Alcina advanced, and greeted him with an air at once dignified and courteous. All her court surrounded the paladin, and rendered him the most flattering attentions. The castle was less admirable for its magnificence than for the charms of those who inhabited it. They were of either sex, well matched in beauty, youth, and grace; but among this charming group the brilliant Alcina shone, as the sun outshines the stars. The young warrior was fascinated. All that he had heard from the myrtle-tree appeared to him but a vile calumny. How could he suspect that falsehood and treason veiled themselves under smiles and the ingenuous air of truth? He doubted not that Astolpho had deserved his fate, and perhaps a punishment more severe; he regarded all his stories as dictated by a disappointed spirit, and a thirst for revenge. But we must not condemn Rogero too harshly, for he was the victim of magic power.

They seated themselves at table, and immediately harmonious lyres and harps waked the air with the most ravishing notes. The charms of poetry were added in entertaining recitals; the magnificence of the feast would have done credit to a royal board. The traitress forgot nothing which might charm the paladin, and attach him to the spot, meaning, when she should grow tired of him, to metamorphose him as she had done others. In the same manner passed each succeeding day. Games of pleasant exercise, the chase, the dance, or rural sports, made the hours pass quickly; while they gave zest to the refreshment of the bath, or sleep.

Thus Rogero led a life of ease and luxury, while Charlemagne and Agramant were struggling for empire. But I cannot linger with him while the amiable and courageous Bradamante is night and day directing her uncertain steps to every spot where the slightest chance invites her, in the hope of recovering Rogero.

I will therefore say that, having sought him in vain in fields and in cities, she knew not whither next to direct her steps. She did not apprehend the death of Rogero. The fall of such a hero would have reechoed from the Hydaspes to the farthest river of the West; but, not knowing whether he was on the earth or in the air, she concluded, as a last resource, to return to the cavern which contained the tomb of Merlin, to ask of him some sure direction to the object of her search.

While this thought occupied her mind, Melissa, the sage enchantress, suddenly appeared before her. This virtuous and beneficent magician had discovered by her spells that Rogero was passing his time in pleasure and idleness, forgetful of his honor and his sovereign. Not able to endure the thought that one who was born to be a hero should waste his years in base repose, and leave a sullied reputation in the memory of survivors, she saw that vigorous measures must be employed to draw him forth into the paths of virtue. Melissa was not blinded by her affection for the amiable paladin, like Atlantes, who, intent only on preserving Rogero's life, cared nothing for his fame. It was that old enchanter whose arts had guided the Hippogriff to the isle of the too charming Alcina, where he hoped his favorite would learn to forget honor, and lose the love of glory.

At the sight of Melissa joy lighted up the countenance of Bradamante, and hope animated her breast. Melissa concealed nothing from her, but told her how Rogero was in the toils of Alcina. Bradamante was plunged in grief and terror; but the kind enchantress calmed her, dispelled her fears, and promised that before many days she would lead back the paladin to her feet.

"My daughter," she said, "give me the ring which you wear, and which possesses the power to overcome enchantments. By means of it I doubt not but that I may enter the stronghold where the false Alcina holds Rogero in durance, and may succeed in vanquishing her and liberating him." Bradamante unhesitatingly delivered her the ring, recommending Rogero to her best efforts. Melissa then summoned by her art a huge palfrey, black as jet, excepting one foot, which was bay. Mounted upon this animal, she rode with such speed that by the next morning she had reached the abode of Alcina.

She here transformed herself into the perfect resemblance of the old magician Atlantes, adding a palm-breadth to her height, and enlarging her whole figure. Her chin she covered with a long beard, and seamed her whole visage well with wrinkles. She assumed also his voice and manner, and watched her chance to find Rogero alone. At last she found him, dressed in a rich tunic of silk and gold, a collar of precious stones about his neck, and his arms, once so rough with exercise, decorated with bracelets.

His air and his every motion indicated effeminacy, and he seemed to retain nothing of Rogero but the name; such power had the enchantress obtained over him.

Melissa, under the form of his old instructor, presented herself before him, wearing a stern and serious visage. "Is this, then," she said, "the fruit of all my labors? Is it for this that I fed you on the marrow of bears and lions, that I taught you to subdue dragons, and, like Hercules, strangle serpents in your youthful grasp, only to make you, by all my cares, a feeble Adonis? My nightly watchings of the stars, of the yet warm fibres of animals, the lots I have cast, the points of nativity that I have calculated, have they all falsely indicated that you were born for greatness? Who could have believed that you would become the slave of a base enchantress? O Rogero, learn to know this Alcina, learn to understand her arts and to countervail them. Take this ring, place it on your finger, return to her presence, and see for yourself what are her real charms."

At these words, Rogero, confused, abashed, cast his eyes upon the ground, and knew not what to answer. Melissa seized the moment, slipped the ring on his finger, and the paladin was himself again. What a thunderclap to him! Overcome by shame, he dared not to encounter the looks of his instructor. When at last he raised his eyes he beheld not that venerable form, but the priestess Melissa, who in virtue of the ring now appeared in her true person. She told him of the motives which had led her to come to his rescue, of the griefs and regrets of Bradamante, and of her unwearied search for him. "That charming Amazon," she said, "sends you this ring, which is a sovereign antidote to all enchantments. She would have sent you her heart in my hands, if it would have had greater power to serve you."

It was needless for Melissa to say more. Rogero's love for Alcina, being but the work of enchantment, vanished as soon as the enchantment was withdrawn, and he now hated her with an equal intensity, seeing no longer anything in her but her vices, and feeling only resentment for the shame that she had put upon him.

His surprise when he again beheld Alcina was no less than his indignation. Fortified by his ring from her enchantments, he saw her as she was, a monster of ugliness. All her charms were artificial, and, truly viewed, were rather deformities. She was, in fact, older than Hecuba or the Sibyl of Cumae; but an art, which it is to be regretted our times have lost, enabled her to appear charming, and to clothe herself in all the attractions of youth. Rogero now saw all this, but, governed by the counsels of Melissa, he concealed his surprise, assumed under some pretext his armor, long neglected, and bound to his side Belisarda, his trusty sword, taking also the buckler of Atlantes, covered with its veil.

He then selected a horse from the stables of Alcina, without exciting her suspicions; but he left the Hippogriff, by the advice of Melissa, who promised to take him in charge, and train him to a more manageable state. The horse he took was Rabican, which belonged to Astolpho. He restored the ring to Melissa.

Rogero had not ridden far when he met one of the huntsmen of Alcina, bearing a falcon on his wrist, and followed by a dog. The huntsman was mounted on a powerful horse, and came boldly up to the paladin, demanding, in a somewhat imperious manner, whither he was going so rapidly. Rogero disdained to stop or to reply; whereupon the huntsman, not doubting that he was about making his escape, said, "What if I, with my falcon, stop your ride?" So saying, he threw off the bird, which even Rabican could not equal in speed. The huntsman then leapt from his horse, and the animal, open-mouthed, darted after Rogero with the swiftness of an arrow. The huntsman also ran as if the wind or fire bore him, and the dog was equal to Rabican in swiftness. Rogero, finding flight impossible, stopped and faced his pursuers; but his sword was useless against such foes. The insolent huntsman assailed him with words, and struck him with his whip, the only weapon he had; the dog bit his feet, and the horse drove at him with his hoofs. At the same time the falcon flew over his head and over Rabican's and attacked them with claws and wings, so that the horse in his fright began to be unmanageable. At that moment the sound of trumpets and cymbals was heard in the valley, and it was evident that Alcina had ordered out all her array to go in pursuit. Rogero felt that there was no time to be lost, and luckily remembered the shield of Atlantes, which he bore suspended from his neck. He unveiled it, and the charm worked wonderfully. The huntsman, the dog, the horse, fell flat; the trembling wings of the falcon could no longer sustain her, and she fell senseless to the ground. Rogero, rid of their annoyances, left them in their trance, and rode away.

Meanwhile Alcina, with all the force she could muster, sallied forth from her palace in pursuit. Melissa, left behind, took advantage of the opportunity to ransack all the rooms, protected by the ring. She undid one by one all the talismans and spells which she found, broke the seals, burned the images, and untied the hagknots. Thence, hurrying through the fields, she disenchanted the victims changed into trees, fountains, stones, or brutes; all of whom recovered their liberty, and vowed eternal gratitude to their deliverer. They made their escape, with all possible despatch, to the realms of the good Logestilla, whence they departed to their several homes.

Astolpho was the first whom Melissa liberated, for Rogero had particularly recommended him to her care. She aided him to recover his arms, and particularly that precious golden-headed lance which once was Argalia's. The enchantress mounted with him upon the winged horse, and in a short time arrived through the air at the castle of Logestilla, where Rogero joined them soon after.

In this abode the friends passed a short period of delightful and improving intercourse with the sage Logestilla and her virtuous court; and then each departed, Rogero with the Hippogriff, ring, and buckler; Astolpho with his golden lance, and mounted on Rabican, the fleetest of steeds. To Rogero Logestilla gave a bit and bridle suited to govern the Hippogriff; and to Astolpho a horn of marvellous powers, to be sounded only when all other weapons were unavailing.

THE ORC

We left the charming Angelica at the moment when, in her flight from her contending lovers, Sacripant and Rinaldo, she met an aged hermit. We have seen that her request to the hermit was to furnish her the means of gaining the sea-coast, eager to avoid Rinaldo, whom she hated, by leaving France and Europe itself. The pretended hermit, who was no other than a vile magician, knowing well that it would not be agreeable to his false gods to aid Angelica in this undertaking, feigned to comply with her desire. He supplied her a horse, into which he had by his arts caused a subtle devil to enter, and, having mounted Angelica on the animal, directed her what course to take to reach the sea.

Angelica rode on her way without suspicion, but when arrived at the shore, the demon urged the animal headlong into the water. Angelica in vain attempted to turn him back to the land; he continued his course till, as night approached, he landed with his burden on a sandy headland.

Angelica, finding herself alone, abandoned in this frightful solitude, remained without movement, as if stupefied, with hands joined and eyes turned towards heaven, till at last, pouring forth a torrent of tears, she exclaimed: "Cruel fortune, have you not yet exhausted your rage against me? To what new miseries do you doom me? Alas! then finish your work! Deliver me a prey to some ferocious beast, or by whatever fate you choose bring me to an end. I will be thankful to you for terminating my life and my misery." At last, exhausted by her sorrows, she fell asleep, and sunk prostrate on the sand.

Before recounting what next befell, we must declare what place it was upon which the unhappy lady was now thrown. In the sea that washes the coast of Ireland there is an island called Ebuda, whose inhabitants, once numerous, had been wasted by the anger of Proteus till there were now but few left. This deity was incensed by some neglect of the usual honors which he had in old times received from the inhabitants of the land, and, to execute his vengeance, had sent a horrid sea-monster, called an Orc, to devour them. Such were the terrors of his ravages that the whole people of the isle had shut themselves up in the principal town, and relied on their walls alone to protect them. In this distress they applied to the Oracle for advice, and were directed to appease the wrath of the sea-monster by offering to him the fairest virgin that the country could produce.

Now it so happened that the very day when this dreadful oracle was announced, and when the fatal mandate had gone forth to seek among the fairest maidens of the land one to be offered to the monster, some sailors, landing on the beach where Angelica was, beheld that beauty as she lay asleep.

O blind Chance! whose power in human affairs is but too great, canst thou then abandon to the teeth of a horrible monster those charms which different sovereigns took arms against one another to possess? Alas! the lovely Angelica is destined to be the victim of those cruel islanders.

Still asleep, she was bound by the Ebudians, and it was not until she was carried on board the vessel that she came to a knowledge of her situation. The wind filled the sails and wafted the ship swiftly to the port, where all that beheld her agreed that she was unquestionably the victim selected by Proteus himself to be his prey. Who can tell the screams, the mortal anguish of this unhappy maiden, the reproaches she addressed even to the heavens themselves, when the dreadful information of her cruel fate was made known to her? I cannot; let me rather turn to a happier part of my story.

Rogero left the palace of Logestilla, careering on his flying courser far above the tops of the mountains, and borne westward by the Hippogriff, which he guided with ease, by means of the bridle that Melissa had given him. Anxious as he was to recover Bradamante, he could not fail to be delighted at the view his rapid flight presented of so many vast regions and populous countries as he passed over in his career. At last he approached the shores of England, and perceived an immense army in all the splendor of military pomp, as if about to go forth flushed with hopes of victory. He caused the Hippogriff to alight not far from the scene, and found himself immediately surrounded by admiring spectators, knights and soldiers, who could not enough indulge their curiosity and wonder. Rogero learned, in reply to his questions, that the fine array of troops before him was the army destined to go to the aid of the French Emperor, in compliance with the request presented by the illustrious Rinaldo, as ambassador of King Charles, his uncle.

By this time the curiosity of the English chevaliers was partly gratified in beholding the Hippogriff at rest, and Rogero, to renew their surprise and delight, remounted the animal, and, slapping spurs to his sides, made him launch into the air with the rapidity of a meteor, and directed his flight still westwardly, till he came within sight of the coasts of Ireland. Here he descried what seemed to be a fair damsel, alone, fast chained to a rock which projected into the sea. What was his astonishment when, drawing nigh, he beheld the beautiful princess Angelica! That day she had been led forth and bound to the rock, there to wait till the sea-monster should come to devour her. Rogero exclaimed as he came near, "What cruel hands, what barbarous soul, what fatal chance can have loaded thee with those chains?" Angelica replied by a torrent of tears, at first her only response; then, in a trembling voice, she disclosed to him the horrible destiny for which she was there exposed. While she spoke, a terrible roaring was heard far off on the sea. The huge monster soon came in sight, part of his body appearing above the waves and part concealed. Angelica, half dead with fear, abandoned herself to despair.

Rogero, lance in rest, spurred his Hippogriff toward the Orc, and gave him a thrust. The horrible monster was like nothing that nature produces. It was but one mass of tossing and twisting body, with nothing of the animal but head, eyes, and mouth, the last furnished with tusks like those of the wild boar. Rogero's lance had struck him between the eyes; but rock and iron are not more impenetrable than were his scales. The knight, seeing the fruitlessness of the first blow, prepared to give a second. The animal, beholding upon the water the shadow of the great wings of the Hippogriff, abandoned his prey, and turned to seize what seemed nearer. Rogero took the opportunity, and dealt him furious blows on various parts of his body, taking care to keep clear of his murderous teeth; but the scales resisted every attack. The Orc beat the water with his tail till he raised a foam which enveloped Rogero and his steed, so that the knight hardly knew whether he was in the water or the air. He began to fear that the wings of the Hippogriff would be so drenched with water that they would cease to sustain him. At that moment Rogero bethought him of the magic shield which hung at his saddle-bow; but the fear that Angelica would also be blinded by its glare discouraged him from employing it. Then he remembered the ring which Melissa had given him, the power of which he had so lately proved. He hastened to Angelica and placed it on her finger. Then, uncovering the buckler, he turned its bright disk full in the face of the detestable Orc. The effect was instantaneous. The monster, deprived of sense and motion, rolled over on the sea, and lay floating on his back. Rogero would fain have tried the effect of his lance on the now exposed parts, but Angelica implored him to lose no time in delivering her from her chains before the monster should revive. Rogero, moved with her entreaties, hastened to do so, and, having unbound her, made her mount behind him on the Hippogriff. The animal, spurning the earth, shot up into the air, and rapidly sped his way through it. Rogero, to give time to the princess to rest after her cruel agitations, soon sought the earth again, alighting on the shore of Brittany. Near the shore a thick wood presented itself, which resounded with the songs of birds. In the midst, a fountain of transparent water bathed the turf of a little meadow. A gentle hill rose near by. Rogero, making the Hippogriff alight in the meadow, dismounted, and took Angelica from the horse.

When the first tumults of emotion had subsided Angelica, casting her eyes downward, beheld the precious ring upon her finger, whose virtues she was well acquainted with, for it was the very ring which the Saracen Brunello had robbed her of. She drew it from her finger and placed it in her mouth, and, quicker than we can tell it, disappeared from the sight of the paladin.

Rogero looked around him on all sides, like one frantic, but soon remembered the ring which he had so lately placed on her finger. Struck with the ingratitude which could thus recompense his services, he exclaimed: "Thankless beauty, is this then the reward you make me? Do you prefer to rob me of my ring rather than receive it as a gift? Willingly would I have given it to you, had you but asked it." Thus he said, searching on all sides with arms extended like a blind man, hoping to recover by the touch what was lost to sight; but he sought in vain. The cruel beauty was already far away.

Though sensible of her obligations to her deliverer, her first necessity was for clothing, food, and repose. She soon reached a shepherd's hut, where, entering unseen, she found what sufficed for her present relief. An old herdsman inhabited the hut, whose charges consisted of a drove of mares. When recruited by repose Angelica selected one of the mares from the flock, and, mounting the animal, felt the desire revive in her mind of returning to her home in the East, and for that purpose would gladly have accepted the protection of Orlando or of Sacripant across those wide regions which divided her from her own country. In hopes of meeting with one or the other of them she pursued her way.

Meanwhile Rogero, despairing of seeing Angelica again, returned to the tree where he had left his winged horse, but had the mortification to find that the animal had broken his bridle and escaped. This loss, added to his previous disappointment, overwhelmed him with vexation. Sadly he gathered up his arms, threw his buckler over his shoulders, and, taking the first path that offered, soon found himself within the verge of a dense and widespread forest.

He had proceeded for some distance when he heard a noise on his right, and, listening attentively, distinguished the clash of arms. He made his way toward the place whence the sound proceeded, and found two warriors engaged in mortal combat. One of them was a knight of a noble and manly bearing, the other a fierce giant. The knight appeared to exert consummate address in defending herself against the massive club of the giant, evading his strokes, or parrying them with sword or shield. Rogero stood spectator of the combat, for he did not allow himself to interfere in it, though a secret sentiment inclined him strongly to take part with the knight. At length he saw with grief the massive club fall directly on the head of the knight, who yielded to the blow, and fell prostrate. The giant sprang forward to despatch him, and for that purpose unlaced his helmet, when Rogero, with dismay, recognized the face of Bradamante. He cried aloud, "Hold, miscreant!" and sprang forward with drawn sword. Whereupon the giant, as if he cared not to enter upon another combat, lifted Bradamante on his shoulders, and ran with her into the forest.

Rogero plunged after him, but the long legs of the giant carried him forward so fast that the paladin could hardly keep him in sight. At length they issued from the wood, and Rogero perceived before him a rich palace, built of marble, and adorned with sculptures executed by a master hand. Into this edifice, through a golden door, the giant passed, and Rogero followed; but, on looking round, saw nowhere either the giant or Bradamante. He ran from room to room, calling aloud on his cowardly foe to turn and meet him; but got no response, nor caught another glimpse of the giant or his prey. In his vain pursuit he met, without knowing them, Ferrau, Florismart, King Gradasso, Orlando, and many others, all of whom had been entrapped like himself into this enchanted castle. It was a new stratagem of the magician Atlantes to draw Rogero into his power, and to secure also those who might by any chance endanger his safety. What Rogero had taken for Bradamante was a mere phantom. That charming lady was far away, full of anxiety for her Rogero, whose coming she had long expected.

The Emperor had committed to her charge the city and garrison of Marseilles, and she held the post against the infidels with valor and discretion. One day Melissa suddenly presented herself before her. Anticipating her questions, she said, "Fear not for Rogero; he lives, and is as ever true to you; but he has lost his liberty. The fell enchanter has again succeeded in making him a prisoner. If you would deliver him, mount your horse and follow me." She told her in what manner Atlantes had deceived Rogero, in deluding his eyes with the phantom of herself in peril. "Such," she continued, "will be his arts in your own case, if you penetrate the forest and approach that castle. You will think you behold Rogero, when, in fact, you see only the enchanter himself. Be not deceived, plunge your sword into his body, and trust me when I tell you that, in slaying him, you will restore not only Rogero, but with him many of the bravest knights of France, whom the wizard's arts have withdrawn from the camp of their sovereign."

Bradamante promptly armed herself, and mounted her horse. Melissa led her by forced journeys, by field and forest, beguiling the way with conversation on the theme which interested her hearer most. When at last they reached the forest, she repeated once more her instructions, and then took her leave, for fear the enchanter might espy her, and be put on his guard.

Bradamante rode on about two miles when suddenly she beheld Rogero, as it appeared to her, hard pressed by two fierce giants. While she hesitated she heard his voice calling on her for help. At once the cautions of Melissa lost their weight. A sudden doubt of the faith and truth of her kind monitress flashed across her mind. "Shall I not believe my own eyes and ears?" she said, and rushed forward to his defence. Rogero fled, pursued by the giants, and Bradamante followed, passing with them through the castle gate. When there, Bradamante was undeceived, for neither giant nor knight was to be seen. She found herself a prisoner, but had not the consolation of knowing that she shared the imprisonment of her beloved. She saw various forms of men and women, but could recognize none of them; and their lot was the same with respect to her. Each viewed the others under some illusion of the fancy, wearing the semblance of giants, dwarfs, or even four-footed animals, so that there was no companionship or communication between them.

ASTOLPHO'S ADVENTURES CONTINUED, AND ISABELLA'S BEGUN

When Astolpho escaped from the cruel Alcina, after a short abode in the realm of the virtuous Logestilla, he desired to return to his native country. Logestilla lent him the best vessel of her fleet to convey him to the mainland. She gave him at parting a wonderful book, which taught the secret of overcoming all manners of enchantments, and begged him to carry it always with him, out of regard for her. She also gave him another gift, which surpassed everything of the kind that mortal workmanship can frame; yet it was nothing in appearance but a simple horn.

Astolpho, protected by these gifts, thanked the good fairy, took leave of her, and set out on his return to France. His voyage was prosperous, and on reaching the desired port he took leave of the faithful mariners, and continued his journey by land. As he proceeded over mountains and through valleys he often met with bands of robbers, wild beasts, and venomous serpents, but he had only to sound his horn to put them all to flight.

Having landed in France, and traversed many provinces on his way to the army, he one day, in crossing a forest, arrived beside a fountain, and alighted to drink. While he stooped at the fountain a young rustic sprang from the copse, mounted Rabican, and rode away. It was a new trick of the enchanter Atlantes. Astolpho, hearing the noise, turned his head just in time to see his loss; and, starting up, pursued the thief, who, on his part, did not press the horse to his full speed, but just kept in sight of his pursuer till they both issued from the forest; and then Rabican and his rider took shelter in a castle which stood near. Astolpho followed, and penetrated without difficulty within the court-yard of the castle, where he looked around for the rider and his horse, but could see no trace of either, nor any person of whom he could make inquiry. Suspecting that enchantment was employed to embarrass him, he bethought him of his book, and on consulting it discovered that his suspicions were well founded. He also learned what course to pursue. He was directed to raise the stone which served as a threshold, under which a spirit lay pent, who would willingly escape, and leave the castle free of access. Astolpho applied his strength to lift aside the stone. Thereupon the magician put his arts in force. The castle was full of prisoners, and the magician caused that to all of them Astolpho should appear in some false guise--to some a wild beast, to others a giant, to others a bird of prey. Thus all assailed him, and would quickly have made an end of him, if he had not bethought him of his horn. No sooner had he blown a blast than, at the horrid larum, fled the cavaliers and the necromancer with them, like a flock of pigeons at the sound of the fowler's gun. Astolpho then renewed his efforts on the stone, and turned it over. The under face was all inscribed with magical characters, which the knight defaced, as directed by his book; and no sooner had he done so, than the castle, with its walls and turrets, vanished into smoke.

The knights and ladies set at liberty were, besides Rogero and Bradamante, Orlando, Gradasso, Florismart, and many more. At the sound of the horn they fled, one and all, men and steeds, except Rabican, which Astolpho secured, in spite of his terror. As soon as the sound had ceased Rogero recognized Bradamante, whom he had daily met during their imprisonment, but had been prevented from knowing by the enchanter's arts. No words can tell the delight with which they recognized each other, and recounted mutually all that had happened to each since they were parted. Rogero took advantage of the opportunity to press his suit, and found Bradamante as propitious as he could wish, were it not for a single obstacle, the difference of their faiths. "If he would obtain her in marriage," she said, "he must in due form demand her of her father, Duke Aymon, and must abandon his false prophet, and become a Christian." The latter step was one which Rogero had for some time intended taking, for reasons of his own. He therefore gladly accepted the terms, and proposed that they should at once repair to the abbey of Vallombrosa, whose towers were visible at no great distance. Thither they turned their horses' heads, and we will leave them to find their way without our company.

I know not if my readers recollect that at the moment when Rogero had just delivered Angelica from the voracious Orc that scornful beauty placed her ring in her mouth, and vanished out of sight. At the same time the Hippogriff shook off his bridle, soared away, and flew to rejoin his former master, very naturally returning to his accustomed stable. Here Astolpho found him, to his very great delight. He knew the animal's powers, having seen Rogero ride him, and he longed to fly abroad over all the earth, and see various nations and peoples from his airy course. He had heard Logestilla's directions how to guide the animal, and saw her fit a bridle to his head. He therefore was able, out of all the bridles he found in the stable, to select one suitable, and, placing Rabican's saddle on the Hippogriff's back, nothing seemed to prevent his immediate departure. Yet before he went he bethought him of placing Rabican in hands where he would be safe, and whence he might recover him in time of need. While he stood deliberating where he should find a messenger, he saw Bradamante approach. That fair warrior had been parted from Rogero on their way to the abbey of Vallombrosa, by an inopportune adventure which had called the knight away. She was now returning to Montalban, having arranged with Rogero to join her there. To Bradamante, therefore, his fair cousin, Astolpho committed Rabican, and also the lance of gold, which would only be an incumbrance in his aerial excursion. Bradamante took charge of both; and Astolpho, bidding her farewell, soared in air.

Among those delivered by Astolpho from the magician's castle was Orlando. Following the guide of chance, the paladin found himself at the close of day in a forest, and stopped at the foot of a mountain. Surprised to discern a light which came from a cleft in the rock, he approached, guided by the ray, and discovered a narrow passage in the mountain-side, which led into a deep grotto.

Orlando fastened his horse, and then, putting aside the bushes that resisted his passage, stepped down from rock to rock till he reached a sort of cavern. Entering it, he perceived a lady, young and handsome, as well as he could discover through the signs of distress which agitated her countenance. Her only companion was an old woman, who seemed to be regarded by her young partner with terror and indignation. The courteous paladin saluted the women respectfully, and begged to know by whose barbarity they had been subjected to such imprisonment.

The younger lady replied, in a voice often broken with sobs:

"Though I know well that my recital will subject me to worse treatment by the barbarous man who keeps me here, to whom this woman will not fail to report it, yet I will not hide from you the facts. Ah! why should I fear his rage? If he should take my life, I know not what better boon than death I can ask.

"My name is Isabella. I am the daughter of the king of Galicia, or rather I should say misfortune and grief are my parents. Young, rich, modest, and of tranquil temper, all things appeared to combine to render my lot happy. Alas! I see myself to-day poor, humbled, miserable, and destined perhaps to yet further afflictions. It is a year since, my father having given notice that he would open the lists for a tournament at Bayonne, a great number of chevaliers from all quarters came together at our court. Among these Zerbino, son of the king of Scotland, victorious in all combats, eclipsed by his beauty and his valor all the rest. Before departing from the court of Galicia he testified the wish to espouse me, and I consented that he should demand my hand of the king, my father. But I was a Mahometan, and Zerbino a Christian, and my father refused his consent. The prince, called home by his father to take command of the forces destined to the assistance of the French Emperor, prevailed on me to be married to him secretly, and to follow him to Scotland. He caused a galley to be prepared to receive me, and placed in command of it the chevalier Oderic, a Biscayan, famous for his exploits both by land and sea. On the day appointed, Oderic brought his vessel to a seaside resort of my father's, where I embarked. Some of my domestics accompanied me, and thus I departed from my native land.

"Sailing with a fair wind, after some hours we were assailed by a violent tempest. It was to no purpose that we took in all sail; we were driven before the wind directly upon the rocky shore. Seeing no other hopes of safety, Oderic placed me in a boat, followed himself with a few of his men, and made for land. We reached it through infinite peril, and I no sooner felt the firm land beneath my feet, than I knelt down and poured out heartfelt thanks to the Providence that had preserved me.

"The shore where we landed appeared to be uninhabited. We saw no dwelling to shelter us, no road to lead us to a more hospitable spot. A high mountain rose before us, whose base stretched into the sea. It was here the infamous Oderic, in spite of my tears and entreaties, sold me to a band of pirates, who fancied I might be an acceptable present to their prince, the Sultan of Morocco. This cavern is their den, and here they keep me under the guard of this woman, until it shall suit their convenience to carry me away."

Isabella had hardly finished her recital when a troop of armed men began to enter the cavern. Seeing the prince Orlando, one said to the rest, "What bird is this we have caught, without even setting a snare for him?" Then addressing Orlando, "It was truly civil in you, friend, to come hither with that handsome coat of armor and vest, the very things I want." "You shall pay for them, then," said Orlando; and seizing a half-burnt brand from the fire, he hurled it at him, striking his head, and stretching him lifeless on the floor.

There was a massy table in the middle of the cavern, used for the pirates' repasts. Orlando lifted it and hurled it at the robbers as they stood clustered in a group toward the entrance. Half the gang were laid prostrate, with broken heads and limbs; the rest got away as nimbly as they could.

Leaving the den and its inmates to their fate, Orlando, taking Isabella under his protection, pursued his way for some days, without meeting with any adventure.

One day they saw a band of men advancing, who seemed to be guarding a prisoner, bound hand and foot, as if being carried to execution. The prisoner was a youthful cavalier, of a noble and ingenuous appearance. The band bore the ensigns of Count Anselm, head of the treacherous house of Maganza. Orlando desired Isabella to wait, while he rode forward to inquire the meaning of this array. Approaching, he demanded of the leader who his prisoner was, and of what crime he had been guilty. The man replied that the prisoner was a murderer, by whose hand Pinabel, the son of Count Anselm, had been treacherously slain. At these words the prisoner exclaimed, "I am no murderer, nor have I been in any way the cause of the young man's death." Orlando, knowing the cruel and ferocious character of the chiefs of the house of Maganza, needed no more to satisfy him that the youth was the victim of injustice. He commanded the leader of the troop to release his victim, and, receiving an insolent reply, dashed him to the earth with a stroke of his lance; then by a few vigorous blows dispersed the band, leaving deadly marks on those who were slowest to quit the field.

Orlando then hastened to unbind the prisoner, and to assist him to reclothe himself in his armor, which the false Magencian had dared to assume. He then led him to Isabella, who now approached the scene of action. How can we picture the joy, the astonishment, with which Isabella recognized in him Zerbino, her husband, and the prince discovered her whom he had believed overwhelmed in the waves! They embraced one another, and wept for joy. Orlando, sharing in their happiness, congratulated himself in having been the instrument of it. The princess recounted to Zerbino what the illustrious paladin had done for her, and the prince threw himself at Orlando's feet, and thanked him as having twice preserved his life.

While these exchanges of congratulation and thankfulness were going on, a sound in the underwood attracted their attention, and caused the two knights to brace their helmets and stand on their guard. What the cause of the interruption was we shall record in another chapter.

MEDORO

France was at this time the theatre of dreadful events. The Saracens and the Christians, in numerous encounters, slew one another. On one occasion Rinaldo led an attack on the infidel columns, broke and scattered them, till he found himself opposite to a knight whose armor (whether by accident or by choice, it matters not) bore the blazon of Orlando. It was Dardinel, the young and brave prince of Zumara, and Rinaldo remarked him by the slaughter he spread all around. "Ah," said he to himself, "let us pluck up this dangerous plant before it has grown to its full height."

As Rinaldo advanced, the crowd opened before him, the Christians to let his sword have free course, the Pagans to escape its sweep. Dardinel and he stood face to face. Rinaldo exclaimed, fiercely, "Young man, whoever gave you that noble buckler to bear made you a dangerous gift; I should like to see how you are able to defend those quarterings, red and white. If you cannot defend them against me, how pray will you do so when Orlando challenges them?" Dardinel replied: "Thou shalt learn that I can defend the arms I bear, and shed new glory upon them. No one shall rend them from me but with life." Saying these words, Dardinel rushed upon Rinaldo with sword uplifted. The chill of mortal terror filled the souls of the Saracens when they beheld Rinaldo advance to attack the prince, like a lion against a young bull. The first blow came from the hand of Dardinel, and the weapon rebounded from Mambrino's helmet without effect. Rinaldo smiled, and said, "I will now show you if my strokes are more effectual." At these words he thrust the unfortunate

Dardinel in the middle of his breast. The blow was so violent that the cruel weapon pierced the body, and came out a palm-breadth behind his back. Through this wound the life of Dardinel issued with his blood, and his body fell helpless to the ground.

As a flower which the passing plough has uprooted languishes, and droops its head, so Dardinel, his visage covered with the paleness of death, expires, and the hopes of an illustrious race perish with him.

Like waters kept back by a dike, which, when the dike is broken, spread abroad through all the country, so the Moors, no longer kept in column by the example of Dardinel, fled in all directions. Rinaldo despised too much such easy victories to pursue them; he wished for no combats but with brave men. At the same time, the other paladins made terrible slaughter of the Moors. Charles himself, Oliver, Guido, and Ogier the Dane, carried death into their ranks on all sides.

The infidels seemed doomed to perish to a man on that dreadful day; but the wise king, Marsilius, at last put some slight degree of method into the general rout. He collected the remnant of the troops, formed them into a battalion, and retreated in tolerable order to his camp. That camp was well fortified by intrenchments and a broad ditch. Thither the fugitives hastened, and by degrees all that remained of the Moorish army was brought together there.

The Emperor might perhaps that night have crushed his enemy entirely; but not thinking it prudent to expose his troops, fatigued as they were, to an attack upon a camp so well fortified, he contented himself with encompassing the enemy with his troops, prepared to make a regular siege. During the night the Moors had time to see the extent of their loss. Their tents resounded with lamentations. This warrior had to mourn a brother, that a friend;

many suffered with grievous wounds, all trembled at the fate in store for them.

There were two young Moors, both of humble rank, who gave proof at that time of attachment and fidelity rare in the history of man. Cloridan and Medoro had followed their prince, Dardinel, to the wars of France. Cloridan, a bold huntsman, combined strength with activity. Medoro was a mere youth, his cheeks yet fair and blooming. Of all the Saracens, no one united so much grace and beauty. His light hair was set off by his black and sparkling eyes. The two friends were together on guard at the rampart. About midnight they gazed on the scene in deep dejection. Medoro, with tears in his eyes, spoke of the good prince Dardinel, and could not endure the thought that his body should be cast out on the plain, deprived of funeral honors. "O my friend," said he, "must then the body of our prince be the prey of wolves and ravens? Alas! when I remember how he loved me, I feel that if I should sacrifice my life to do him honor, I should not do more than my duty. I wish, dear friend, to seek out his body on the battlefield, and give it burial, and I hope to be able to pass through King Charles's camp without discovery, as they are probably all asleep. You, Cloridan, will be able to say for me, if I should die in the adventure, that gratitude and fidelity to my prince were my inducements."

Cloridan was both surprised and touched with this proof of the young man's devotion. He loved him tenderly, and tried for a long time every effort to dissuade him from his design; but he found Medoro determined to accomplish his object or die in the endeavor.

Cloridan, unable to change his purpose, said, "I will go with you, Medoro, and help you in this generous enterprise. I value not life compared with honor, and if I did, do you suppose, dear friend, that I could live without you? I would rather fall by the arms of our enemies than die of grief for the loss of you."

When the two friends were relieved from their guard duty they went without any followers into the camp of the Christians. All there was still; the fires were dying out; there was no fear of any attempt on the part of the Saracens, and the soldiers, overcome by fatigue or wine, slept secure, lying upon the ground in the midst of their arms and equipage. Cloridan stopped, and said, "Medoro, I am not going to quit this camp without taking vengeance for the death of our prince. Keep watch, be on your guard that no one shall surprise us; I mean to mark a road with my sword through the ranks of our enemies." So saying, he entered the tent where Alpheus slept, who a year before had joined the camp of Charles, and pretended to be a great physician and astrologer. But his science had deceived him, if it gave him hope of dying peacefully in his bed at a good old age; his lot was to die with little warning. Cloridan ran his sword through his heart. A Greek and a German followed, who had been playing late at dice: fortunate if they had continued their game a little longer; but they never reckoned a throw like this among their chances. Cloridan next came to the unlucky Grillon, whose head lay softly on his pillow. He dreamed probably of the feast from which he had but just retired; for when Cloridan cut off his head wine flowed forth with the blood.

The two young Moors might have penetrated even to the tent of Charlemagne; but knowing that the paladins encamped around him kept watch by turns, and judging that it was impossible they should all be asleep, they were afraid to go too near. They might also have obtained rich booty; but, intent only on their object, they crossed the camp, and arrived at length at the bloody field, where bucklers, lances, and swords lay scattered in the midst of corpses of poor and rich, common soldier and prince, horses and pools of blood. This terrible scene of carnage would have destroyed all hope of finding what they were in search of until dawn of day, were it not that the moon lent the aid of her uncertain rays.

Medoro raised his eyes to the planet, and exclaimed, "O holy goddess, whom our fathers have adored under three different forms,--thou who displayest thy power in heaven, on earth, and in the underworld,--thou who art seen foremost among the nymphs chasing the beasts of the forest,--cause me to see, I implore thee, the spot where my dear master lies, and make me all my life long follow the example which thou dost exhibit of works of charity and love."

Either by accident, or that the moon was sensible of the prayer of Medoro, the cloud broke away, and the moonlight burst forth as bright as day. The rays seemed especially to gild the spot where lay the body of Prince Dardinel; and Medoro, bathed in tears and with bleeding heart, recognized him by the quarterings of red and white on his shield.

With groans stifled by his tears, and lamentations in accents suppressed, not from any fear for himself, for he cared not for life, but lest any one should be roused to interrupt their pious duty while yet incomplete, he proposed to his companion that they should together bear Dardinel on their shoulders, sharing the burden of the beloved remains.

Marching with rapid strides under their precious load, they perceived that the stars began to grow pale, and that the shades of night would soon be dispersed by the dawn. Just then Zerbino, whose extreme valor had urged him far from the camp in pursuit of the fugitives, returning, entered the wood in which they were. Some knights in his train perceived at a distance the two brothers-in-arms. Cloridan saw the troop, and, observing that they dispersed themselves over the plain as if in search of booty, told Medoro to lay down the body, and let each save himself by flight. He dropped his part, thinking that Medoro would do the same; but the good youth loved his prince too well to abandon him, and continued to carry his load singly as well as he might, while Cloridan made his escape. Near by there was a part of the wood tufted as if nothing but wild animals had ever penetrated it. The unfortunate youth, loaded with the weight of his dead master, plunged into its recesses.

Cloridan, when he perceived that he had evaded his foes, discovered that Medoro was not with him. "Ah!" exclaimed he, "how could I, dear Medoro, so forget myself as to consult my own safety without heeding yours?" So saying, he retraced the tangled passes of the wood toward the place from whence he had fled. As he approached he heard the noise of horses, and the menacing voices of armed men. Soon he perceived Medoro, on foot, with the cavaliers surrounding him. Zerbino, their commander, bade them seize him. The unhappy Medoro turned now this way, now that, trying to conceal himself behind an oak or a rock, still bearing the body, which he would by no means leave. Cloridan not knowing how to help him, but resolved to perish with him, if he must perish, takes an arrow, fits it to his bow, discharges it, and pierces the breast of a Christian knight, who falls helpless from his horse. The others look this way and that, to discover whence the fatal bolt was sped. One, while demanding of his comrades in what direction the arrow came, received a second in his throat, which stopped his words, and soon closed his eyes to the scene.

Zerbino, furious at the death of his two comrades, ran upon Medoro, seized his golden hair, and dragged him forward to slay him. But the sight of so much youth and beauty commanded pity. He stayed his arm. The young man spoke in suppliant tones. "Ah! signor," said he, "I conjure you by the God whom you serve, deprive me not of life until I shall have buried the body of the prince, my master. Fear not that I will ask you any other favor; life is not dear to me; I desire death as soon as I shall have performed this sacred duty. Do with me then as you please. Give my limbs a prey to the birds and beasts; only let me first bury my prince." Medoro pronounced these words with an air so sweet and tender that a heart of stone would have been moved by them.

Zerbino was so to the bottom of his soul. He was on the point of uttering words of mercy, when a cruel subaltern, forgetting all respect to his commander, plunged his lance into the breast of the young Moor. Zerbino, enraged at his brutality, turned upon the wretch to take vengeance, but he saved himself by a precipitate flight.

Cloridan, who saw Medoro fall, could contain himself no longer. He rushed from his concealment, threw down his bow, and, sword in hand, seemed only desirous of vengeance for Medoro, and to die with him. In a moment, pierced through and through with many wounds, he exerts the last remnant of his strength in dragging himself to Medoro, to die embracing him. The cavaliers left them thus to rejoin Zerbino, whose rage against the murderer of Medoro had drawn him away from the spot.

Cloridan died; and Medoro, bleeding copiously, was drawing near his end when help arrived.

A young maiden approached the fallen knights at this critical moment. Her dress was that of a peasant-girl, but her air was noble, and her beauty celestial; sweetness and goodness reigned in her lovely countenance. It was no other than Angelica, the Princess of Cathay.

When she had recovered that precious ring, as we have before related, Angelica, knowing its value, felt proud in the power it conferred, travelled alone without fear, not without a secret shame that she had ever been obliged to seek protection in her wanderings of the Count Orlando and of Sacripant. She reproached herself too as with a weakness that she had ever thought of marrying Rinaldo; in fine, her pride grew so high as to persuade her that no man living was worthy to aspire to her hand.

Moved with pity at the sight of the young man wounded, and melted to tears at hearing the cause, she quickly recalled to remembrance the knowledge she had acquired in India, where the virtues of plants and the art of healing formed part of the education even of princesses. The beautiful queen ran into the adjoining meadow to gather plants of virtue to staunch the flow of blood. Meeting on her way a countryman on horseback seeking a strayed heifer, she begged him to come to her assistance, and endeavor to remove the wounded man to a more secure asylum.

Angelica, having prepared the plants by bruising them between two stones, laid them with her fair hand on Medoro's wound. The remedy soon restored in some degree the strength of the wounded man, who, before he would quit the spot, made them cover with earth and turf the bodies of his friend and of the prince. Then surrendering himself to the pity of his deliverers, he allowed them to place him on the horse of the shepherd, and conduct him to his cottage. It was a pleasant farmhouse on the borders of the wood, bearing marks of comfort and competency. There the shepherd lived with his wife and children. There Angelica tended Medoro, and there, by the devoted care of the beautiful queen, his sad wound closed over, and he recovered his perfect health.

O Count Rinaldo, O King Sacripant! what availed it you to possess so many virtues and such fame? What advantage have you derived from all your high deserts? O hapless king, great Agrican! if you could return to life, how would you endure to see yourself rejected by one who will bow to the yoke of Hymen in favor of a young soldier of humble birth? And thou, Ferrau, and ye numerous others who a hundred times have put your lives at hazard for this cruel beauty, how bitter will it be to you to see her sacrifice you all to the claims of the humble Medoro!

There, under the low roof of a shepherd, the flame of Hymen was lighted for this haughty queen. She takes the shepherd's wife to serve in place of mother, the shepherd and his children for witnesses, and marries the happy Medoro.

Angelica, after her marriage, wishing to endow Medoro with the sovereignty of the countries which yet remained to her, took with him the road to the East. She had preserved through all her adventures a bracelet of gold enriched with precious stones, the present of the Count Orlando. Having nothing else wherewith to reward the good shepherd and his wife, who had served her with so much care and fidelity, she took the bracelet from her arm and gave it to them, and then the newly-married couple directed their steps toward those mountains which separate France and Spain, intending to wait at Barcelona a vessel which should take them on their way to the East.

ORLANDO MAD

Orlando, on the loss of Angelica, laid aside his crest and arms, and arrayed himself in a suit of black armor expressive of his despair. In this guise he carried such slaughter among the ranks of the infidels that both armies were astonished at the achievements of the stranger knight. Mandricardo, who had been absent from the battle, heard the report of these achievements and determined to test for himself the valor of the knight so extolled. He it was who broke in upon the conference of Zerbino and Isabella, and their benefactor Orlando, as they stood occupied in mutual felicitations, after the happy reunion of the lovers by the prowess of the paladin.

Mandricardo, after contemplating the group for a moment, addressed himself to Orlando in these words: "Thou must be the man I seek. For ten days and more I have been on thy track. The fame of thy exploits has brought me hither, that I may measure my strength with thine. Thy crest and shield prove thee the same who spread such slaughter among our troops. But these marks are superfluous, and if I saw thee among a hundred I should know thee by thy martial bearing to be the man I seek."

"I respect thy courage," said Orlando; "such a design could not have sprung up in any but a brave and generous soul. If the desire to see me has brought thee hither, I would, if it were possible, show thee my inmost soul. I will remove my visor, that you may satisfy your curiosity; but when you have done so I hope that you will also try and see if my valor corresponds to my appearance." "Come on," said the Saracen, "my first wish was to see and know thee; I will not gratify my second."

Orlando, observing Mandricardo was surprised to see no sword at his side, nor mace at his saddle-bow. "And what weapon hast thou," said he, "if thy lance fail thee?"

"Do not concern yourself about that," said Mandricardo; "I have made many good knights give ground with no other weapon than you see. Know that I have sworn an oath never to bear a sword until I win back that famous Durindana that Orlando, the paladin, carries. That sword belongs to the suit of armor which I wear; that only is wanting. Without doubt it was stolen, but how it got into the hands of Orlando I know not. But I will make him pay dearly for it when I find him I seek him the more anxiously that I may avenge with his blood the death of King Agrican, my father, whom he treacherously slew. I am sure he must have done it by treachery, for it was not in his power to subdue in fair fight such a warrior as my father."

"Thou liest," cried Orlando; "and all who say so lie. I am Orlando, whom you seek; yes, I am he who slew your father honorably. Hold, here is the sword: you shall have it if your courage avails to merit it. Though it belongs to me by right, I will not use it in this dispute. See, I hang it on this tree; you shall be master of it, if you bereave me of life; not else."

At these words Orlando drew Durindana, and hung it on one of the branches of a tree near by.

Both knights, boiling with equal ardor, rode off in a semicircle; then rushed together with reins thrown loose, and struck one another with their lances. Both kept their seats, immovable. The splinters of their lances flew into the air, and no weapon remained for either but the fragment which he held in his hand. Then those two knights, covered with iron mail, were reduced to the necessity of fighting with staves, in the manner of two rustics, who dispute the boundary of a meadow, or the possession of a spring.

These clubs could not long keep whole in the hands of such sturdy smiters, who were soon reduced to fight with naked fists. Such warfare was more painful to him that gave than to him that received the blows. They next clasped, and strained each his adversary, as Hercules did Antaeus. Mandricardo, more enraged than Orlando, made violent efforts to unseat the paladin, and dropped the rein of his horse. Orlando, more calm, perceived it. With one hand he resisted Mandricardo, with the other he twitched the horse's bridle over the ears of the animal. The Saracen dragged Orlando with all his might, but Orlando's thighs held the saddle like a vise. At last the efforts of the Saracen broke the girths of Orlando's horse; the saddle slipped; the knight, firm in his stirrups, slipped with it, and came to the ground hardly conscious of his fall. The noise of his armor in falling startled Mandricardo's horse, now without a bridle. He started off in full career, heeding neither trees nor rocks nor broken ground. Urged by fright, he ran with furious speed, carrying his master, who, almost distracted with rage, shouted and beat the animal with his fists, and thereby impelled his flight. After running thus three miles or more, a deep ditch opposed their progress. The horse and rider fell headlong into it, and did not find the bottom covered with feather-beds or roses. They got sadly bruised; but were lucky enough to escape without any broken limbs.

Mandricardo, as soon as he gained his feet, seized the horse by his mane with fury; but, having no bridle, could not hold him. He looked round in hopes of finding something that would do for a rein. Just then fortune, who seemed willing to help him at last, brought that way a peasant with a bridle in his hand, who was in search of his farm horse that had strayed away.

Orlando, having speedily repaired his horse's girths, remounted, and waited a good hour for the Saracen to return. Not seeing him, he concluded to go in search of him. He took an affectionate leave of Zerbino and Isabella, who would willingly have followed him; but this the brave paladin would by no means permit. He held it unknightly to go in search of an enemy accompanied by a friend, who might act as a defender. Therefore, desiring them to say to Mandricardo, if they should meet him, that his purpose was to tarry in the neighborhood three days, and then repair to the camp of Charlemagne, he took down Durindana from the tree, and proceeded in the direction which the Saracen's horse had taken. But the animal, having no guide but its terror, had so doubled and confused its traces that Orlando, after two days spent in the search, gave up the attempt.

It was about the middle of the third day when the paladin arrived on the pleasant bank of a stream which wound through a meadow enamelled with flowers. High trees, whose tops met and formed an arbor, over-shadowed the fountain; and the breeze which blew through their foliage tempered the heat. Hither the shepherds used to resort to quench their thirst, and to enjoy the shelter from the midday sun. The air, perfumed with the flowers, seemed to breathe fresh strength into their veins. Orlando felt the influence, though covered with his armor. He stopped in this delicious arbor, where everything seemed to invite to repose. But he could not have chosen a more fatal asylum. He there spent the most miserable moments of his life.

He looked around, and noted with pleasure all the charms of the spot. He saw that some of the trees were carved with inscriptions--he drew near, and read them, and what was his surprise to find that they composed the name of Angelica! Farther on he found the name of Medoro mixed with hers. The paladin thought he dreamed. He stood like one amazed--like a bird that, rising to fly, finds its feet caught in a net.

Orlando followed the course of the stream, and came to one of its turns where the rocks of the mountain bent in such a way as to form a sort of grotto. The twisted stems of ivy and the wild vine draped the entrance of this recess, scooped by the hand of nature.

The unhappy paladin, on entering the grotto, saw letters which appeared to have been lately carved. They were verses which Medoro had written in honor of his happy nuptials with the beautiful queen. Orlando tried to persuade himself it must be some other Angelica whom those verses celebrated, and as for Medoro, he had never heard his name. The sun was now declining, and Orlando remounted his horse, and went on his way. He soon saw the roof of a cottage whence the smoke ascended; he heard the barking of dogs and the lowing of cattle, and arrived at a humble dwelling which seemed to offer an asylum for the night. The inmates, as soon as they saw him, hastened to tender him service. One took his horse, another his shield and cuirass, another his golden spurs. This cottage was the very same where Medoro had been carried, deeply wounded,--where Angelica had tended him, and afterwards married him. The shepherd who lived in it loved to tell everybody the story of this marriage, and soon related it, with all its details, to the miserable Orlando.

Having finished it, he went away, and returned with the precious bracelet which Angelica, grateful for his services, had given him as a memorial. It was the one which Orlando had himself given her.

This last touch was the finishing stroke to the excited paladin. Frantic, exasperated, he exclaimed against the ungrateful and cruel princess who had disdained him, the most renowned, the most indomitable of all the paladins of France,--him, who had rescued her from the most alarming perils,--him, who had fought the most terrible battles for her sake,--she to prefer to him a young Saracen! The pride of the noble Count was deeply wounded. Indignant, frantic, a victim to ungovernable rage, he rushed into the forest, uttering the most frightful shrieks.

"No, no!" cried he, "I am not the man they take me for! Orlando is dead! I am only the wandering ghost of that unhappy Count, who is now suffering the torments of hell!"

Orlando wandered all night, as chance directed, through the wood, and at sunrise his destiny led him to the fountain where Medoro had engraved the fatal inscription. The frantic paladin saw it a second time with fury, drew his sword, and hacked it from the rock.

Unlucky grotto! you shall no more attract by your shade and coolness, you shall no more shelter with your arch either shepherd or flock. And you, fresh and pure fountain, you may not escape the rage of the furious Orlando! He cast into the fountain branches, trunks of trees which he tore up, pieces of rocks which he broke off, plants uprooted, with the earth adhering, and turf and brushes, so as to choke the fountain, and destroy the purity of its waters. At length, exhausted by his violent exertions, bathed in sweat, breathless, Orlando sunk panting upon the earth, and lay there insensible three days and three nights.

The fourth day he started up and seized his arms. His helmet, his buckler, he cast far from him; his hauberk and his clothes he rent asunder; the fragments were scattered through the wood. In fine, he became a furious madman. His insanity was such that he cared not to retain even his sword. But he had no need of Durindana, nor of other arms, to do wonderful things. His prodigious strength sufficed. At the first wrench of his mighty arm he tore up a pine-tree by the roots. Oaks, beeches, maples, whatever he met in his path, yielded in like manner. The ancient forest soon became as bare as the borders of a morass, where the fowler has cleared away the bushes to spread his nets. The shepherds, hearing the horrible crashing in the forest, abandoned their flocks to run and see the cause of this unwonted uproar. By their evil star, or for their sins, they were led thither. When they saw the furious state the Count was in, and his incredible force, they would fain have fled out of his reach, but in their fears lost their presence of mind. The madman pursued them, seized one and rent him limb from limb, as easily as one would pull ripe apples from a tree. He took another by the feet, and used him as a club to knock down a third. The shepherds fled; but it would have been hard for any to escape, if he had not at that moment left them to throw himself with the same fury upon their flocks. The peasants, abandoning their ploughs and harrows, mounted on the roofs of buildings and pinnacles of the rocks, afraid to trust themselves even to the oaks and pines. From such heights they looked on, trembling at the raging fury of the unhappy Orlando. His fists, his teeth, his nails, his feet, seize, break, and tear cattle, sheep, and swine; the most swift in flight alone being able to escape him.

When at last terror had scattered everything before him, he entered a cottage which was abandoned by its inhabitants, and there found that which served for food. His long fast had caused him to feel the most ravenous hunger. Seizing whatever he found that was eatable, whether roots, acorns, or bread, raw meat or cooked, he gorged it indiscriminately.

Issuing thence again, the frantic Orlando gave chase to whatever living thing he saw, whether men or animals. Sometimes he pursued the deer and hind, sometimes he attacked bears and wolves, and with his naked hands killed and tore them, and devoured their flesh.

Thus he wandered, from place to place, through France, imperilling his life a thousand ways, yet always preserved by some mysterious providence from a fatal result. But here we leave

Orlando for a time, that we may record what befell Zerbino and Isabella after their parting with him.

The prince and his fair bride waited, by Orlando's request, near the scene of the battle for three days, that, if Mandricardo should return, they might inform him where Orlando would give him another meeting. At the end of that time their anxiety to know the issue led them to follow Orlando's traces, which led them at last to the wood where the trees were inscribed with the names of Angelica and Medoro. They remarked how all these inscriptions were defaced, and how the grotto was disordered, and the fountain clogged with rubbish. But that which surprised them and distressed them most of all was to find on the grass the cuirass of Orlando, and not far from it his helmet, the same which the renowned Almontes once wore.

Hearing a horse neigh in the forest, Zerbino turned his eyes in that direction, and saw Brigliadoro, with the bridle yet hanging at the saddle-bow. He looked round for Durindana, and found that famous sword, without the scabbard, lying on the grass. He saw also the fragments of Orlando's other arms and clothing scattered on all sides over the plain.

Zerbino and Isabella stood in astonishment and grief, not knowing what to think, but little imagining the true cause. If they had found any marks of blood on the arms or on the fragments of the clothing, they would have supposed him slain, but there were none. While they were in this painful uncertainty they saw a young peasant approach. He, not yet recovered from the terror of the scene, which he had witnessed from the top of a rock, told them the whole of the sad events.

Zerbino, with his eyes full of tears, carefully collected all the scattered arms. Isabella also dismounted to aid him in the sad duty. When they had collected all the pieces of that rich armor they hung them like a trophy on a pine; and to prevent their being violated by any passers-by, Zerbino inscribed on the bark this caution: "These are the arms of the Paladin Orlando."

Having finished this pious work, he remounted his horse, and just then a knight rode up, and requested Zerbino to tell him the meaning of the trophy. The prince related the facts as they had happened; and Mandricardo, for it was that Saracen knight, full of joy, rushed forward, and seized the sword, saying, "No one can censure me for what I do; this sword is mine; I can take my own wherever I find it. It is plain that Orlando, not daring to defend it against me, has counterfeited madness to excuse him in surrendering it."

Zerbino vehemently exclaimed, "Touch not that sword. Think not to possess it without a contest. If it be true that the arms you wear are those of Hector, you must have got them by theft, and not by prowess."

Immediately they attacked one another with the utmost fury. The air resounded with thick-falling blows. Zerbino, skilful and alert, evaded for a time with good success the strokes of Durindana; but at length a terrible blow struck him on the neck. He fell from his horse, and the Tartar king, possessed of the spoils of his victory, rode away.

ZERBINO AND ISABELLA

Zerbino's pain at seeing the Tartar prince go off with the sword surpassed the anguish of his wound; but now the loss of blood so reduced his strength that he could not move from where he fell. Isabella, not knowing whither to resort for help, could only bemoan him, and chide her cruel fate. Zerbino said, "If I could but leave thee, my best beloved, in some secure abode, it would not distress me to die; but to abandon thee so, without protection, is sad indeed." She replied, "Think not to leave me, dearest; our souls shall not be parted; this sword will give me the means to follow thee." Zerbino's last words implored her to banish such a thought, but live, and be true to his memory. Isabella promised, with many tears, to be faithful to him so long as life should last.

When he ceased to breathe, Isabella's cries resounded through the forest, and reached the ears of a reverend hermit, who hastened to the spot. He soothed and calmed her, urging those consolations which the word of God supplies; and at last brought her to wish for nothing else but to devote herself for the rest of life wholly to religion.

As she could not bear the thoughts of leaving her dead lord abandoned, the body was, by the good hermit's aid, placed upon the horse, and taken to the nearest inhabited place, where a chest was made for it, suitable to be carried with them on their way. The hermit's plan was to escort his charge to a monastery, not many days' journey distant, where Isabella resolved to spend the remainder of her days. Thus they travelled day after day, choosing the most retired ways, for the country was full of armed men. One day a cavalier met them, and barred their way. It was no other than Rodomont, king of Algiers, who had just left the camp of Agramant, full of indignation at the treatment he had received from Doralice. At sight of the lovely lady and her reverend attendant, with their horse laden with a burden draped with black, he asked the meaning of their journey. Isabella told him her affliction, and her resolution to renounce the world and devote herself to religion, and to the memory of the friend she had lost. Rodomont laughed scornfully at this, and told her that her project was absurd; that charms like hers were meant to be enjoyed, not buried, and that he himself would more than make amends for her dead lover. The monk, who promptly interposed to rebuke this impious talk, was commanded to hold his peace; and still persisting was seized by the knight and hurled over the edge of the cliff, where he fell into the sea, and was drowned.

Rodomont, when he had got rid of the hermit, again applied to the sad lady, heartless with affright, and, in the language used by lovers, said, "she was his very heart, his life, his light." Having laid aside all violence, he humbly sued that she would accompany him to his retreat, near by. It was a ruined chapel from which the monks had been driven by the disorders of the time, and which Rodomont had taken possession of. Isabella, who had no choice but to obey, followed him, meditating as she went what resource she could find to escape out of his power, and keep her vow to her dead husband, to be faithful to his memory as long as life should last. At length she said, "If, my lord, you will let me go and fulfil my vow, and my intention, as I have already declared it, I will bestow upon you what will be to you of more value than a hundred women's hearts. I know an herb, and I have seen it on our way, which, rightly prepared, affords a juice of such power, that the flesh, if laved with it, becomes impenetrable to sword or fire. This liquor I can make, and will, to-day, if you will accept my offer; and when you have seen its virtue you will value it more than if all Europe were made your own."

Rodomont, at hearing this, readily promised all that was asked, so eager was he to learn a secret that would make him as Achilles was of yore. Isabella, having collected such herbs as she thought proper, and boiled them, with certain mysterious signs and words, at length declared her labor done, and, as a test, offered to try its virtue on herself. She bathed her neck and bosom with the liquor, and then called on Rodomont to smite with all his force, and see whether his sword had power to harm. The pagan, who during the preparations had taken frequent draughts of wine, and scarce knew what he did, drew his sword at the word, and struck across her neck with all his might, and the fair head leapt sundered from the snowy neck and breast.

Rude and unfeeling as he was, the pagan knight lamented bitterly this sad result. To honor her memory he resolved to do a work as unparalleled as her devotion. From all parts round he caused laborers to be brought, and had a tower built to enclose the chapel, within which the remains of Zerbino and Isabella were entombed. Across the stream which flowed near by he built a bridge, scarce two yards wide, and added neither parapet nor rail. On the top of the tower a sentry was placed, who, when any traveller approached the bridge, gave notice to his master. Rodomont thereupon sallied out, and defied the approaching knight to fight him upon the bridge, where any chance step a little aside would plunge the rider headlong in the stream. This bridge he vowed to keep until a thousand suits of armor should be won from conquered knights, wherewith to build a trophy to his victim and her lord.

Within ten days the bridge was built, and the tower was in progress. In a short time many knights, either seeking the shortest route, or tempted by a desire of adventure, had made the attempt to pass the bridge. All, without exception, had lost either arms or life, or both; some falling before Rodomont's lance, others precipitated into the river. One day, as Rodomont stood urging his workmen, it chanced that Orlando in his furious mood came thither, and approached the bridge. Rodomont halloed to him, "Halt, churl; presume not to set foot upon that bridge; it was not made for such as you!" Orlando took no notice, but pressed on. Just then a gentle damsel rode up. It was Flordelis, who was seeking her Florismart. She saw Orlando, and, in spite of his strange appearance, recognized him. Rodomont, not used to have his commands disobeyed, laid hands on the madman, and would have thrown him into the river, but to his astonishment found himself in the gripe of one not so easily disposed of. "How can a fool have such strength?" he growled between his teeth. Flordelis stopped to see the issue, where each of these two puissant warriors strove to throw the other from the bridge. Orlando at last had strength enough to lift his foe with all his armor, and fling him over the side, but had not wit to clear himself from him, so both fell together. High flashed the wave as they together smote its surface. Here Orlando had the advantage; he was naked, and could swim like a fish. He soon reached the bank, and, careless of praise or blame, stopped not to see what came of the adventure. Rodomont, entangled with his armor, escaped with difficulty to the bank. Meantime, Flordelis passed the bridge unchallenged.

After long wandering without success she returned to Paris, and there found the object of her search; for Florismart, after the fall of Albracca, had repaired thither. The joy of meeting was clouded to Florismart by the news which Flordelis brought of Orlando's wretched plight. The last she had seen of him was when he fell with Rodomont into the stream. Florismart, who loved Orlando like a brother, resolved to set out immediately, under the guidance of the lady, to find him, and bring him where he might receive the treatment suited to his case. A few days brought them to the place where they found the Tartar king still guarding the bridge. The usual challenge and defiance was made, and the knights rode to encounter one another on the bridge. At the first encounter both horses were overthrown; and, having no space to regain their footing, fell with their riders into the water. Rodomont, who knew the soundings of the stream, soon recovered the land; but Florismart was carried downward by the current, and landed at last on a bank of mud where his horse could hardly find footing. Flordelis, who watched the battle from the bridge, seeing her lover in this piteous case, exclaimed aloud, "Ah! Rodomont, for love of her whom dead you honor, have pity on me, who love this knight, and slay him not. Let it suffice he yields his armor to the pile, and none more glorious will it bear than his." Her prayer, so well directed, touched the pagan's heart, though hard to move, and he lent his aid to help the knight to land. He kept him a prisoner, however, and added his armor to the pile. Flordelis, with a heavy heart, went her way.

We must now return to Rogero, who, when we parted with him, was engaged in an adventure which arrested his progress to the monastery whither he was bound with the intention of receiving baptism, and thus qualifying himself to demand Bradamante as his bride. On his way he met with Mandricardo, and the quarrel was revived respecting the right to wear the badge of Hector. After a warm discussion both parties agreed to submit the question to King Agramant, and for that purpose took their way to the Saracen camp. Here they met Gradasso, who had his controversy also with Mandricardo. This warrior claimed the sword of Orlando, denying the right of Mandricardo to possess it in virtue of his having found it abandoned by its owner. King Agramant strove in vain to reconcile these quarrels, and was forced at last to consent that the points in dispute should be settled by one combat, in which Mandricardo should meet one of the other champions, to whom should be committed the cause of both. Rogero was chosen by lot to maintain Gradasso's cause and his own. Great preparations were made for this signal contest. On the appointed day it was fought in the presence of Agramant, and of the whole army. Rogero won it; and Mandricardo, the conqueror of Hector's arms, the challenger of Orlando, and the slayer of Zerbino, lost his life. Gradasso received Durindana as his prize, which lost half its value in his eyes, since it was won by another's prowess, not his own.

Rogero, though victorious, was severely wounded, and lay helpless many weeks in the camp of Agramant, while Bradamante, ignorant of the cause of his delay, expected him at Montalban. Thither he had promised to repair in fifteen days, or twenty at furthest, hoping to have obtained by that time an honorable discharge from his obligations to the Saracen commander. The twenty days were passed, and a month more, and still Rogero came not, nor did any tidings reach Bradamante accounting for his absence. At the end of that time, a wandering knight brought news of the famous combat, and of Rogero's wound. He added, what alarmed Bradamante still more, that Marphisa, a female warrior, young and fair, was in attendance on the wounded knight. He added that the whole army expected that, as soon as

Rogero's wounds were healed, the pair would be united in marriage.

Bradamante, distressed by this news, though she believed it but in part, resolved to go immediately and see for herself. She mounted Rabican, the horse of Astolpho, which he had committed to her care, and took with her the lance of gold, though unaware of its wonderful powers. Thus accoutred, she left the castle, and took the road toward Paris and the camp of the Saracens.

Marphisa, whose devotion to Rogero in his illness had so excited the jealousy of Bradamante, was the twin sister of Rogero. She, with him, had been taken in charge when an infant by Atlantes, the magician, but while yet a child she had been stolen away by an Arab tribe. Adopted by their chief, she had early learned horsemanship and skill in arms, and at this time had come to the camp of Agramant with no other view than to see and test for herself the prowess of the warriors of either camp, whose fame rang through the world. Arriving at the very moment of the late encounter, the name of Rogero, and some few facts of his story which she learned, were enough to suggest the idea that it was her brother whom she saw victorious in the single combat. Inquiry satisfied the two of their near kindred, and from that moment Marphisa devoted herself to the care of her new-found and much-loved brother.

In those moments of seclusion Rogero informed his sister of what he had learned of their parentage from old Atlantes. Rogero, their father, a Christian knight, had won the heart of Galaciella, daughter of the Sultan of Africa, and sister of King Agramant, converted her to the Christian faith, and secretly married her. The Sultan, enraged at his daughter's marriage, drove her husband into exile, and caused her with her infant children, Rogero and Marphisa, to be placed in a boat and committed to the winds and waves, to perish; from which fate they were saved by Atlantes. On hearing this, Marphisa exclaimed, "How can you, brother, leave our parents unavenged so long, and even submit to serve the son of the tyrant who so wronged them?" Rogero replied that it was but lately he had learned the full truth; that when he learned it he was already embarked with Agramant, from whom he had received knighthood, and that he only waited for a suitable opportunity when he might with honor desert his standard, and at the same time return to the faith of his fathers. Marphisa hailed this resolution with joy, and declared her intention to join with him in embracing the Christian faith.

We left Bradamante when, mounted on Rabican and armed with Astolpho's lance, she rode forth, determined to learn the cause of Rogero's long absence. One day, as she rode, she met a damsel, of visage and of manners fair, but overcome with grief. It was Flordelis, who was seeking far and near a champion capable of liberating and avenging her lord. Flordelis marked the approaching warrior, and, judging from appearances, thought she had found the champion she sought. "Are you, Sir Knight," she said, "so daring and so kind as to take up my cause against a fierce and cruel warrior who has made prisoner of my lord, and forced me thus to be a wanderer and a suppliant?" Then she related the events which had happened at the bridge. Bradamante, to whom noble enterprises were always welcome, readily embraced this, and the rather as in her gloomy forebodings she felt as if Rogero was forever lost to her.

Next day the two arrived at the bridge. The sentry descried them approaching, and gave notice to his lord, who thereupon donned his armor and went forth to meet them. Here, as usual, he called on the advancing warrior to yield his horse and arms an oblation to the tomb. Bradamante replied, asking by what right he called on the innocent to do penance for his crime. "Your life and your armor," she added, "are the fittest offering to her tomb, and I, a woman, the fittest champion to take them." With that she couched her spear, spurred her horse, and ran to the encounter. King Rodomont came on with speed. The trampling sounded on the bridge like thunder. It took but a moment to decide the contest. The golden lance did its office, and that fierce Moor, so renowned in tourney, lay extended on the bridge. "Who is the loser now?" said Bradamante; but Rodomont, amazed that a woman's hand should have laid him low, could not or would not answer. Silent and sad, he raised himself, unbound his helm and mail, and flung them against the tomb; then, sullen and on foot, left the ground; but first gave orders to one of his squires to release all his prisoners. They had been sent off to Africa. Besides Florismart, there were Sansonnet and Oliver, who had ridden that way in quest of Orlando, and had both in turn been overthrown in the encounter.

Bradamante after her victory resumed her route, and in due time reached the Christian camp, where she readily learned an explanation of the mystery which had caused her so much anxiety. Rogero and his fair and brave sister, Marphisa, were too illustrious by their station and exploits not to be the frequent topic of discourse even among their adversaries, and all that Bradamante was anxious to know reached her ear, almost without inquiry.

We now return to Gradasso, who by Rogero's victory had been made possessor of Durindana. There now only remained to him to seek the horse of Rinaldo; and the challenge, given and accepted, was yet to be fought with that warrior, for it had been interrupted by the arts of Malagigi. Gradasso now sought another meeting with Rinaldo, and met with no reluctance on his part. As the combat was for the possession of Bayard, the knights dismounted and fought on foot. Long time the battle lasted. Rinaldo, knowing well the deadly stroke of Durindana, used all his art to parry or avoid its blow. Gradasso struck with might and main, but wellnigh all his strokes were spent in air, or if they smote they fell obliquely and did little harm.

Thus had they fought long, glancing at one another's eyes, and seeing naught else, when their attention was arrested perforce by a strange noise. They turned, and beheld the good Bayard attacked by a monstrous bird. Perhaps it was a bird, for such it seemed; but when or where such a bird was ever seen I have nowhere read, except in Turpin; and I am inclined to believe that it was not a bird, but a fiend, evoked from underground by Malagigi, and thither sent on purpose to interrupt the fight. Whether a fiend or a fowl, the monster flew right at Bayard, and clapped his wings in his face. Thereat the steed broke loose, and ran madly across the plain, pursued by the bird, till Bayard plunged into the wood, and was lost to sight.

Rinaldo and Gradasso, seeing Bayard's escape, agreed to suspend their battle till they could recover the horse, the object of contention. Gradasso mounted his steed, and followed the footmarks of Bayard into the forest. Rinaldo, never more vexed in spirit, remained at the spot, Gradasso having promised to return thither with the horse, if he found him. He did find him, after long search, for he had the good fortune to hear him neigh. Thus he became possessed of both the objects for which he had led an army from his own country, and invaded France. He did not forget his promise to bring Bayard back to the place where he had left Rinaldo, but only muttering, "Now I have got him, he little knows me who expects me to give him up; if Rinaldo wants the horse let him seek him in India, as I have sought him in France,"-- he made the best of his way to Arles, where his vessels lay; and in possession of the two objects of his ambition, the horse and the sword, sailed away to his own country.

ASTOLPHO IN ABYSSINIA

When we last parted with the adventurous paladin Astolpho, he was just commencing that flight over the countries of the world from which he promised himself so much gratification. Our readers are aware that the eagle and the falcon have not so swift a flight as the Hippogriff on which Astolpho rode. It was not long, therefore, before the paladin, directing his course toward the southeast, arrived over that part of Africa where the great river Nile has its source. Here he alighted, and found himself in the neighborhood of the capital of Abyssinia, ruled by Senapus, whose riches and power were immense. His palace was of surpassing splendor; the bars of the gates, the hinges and locks, were all of pure gold; in fact, this metal, in that country, is put to all those uses for which we employ iron. It is so common that they prefer for ornamental purposes rock crystal, of which all the columns were made. Precious stones of different kinds, rubies, emeralds, sapphires, and topazes were set in ornamental designs, and the walls and ceilings were adorned with pearls.

It is in this country those famous balms grow of which there are some few plants in that part of Judaea called Gilead. Musk, ambergris, and numerous gums, so precious in Europe, are here in their native climate. It is said the Sultan of Egypt pays a vast tribute to the monarch of this country to hire him not to cut off the source of the Nile, which he might easily do, and cause the river to flow in some other direction, thus depriving Egypt of the source of its fertility.

At the time of Astolpho's arrival in his dominions, this monarch was in great affliction. In spite of his riches and the precious productions of his country, he was in danger of dying of hunger. He was a prey to a flock of obscene birds called Harpies, which attacked him whenever he sat at meat, and with their claws snatched, tore, and scattered everything, overturning the vessels, devouring the food, and infecting what they left with their filthy touch. It was said this punishment was inflicted upon the king because when young, and filled with pride and presumption, he had attempted to invade with an army the terrestrial paradise, which is situated on the top of a mountain whence the Nile draws its source. Nor was this his only punishment. He was struck blind.

Astolpho, on arriving in the dominions of this monarch, hastened to pay him his respects. King Senapus received him graciously, and ordered a splendid repast to be prepared in honor of his arrival. While the guests were seated at table, Astolpho filling the place of dignity at the king's right hand, the horrid scream of the Harpies was heard in the air, and soon they approached, hovering over the tables, seizing the food from the dishes, and overturning everything with the flapping of their broad wings. In vain the guests struck at them with knives and any weapons which they had, and Astolpho drew his sword and gave them repeated blows, which seemed to have no more effect upon them than if their bodies had been made of tow.

At last Astolpho thought of his horn. He first gave warning to the king and his guests to stop their ears; then blew a blast. The Harpies, terrified at the sound, flew away as fast as their wings could carry them. The paladin mounted his Hippogriff, and pursued them, blowing his horn as often as he came near them. They stretched their flight towards the great mountain, at the foot of which there is a cavern, which is thought to be the mouth of the infernal abodes. Hither those horrid birds flew, as if to their home. Having seen them all disappear in the recess, Astolpho cared not to pursue them farther, but alighting, rolled huge stones into the mouth of the cave, and piled branches of trees therein, so that he effectually barred their passage out, and we have no evidence of their ever having been seen since in the outer air.

After this labor Astolpho refreshed himself by bathing in a fountain whose pure waters bubbled from a cleft of the rock. Having rested awhile, an earnest desire seized him of ascending the mountain which towered above him. The Hippogriff bore him swiftly upwards, and landed him on the top of the mountain, which he found to be an extensive plain.

A splendid palace rose in the middle of this plain, whose walls shone with such brilliancy that mortal eyes could hardly bear the sight. Astolpho guided the winged horse towards this edifice, and made him poise himself in the air while he took a leisurely survey of this favored spot and its environs. It seemed as if nature and art had striven with one another to see which could do the most for its embellishment.

Astolpho, on approaching the edifice, saw a venerable man advance to meet him. This personage was clothed in a long vesture as white as snow, while a mantle of purple covered his shoulders, and hung down to the ground. A white beard descended to his middle, and his hair, of the same color, overshadowed his shoulders. His eyes were so brilliant that Astolpho felt persuaded that he was a blessed inhabitant of the heavenly mansions.

The sage, smiling benignantly upon the paladin, who from respect had dismounted from his horse, said to him: "Noble chevalier, know that it is by the Divine will you have been brought to the terrestrial paradise. Your mortal nature could not have borne to scale these heights and reach these seats of bliss if it were not the will of Heaven that you should be instructed in the means to succor Charles, and to sustain the glory of our holy faith. I am prepared to impart the needed counsels; but before I begin let me welcome you to our sojourn. I doubt not your long fast and distant journey have given you a good appetite."

The aspect of the venerable man filled the prince with admiration; but his surprise ceased when he learned from him that he was that one of the Apostles of our Lord to whom he said, "I will that thou tarry till I come."

St. John, conducting Astolpho, rejoined his companions. These were the patriarch Enoch and the prophet Elijah; neither of whom had yet seen his dying day, but, taken from our lower world, were dwelling in a region of peace and joy, in a climate of eternal spring, till the last trumpet shall sound.

The three holy inhabitants of the terrestrial paradise received Astolpho with the greatest kindness, carried him to a pleasant apartment, and took great care of the Hippogriff, to whom they gave such food as suited him, while to the prince they presented fruits so delicious that he felt inclined to excuse our first parents for their sin in eating them without permission.

Astolpho, having recruited his strength, not only by these excellent fruits, but also by sweet sleep, roused himself at the first blush of dawn, and as soon as he left his chamber met the beloved Apostle coming to seek him. St. John took him by the hand, and told him many things relating to the past and the future. Among others, he said, "Son, let me tell you what is now going on in France. Orlando, the illustrious prince who received at his birth the endowment of strength and courage more than mortal, raised up as was Samson of old to be the champion of the true faith, has been guilty of the basest ingratitude in leaving the Christian camp when it most needed the support of his arm, to run after a Saracen princess, whom he would fain marry, though she scorns him. To punish him his reason has been taken away, so that he runs naked through the land, over mountains and through valleys, without a ray of intelligence. The duration of his punishment has been fixed at three months, and that time having nearly expired, you have been brought hither to learn from us the means by which the reason of Orlando may be restored. True, you will be obliged to make a journey with me, and we must even leave the earth, and ascend to the moon, for it is in that planet we are to seek the remedy for the madness of the paladin. I propose to make our journey this evening, as soon as the moon appears over our head."

As soon as the sun sunk beneath the seas, and the moon presented its luminous disk, the holy man had the chariot brought out in which he was accustomed to make excursions among the stars, the same which was employed long ago to convey Elijah up from earth. The saint made Astolpho seat himself beside him, took the reins, and giving the word to the coursers, they bore them upward with astonishing celerity.

At length they reached the great continent of the Moon. Its surface appeared to be of polished steel, with here and there a spot which, like rust, obscured its brightness. The paladin was astonished to see that the earth, with all its seas and rivers, seemed but an insignificant spot in the distance.

The prince discovered in this region so new to him rivers, lakes, plains, hills, and valleys. Many beautiful cities and castles enriched the landscape. He saw also vast forests, and heard in them the sound of horns and the barking of dogs, which led him to conclude that the nymphs were following the chase.

The knight, filled with wonder at all he saw, was conducted by the saint to a valley, where he stood amazed at the riches strewed all around him. Well he might be so, for that valley was the receptacle of things lost on earth, either by men's fault, or by the effect of time and chance. Let no one suppose we speak here of kingdoms or of treasures; they are the toys of Fortune, which she dispenses in turning her wheel; we speak of things which she can neither give nor take away. Such are reputations, which appear at one time so brilliant, and a short time after are heard of no more. Here, also, are countless vows and prayers for unattainable objects, lovers' sighs and tears, time spent in gaming, dressing, and doing nothing, the leisure of the dull and the intentions of the lazy, baseless projects, intrigues, and plots; these and such like things fill all the valley.

Astolpho had a great desire to understand all that he saw, and which appeared to him so extraordinary. Among the rest, he observed a great mountain of blown bladders, from which issued indistinct noises. The saint told him these were the dynasties of Assyrian and Persian kings, once the wonder of the earth, of which now scarce the name remains.

Astolpho could not help laughing when the saint said to him, "All these hooks of silver and gold that you see are the gifts of courtiers to princes, made in the hope of getting something better in return." He also showed him garlands of flowers in which snares were concealed; these were flatteries and adulations, meant to deceive. But nothing was so comical as the sight of numerous grasshoppers which had burst their lungs with chirping. These, he told him, were sonnets, odes, and dedications, addressed by venal poets to great people.

The paladin beheld with wonder what seemed a lake of spilled milk. "It is," said the saint, "the charity done by frightened misers on their death-beds." It would take too long to tell all that the valley contained: meanness, affectations, pretended virtues, and concealed vices were there in abundance.

Among the rest Astolpho perceived many days of his own lost, and many imprudent sallies which he had made, and would have been glad not to have been reminded of. But he also saw among so many lost things a great abundance of one thing which men are apt to think they all possess, and do not think it necessary to pray for,--good sense. This commodity appeared under the form of a liquor, most light and apt to evaporate. It was therefore kept in vials, firmly sealed. One of these was labelled, "The sense of the Paladin Orlando."

All the bottles were ticketed, and the sage placed one in Astolpho's hand, which he found was his own. It was more than half full. He was surprised to find there many other vials which contained almost the whole of the wits of many persons who passed among men for wise. Ah, how easy it is to lose one's reason! Some lose theirs by yielding to the sway of the passions; some in braving tempests and shoals in search of wealth; some by trusting too much to the promises of the great; some by setting their hearts on trifles. As might have been expected, the bottles which held the wits of astrologers, inventors, metaphysicians, and above all, of poets, were in general the best filled of all.

Astolpho took his bottle, put it to his nose, and inhaled it all; and Turpin assures us that he was for a long time afterwards as sage as one could wish; but the Archbishop adds that there was reason to fear that some of the precious fluid afterwards found its way back into the bottle. The paladin took also the bottle which belonged to Orlando. It was a large one, and quite full.

Before quitting the planetary region Astolpho was conducted to an edifice on the borders of a river. He was shown an immense hall full of bundles of silk, linen, cotton, and wool. A thousand different colors, brilliant or dull, some quite black, were among these skeins. In one part of the hall an old woman was busy winding off yarns from all these different bundles. When she had finished a skein another ancient dame took it and placed it with others; a third selected from the fleeces spun, and mingled them in due proportions. The paladin inquired what all this might be. "These old women," said the saint, "are the Fates, who spin, measure, and terminate the lives of mortals. As long as the thread stretches in one of those skeins, so long does the mortal enjoy the light of day; but nature and death are on the alert to shut the eyes of those whose thread is spun."

Each one of the skeins had a label of gold, silver, or iron, bearing the name of the individual to whom it belonged. An old man, who, in spite of the burden of years, seemed brisk and active, ran without ceasing to fill his apron with these labels, and carried them away to throw them into the river, whose name was Lethe.

When he reached the shore of the river the old man shook out his apron, and the labels sunk to the bottom. A small number only floated for a time, hardly one in a thousand. Numberless birds, hawks, crows, and vultures hovered over the stream, with clamorous cries, and strove to snatch from the water some of these names; but they were too heavy for them, and after a while the birds were forced to let them drop into the river of oblivion. But two beautiful swans, of snowy whiteness, gathered some few of the names, and returned with them to the shore, where a lovely nymph received them from their beaks, and carried them to a temple placed upon a hill, and suspended them for all time upon a sacred column, on which stood the statue of Immortality.

Astolpho was amazed at all this, and asked his guide to explain it. He replied, "The old man is Time. All the names upon the tickets would be immortal if the old man did not plunge them into the river of oblivion. Those clamorous birds which make vain efforts to save certain of the names are flatterers, pensioners, venal rhymesters, who do their best to rescue from oblivion the unworthy names of their patrons; but all in vain; they may keep them from their fate a little while, but ere long the river of oblivion must swallow them all.

"The swans, that with harmonious strains carry certain names to the temple of Eternal Memory, are the great poets, who save from oblivion worse than death the names of those they judge worthy of immortality. Swans of this kind are rare. Let monarchs know the true breed, and fail not to nourish with care such as may chance to appear in their time."

THE WAR IN AFRICA

When Astolpho had descended to the earth with the precious phial, St. John showed him a plant of marvellous virtues, with which he told him he had only to touch the eyes of the king of

Abyssinia to restore him to sight. "That important service," said the saint, "added to your having delivered him from the Harpies, will induce him to give you an army wherewith to attack the Africans in their rear, and force them to return from France to defend their own country." The saint also instructed him how to lead his troops in safety across the great deserts, where caravans are often overwhelmed with moving columns of sand. Astolpho, fortified with ample instructions, remounted the Hippogriff, thanked the saint, received his blessing, and took his flight down to the level country.

Keeping the course of the river Nile, he soon arrived at the capital of Abyssinia, and rejoined Senapus. The joy of the king was great when he heard again the voice of the hero who had delivered him from the Harpies. Astolpho touched his eyes with the plant which he had brought from the terrestrial paradise, and restored their sight. The king's gratitude was unbounded. He begged him to name a reward, promising to grant it, whatever it might be. Astolpho asked an army to go to the assistance of Charlemagne, and the king not only granted him a hundred thousand men, but offered to lead them himself.

The night before the day appointed for the departure of the troops Astolpho mounted his winged horse, and directed his flight towards a mountain, whence the fierce South-wind issues, whose blast raises the sands of the Nubian desert, and whirls them onward in overwhelming clouds. The paladin, by the advice of St. John, had prepared himself with a leather bag, which he placed adroitly, with its mouth open, over the vent whence issues this terrible wind. At the first dawn of morning the wind rushed from its cavern to resume its daily course, and was caught in the bag, and securely tied up. Astolpho, delighted with his prize, returned to his army, placed himself at their head, and commenced his march. The Abyssinians traversed without danger or difficulty those vast fields of sand which separate their country from the kingdoms of Northern Africa, for the terrible South-wind, taken completely captive, had not force enough left to blow out a candle.

Senapus was distressed that he could not furnish any cavalry, for his country, rich in camels and elephants, was destitute of horses. This difficulty the saint had foreseen, and had taught Astolpho the means of remedying. He now put those means in operation. Having reached a place whence he beheld a vast plain and the sea, he chose from his troops those who appeared to be the best made and the most intelligent. These he caused to be arranged in squadrons at the foot of a lofty mountain which bordered the plain, and he himself mounted to the summit to carry into effect his great design. Here he found vast quantities of fragments of rock and pebbles. These he set rolling down the mountain's side, and, wonderful to relate, as they rolled they grew in size, made themselves bodies, legs, necks, and long faces. Next they began to neigh, to curvet, to scamper on all sides over the plain. Some were bay, some roan, some dapple, some chestnut. The troops at the foot of the mountain exerted themselves to catch these new-created horses, which they easily did, for the miracle had been so considerate as to provide all the horses with bridles and saddles. Astolpho thus suddenly found himself supplied with an excellent corps of cavalry, not fewer (as Archbishop Turpin asserts) than eighty thousand strong. With these troops Astolpho reduced all the country to subjection, and at last arrived before the walls of Agramant's capital city, Biserta, to which he laid siege.

We must now return to the camp of the Christians, which lay before Arles, to which city the Saracens had retired after being defeated in a night attack led on by Rinaldo. Agramant here received the tidings of the invasion of his country by a fresh enemy, the Abyssinians, and learned that Biserta was in danger of falling into their hands. He took counsel of his officers, and decided to send an embassy to Charles, proposing that the whole quarrel should be submitted to the combat of two warriors, one from each side, according to the issue of which it should be decided which party should pay tribute to the other, and the war should cease. Charlemagne, who had not heard of the favorable turn which affairs had taken in Africa, readily agreed to this proposal, and Rinaldo was selected on the part of the Christians to sustain the combat.

The Saracens selected Rogero for their champion. Rogero was still in the Saracen camp, kept there by honor alone, for his mind had been opened to the truth of the Christian faith by the arguments of Bradamante, and he had resolved to leave the party of the infidels on the first favorable opportunity, and to join the Christian side. But his honor forbade him to do this while his former friends were in distress; and thus he waited for what time might bring forth, when he was startled by the announcement that he had been selected to uphold the cause of the Saracens against the Christians, and that his foe was to be Rinaldo, the brother of Bradamante.

While Rogero was overwhelmed with this intelligence Bradamante on her side felt the deepest distress at hearing of the proposed combat. If Rogero should fall she felt that no other man living was worthy of her love; and if, on the other hand, Heaven should resolve to punish France by the death of her chosen champion, Bradamante would have to deplore her brother, so dear to her, and be no less completely severed from the object of her affections.

While the fair lady gave herself up to these sad thoughts, the sage enchantress, Melissa, suddenly appeared before her. "Fear not, my daughter," said she, "I shall find a way to interrupt this combat which so distresses you."

Meanwhile Rinaldo and Rogero prepared their weapons for the conflict. Rinaldo had the choice, and decided that it should be on foot, and with no weapons but the battle-axe and poniard. The place assigned was a plain between the camp of Charlemagne and the walls of Arles.

Hardly had the dawn announced the day appointed for this memorable combat, when heralds proceeded from both sides to mark the lists. Erelong the African troops were seen to advance from the city, Agramant at their head; his brilliant arms adorned in the Moorish fashion, his horse a bay, with a white star on his forehead. Rogero marched at his side, and some of the greatest warriors of the Saracen camp attended him, bearing the various parts of his armor and weapons. Charlemagne, on his part, proceeded from his intrenchments, ranged his troops in semicircle, and stood surrounded by his peers and paladins. Some of them bore portions of the armor of Rinaldo, the celebrated Ogier, the Dane, bearing the helmet which Rinaldo took from Mambrino. Duke Namo of Bavaria and Salomon of Bretagne bore two axes, of equal weight, prepared for the occasion.

The terms of the combat were then sworn to with the utmost solemnity by all parties. It was agreed that if from either part any attempt was made to interrupt the battle both combatants should turn their arms against the party which should be guilty of the interruption; and both monarchs assented to the condition that in such case the champion of the offending party should be discharged from his allegiance, and at liberty to transfer his arms to the other side.

When all the preparations were concluded the monarchs and their attendants retired each to his own side, and the champions were left alone. The two warriors advanced with measured steps towards each other, and met in the middle of the space. They attacked one another at the same moment, and the air resounded with the blows they gave. Sparks flew from their battle-axes, while the velocity with which they managed their weapons astonished the beholders. Rogero, always remembering that his antagonist was the brother of his betrothed, could not aim a deadly wound;

he strove only to ward off those levelled against himself. Rinaldo, on the other hand, much as he esteemed Rogero, spared not his blows, for he eagerly desired victory for his own sake, and for the sake of his country and his faith.

The Saracens soon perceived that their champion fought feebly, and gave not to Rinaldo such blows as he received from him. His disadvantage was so marked that anxiety and shame were manifest on the countenance of Agramant. Melissa, one of the most acute enchantresses that ever lived, seized this moment to disguise herself under the form of Rodomont, that rude and impetuous warrior, who had now for some time been absent from the Saracen camp. Approaching Agramant, she said, "How could you, my lord, have the imprudence of selecting a young man without experience to oppose the most redoubtable warrior of France? Surely you must have been regardless of the honor of your arms, and of the fate of your empire! But it is not too late. Break without delay the agreement which is sure to result in your ruin." So saying, she addressed the troops who stood near, "Friends," said she, "follow me; under my guidance every one of you will be a match for a score of those feeble Christians." Agramant, delighted at seeing Rodomont once more at his side, gave his consent, and the Saracens, at the instant, couched their lances, set spurs to their steeds, and swept down upon the French. Melissa, when she saw her work successful, disappeared.

Rinaldo and Rogero, seeing the truce broken, and the two armies engaged in general conflict, stopped their battle; their martial fury ceased at once, they joined hands, and resolved to act no more on either side until it should be clearly ascertained which party had failed to observe its oath. Both renewed their promise to abandon forever the party which had been thus false and perjured.

Meanwhile, the Christians, after the first moment of surprise, met the Saracens with courage redoubled by rage at the treachery of their foes. Guido the Wild, brother and rival of Rinaldo, Griffon and Aquilant, sons of Oliver, and numerous others whose names have already been celebrated in our recitals, beat back the assailants, and at last, after prodigious slaughter, forced them to take shelter within the walls of Arles.

We will now return to Orlando, whom we last heard of as furiously mad, and doing a thousand acts of violence in his senseless rage. One day he came to the borders of a stream which intercepted his course. He swam across it, for he could swim like an otter, and on the other side saw a peasant watering his horse. He seized the animal, in spite of the resistance of the peasant, and rode it with furious speed till he arrived at the sea-coast, where Spain is divided from Africa by only a narrow strait. At the moment of his arrival a vessel had just put off to cross the strait. She was full of people who, with glass in hand, seemed to be taking a merry farewell of the land, wafted by a favorable breeze.

The frantic Orlando cried out to them to stop and take him in; but they, having no desire to admit a madman to their company, paid him no attention. The paladin thought this behavior very uncivil; and by force of blows made his horse carry him into the water in pursuit of the ship. The wretched animal soon had only his head above water; but as Orlando urged him forward, nothing was left for the poor beast but either to die or swim over to Africa.

Already Orlando had lost sight of the bark; distance and the swell of the sea completely hid it from his sight. He continued to press his horse forward, till at last it could struggle no more, and sunk beneath him. Orlando, nowise concerned, stretched out his nervous arms, puffing the salt water from before his mouth, and carried his head above the waves. Fortunately they were not rough, scarce a breath of wind agitated the surface; otherwise, the invincible Orlando would then have met his death. But fortune, which it is said favors fools, delivered him from this danger, and landed him safe on the shore of Ceuta. Here he rambled along the shore till he came to where the black army of Astolpho held its camp.

Now it happened, just before this time, that a vessel filled with prisoners which Rodomont had taken at the bridge had arrived, and, not knowing of the presence of the Abyssinian army, had sailed right into port, where of course the prisoners and their captors changed places, the former being set at liberty and received with all joy, the latter sent to serve in the galleys. Astolpho thus found himself surrounded with Christian knights, and he and his friends were exchanging greetings and felicitations, when a noise was heard in the camp, and seemed to increase every moment.

Astolpho and his friends seized their weapons, mounted their horses, and rode to the quarter whence the noise proceeded. Imagine their astonishment when they saw that the tumult was caused by a single man, perfectly naked, and browned with dirt and exposure, but of a force and fury so terrible that he overturned all that offered to lay hands on him.

Astolpho, Dudon, Oliver, and Florimart gazed at him with amazement. It was with difficulty they knew him. Astolpho, who had been warned of his condition by his holy monitor, was the first to recognize him. As the paladins closed round Orlando, the madman dealt one and another a blow of his fist, which, if they had not been in armor, or he had had any weapon, would probably have despatched them; as it was, Dudon and Astolpho measured their length on the sand. But Florimart seized him from behind, Sansonnet and another grasped his legs, and at last they succeeded in securing him with ropes. They took him to the water-side and washed him well, and then Astolpho, having first bandaged his mouth so that he could not breathe except through his nose, brought the precious phial, uncorked it, and placed it adroitly under his nostrils, when the good Orlando took it all up in one breath. O marvellous prodigy! The paladin recovered in an instant all his intelligence. He felt like one who had awakened from a painful dream, in which he had believed that monsters were about to tear him to pieces. He seemed prostrated, silent, and abashed. Florismart, Oliver, and Astolpho stood gazing upon him, while he turned his eyes around and on himself. He seemed surprised to find himself naked, bound, and stretched on the seashore. After a few moments he recognized his friends, and spoke to them in a tone so tender that they hastened to unbind him, and to supply him with garments. Then they exerted themselves to console him, to diminish the weight with which his spirits were oppressed, and to make him forget the wretched condition into which he had been sunk.

Orlando, in recovering his reason, found himself also delivered from his insane attachment to the queen of Cathay. His heart felt now no further influenced by the recollection of her than to be moved with an ardent desire to retrieve his fame by some distinguished exploit. Astolpho would gladly have yielded to him the chief command of the army, but Orlando would not take from the friend to whom he owed so much the glory of the campaign; but in everything the two paladins acted in concert, and united their counsels. They proposed to make a general assault on the city of Biserta, and were only waiting a favorable moment, when their plan was interrupted by new events.

Agramant, after the bloody battle which followed the infraction of the truce, found himself so weak that he saw it was in vain to attempt to remain in France. So, in concert with Sobrino, the bravest and most trusted of his chiefs, he embarked to return to his own country, having previously sent off his few remaining troops in the same direction. The vessel which carried Agramant and Sobrino approached the shore where the army of Astolpho lay encamped before Biserta, and having discovered this fact before it was too late, the king commanded the pilot to steer eastward, with a view to seek protection of the King of Egypt. But the weather becoming rough, he consented to the advice of his companions, and sought harbor in an island which lies between Sicily and Africa. There he found Gradasso, the warlike king of Sericane, who had come to France to possess himself of the horse Bayard and the sword Durindana; and having procured both these prizes was returning to his own country.

The two kings, who had been companions in arms under the walls of Paris, embraced one another affectionately. Gradasso learned with regret the reverses of Agramant, and offered him his troops and his person. He strongly deprecated resorting to Egypt for aid. "Remember the great Pompey," said he, "and shun that fatal shore. My plan," he continued, "is this: I mean to challenge Orlando to single combat. Possessed of such a sword and steed as mine, if he were made of steel or bronze, he could not escape me. He being removed, there will be no difficulty in driving back the Abyssinians. We will rouse against them the Moslem nations from the other side of the Nile, the Arabians, Persians, and Chaldeans, who will soon make Senapus recall his army to defend his own territories."

Agramant approved this advice except in one particular. "It is for me," said he, "to combat Orlando; I cannot with honor devolve that duty on another."

"Let us adopt a third course," said the aged warrior Sobrino. "I would not willingly remain a simple spectator of such a contest. Let us send three squires to the shore of Africa to challenge Orlando and any two of his companions in arms to meet us three in this island of Lampedusa."

This counsel was adopted; the three squires sped on their way; and now presented themselves, and rehearsed their message to the Christian knights.

Orlando was delighted, and rewarded the squires with rich gifts. He had already resolved to seek Gradasso and compel him to restore Durindana, which he had learned was in his possession. For his two companions the Count chose his faithful friend Florismart and his cousin Oliver.

The three warriors embarked, and sailing with a favorable wind, the second morning showed them, on their right, the island where this important battle was to be fought. Orlando and his two companions, having landed, pitched their tent. Agramant had placed his opposite.

Next morning, as soon as Aurora brightened the edges of the horizon, the warriors of both parties armed themselves and mounted their horses. They took their positions, face to face, lowered their lances, placed them in rest, clapped spurs to their horses, and flew to the charge. Orlando met the charge of Gradasso. The paladin was unmoved, but his horse could not sustain the terrible shock of Bayard. He recoiled, staggered, and fell some paces behind. Orlando tried to raise him, but, finding his efforts unavailing, seized his shield, and drew his famous Balisardo. Meanwhile Agramant and the brave Oliver gained no advantage, one or the other; but Florismart unhorsed the King Sobrino. Having brought his foe to the ground, he would not pursue his victory, but hastened to attack Gradasso, who had overthrown Orlando. Seeing him thus engaged, Orlando would not interfere, but ran with sword upraised upon Sobrino, and with one blow deprived him of sense and motion. Believing him dead, he next turned to aid his beloved Florismart. That brave paladin, neither in horse nor arms equal to his antagonist, could but parry and evade the blows of the terrible Durindana. Orlando, eager to succor him, was delayed for a moment in securing and mounting the horse of the King Sobrino. It was but an instant, and with sword upraised, he rushed upon Gradasso who, noways disconcerted at the onset of this second foe, shouted his defiance, and thrust at him with his sword, but, having miscalculated the distance, scarcely reached him, and failed to pierce his mail. Orlando, in return, dealt him a blow with Balisardo, which wounded as it fell face, breast, and thigh, and, if he had been a little nearer, would have cleft him in twain. Sobrino, by this time recovered from his swoon, though severely wounded, raised himself on his legs, and looked to see how he might aid his friends. Observing Agramant hard pressed by Oliver, he thrust his sword into the bowels of the latter's horse, which fell, and bore down his master, entangling his leg as he fell, so that Oliver could not extricate himself. Florismart saw the danger of his friend, and ran upon Sobrino with his horse, overthrew him, and then turned to defend himself from Agramant. They were not unequally matched, for though Agramant, mounted on Brigliadoro, had an advantage over Florismart, whose horse was but indifferent, yet Agramant had received a serious wound in his encounter with Oliver.

Nothing could exceed the fury of the encounter between Orlando and Gradasso. Durindana, in the hands of Gradasso, clove asunder whatever it struck; but such was the skill of Orlando, who perfectly knew the danger to which he was exposed from a stroke of that weapon, it had not yet struck him in such a way as to inflict a wound. Meanwhile, Gradasso was bleeding from many wounds, and his rage and incaution increased every moment. In his desperation he lifted Durindana with both hands, and struck so terrible a blow full on the helmet of Orlando, that for a moment it stunned the paladin. He dropped the reins, and his frightened horse scoured with him over the plain. Gradasso turned to pursue him, but at that moment saw Florismart in the very act of striking a fatal blow at Agramant, whom he had unhorsed. While Florismart was wholly intent upon completing his victory, Gradasso plunged his sword into his side. Florismart fell from his horse, and bathed the plain with his blood.

Orlando recovered himself just in time to see the deed. Whether rage or grief predominated in his breast, I cannot tell; but, seizing Balisardo with fury, his first blow fell upon Agramant, who was nearest to him, and smote his head from his shoulders. At this sight Gradasso for the first time felt his courage sink, and a dark presentiment of death came over him. He hardly stood on his defence when Orlando cast himself upon him, and gave him a fatal thrust. The sword penetrated his ribs, and came out a palm's breadth on the other side of his body.

Thus fell beneath the sword of the most illustrious paladin of France the bravest warrior of the Saracen host. Orlando then, as if despising his victory, leaped lightly to the ground, and ran to his dear friend Florismart, embraced him, and bathed him with his tears. Florismart still breathed. He could even command his voice to utter a few parting words: "Dear friend, do not forget me,--give me your prayers,--and oh! be a brother to Flordelis." He died in uttering her name.

After a few moments given to grief Orlando turned to look for his other companion and his late foes. Oliver lay oppressed with the weight of his horse, from which he had in vain struggled to liberate himself. Orlando extricated him with difficulty; he then raised Sobrino from the earth, and committed him to his squire, treating him as gently as if he had been his own brother. For this terrible warrior was the most generous of men to a fallen foe. He took Bayard and Brigliadoro, with the arms of the conquered knights; their bodies and their other spoils he remitted to their attendants.

But who can tell the grief of Flordelis when she saw the warriors return, and found not Florismart as usual after absence hasten to her side. She knew by the aspect of the others that her lord was slain. At the thought, and before the question could pass her lips, she fell senseless upon the ground. When life returned, and she learned the truth of her worst fears, she bitterly upbraided herself that she had let him depart without her. "I might have saved him by a single cry when his enemy dealt him that treacherous blow, or I might have thrown myself between and given my worthless life for his. Or if no more, I might have heard his last words, I might have given him a last kiss." So she lamented, and could not be comforted.

ROGERO AND BRADAMANTE

After the interruption of the combat with Rinaldo, as we have related, Rogero was perplexed with doubts what course to take. The terms of the treaty required him to abandon Agramant, who had broken it, and to transfer his allegiance to Charlemagne; and his love for Bradamante called him in the same direction; but unwillingness to desert his prince and leader in the hour of distress forbade this course. Embarking, therefore, for Africa, he took his way to rejoin the Saracen army; but was arrested midway by a storm which drove the vessel on a rock. The crew took to their boat, but that was quickly swamped in the waves, and Rogero with the rest were compelled to swim for their lives. Then while buffeting the waves Rogero bethought him of his sin in so long delaying his Christian profession, and vowed in his heart that, if he should live to reach the land, he would no longer delay to be baptized. His vows were heard and answered; he succeeded in reaching the shore, and was aided and relieved on landing by a pious hermit, whose cell overlooked the sea. From him he received baptism, having first passed some days with him, partaking his humble fare, and receiving instruction in the doctrines of the Christian faith.

While these things were going on, Rinaldo, who had set out on his way to seek Gradasso and recover Bayard from him, hearing on his way of the great things which were doing in Africa, repaired thither to bear his part in them. He arrived too late to do more than join his friends in lamenting the loss of Florismart, and to rejoice with them in their victory over the Pagan knights. On the death of their king the Africans gave up the contest, Biserta submitted, and the Christian knights had only to dismiss their forces, and return home. Astolpho took leave of his Abyssinian army, and sent them back laden with spoil to their own country, not forgetting to intrust to them the bag which held the winds, by means of which they were enabled to cross the sandy desert again without danger, and did not untie it till they reached their own country.

Orlando now, with Oliver, who much needed the surgeon's care, and Sobrino, to whom equal attention was shown, sailed in a swift vessel to Sicily, bearing with him the body of Florismart, to be laid in Christian earth. Rinaldo accompanied them, as did Sansonnet and the other Christian leaders. Arrived at Sicily, the funeral was solemnized with all the rites of religion, and with the profound grief of those who had known Florismart, or had heard of his fame. Then they resumed their course, steering for Marseilles. But Oliver's wound grew worse instead of better, and his sufferings so distressed his friends that they conferred together, not knowing what to do. Then said the pilot, "We are not far from an isle where a holy hermit dwells alone in the midst of the sea. It is said none seek his counsel or his aid in vain. He hath wrought marvellous cures, and if you resort to that holy man without doubt he can heal the knight." Orlando bade him steer thither, and soon the bark was laid safely beside the lonely rock; the wounded man was lowered into their boat, and carried by the crew to the hermit's cell. It was the same hermit with whom Rogero had taken refuge after his shipwreck, by whom he had been baptized, and with whom he was now staying, absorbed in sacred studies and meditations.

The holy man received Orlando and the rest with kindness, and inquired their errand; and being told that they had come for help for one who, warring for the Christian faith, was brought to perilous pass by a sad wound, he straightway undertook the cure. His applications were simple, but they were seconded by his prayers. The paladin was soon relieved from pain, and in a few days his foot was perfectly restored to soundness. Sobrino, as soon as he perceived the holy monk perform that wonder, cast aside his false prophet, and with contrite heart owned the true God, and demanded baptism at his hands. The hermit granted his request, and also by his prayers restored him to health, while all the Christian knights rejoiced in his conversion almost as much as at the restoration of Oliver. More than all Rogero felt joy and gratitude, and daily grew in grace and faith.

Rogero was known by fame to all the Christian knights, but not even Rinaldo knew him by sight, though he had proved his prowess in combat. Sobrino made him known to them, and great was the joy of all when they found one whose valor and courtesy were renowned through the world no longer an enemy and unbeliever, but a convert and champion of the true faith. All press about the knight; one grasps his hand, another locks him fast in his embrace; but more than all the rest, Rinaldo cherished him, for he more than any knew his worth.

It was not long before Rogero confided to his friend the hopes he entertained of a union with his sister, and Rinaldo frankly gave his sanction to the proposal. But causes unknown to the paladin were at that very time interposing obstacles to its success.

The fame of the beauty and worth of Bradamante had reached the ears of the Grecian Emperor, Constantine, and he had sent to Charlemagne to demand the hand of his niece for Leo, his son, and the heir to his dominions. Duke Aymon, her father, had only reserved his consent until he should first have spoken with his son Rinaldo, now absent.

The warriors now prepared to resume their voyage. Rogero took a tender farewell of the good hermit who had taught him the true faith. Orlando restored to him the horse and arms which were rightly his, not even asserting his claim to Balisarda, that sword which he himself had won from the enchantress.

The hermit gave his blessing to the band, and they reembarked. The passage was speedy, and very soon they arrived in the harbor of Marseilles.

Astolpho, when he had dismissed his troops, mounted the Hippogriff, and at one flight shot over to Sardinia, thence to Corsica, thence, turning slightly to the left, hovered over Provence, and alighted in the neighborhood of Marseilles. There he did what he had been commanded to do by the holy saint; he unbridled the Hippogriff, and turned him loose to seek his own retreats, never more to be galled with saddle or bit. The horn had lost its marvellous power ever since the visit to the moon.

Astolpho reached Marseilles the very day when Orlando, Rinaldo, Oliver, Sobrino, and Rogero arrived there. Charles had already heard the news of the defeat of the Saracen kings, and all the accompanying events. On learning the approach of the gallant knights, he sent forward some of his most illustrious nobles to receive them, and himself, with the rest of his court, kings, dukes, and peers, the queen, and a fair and gorgeous band of ladies, set forward from Arles to meet them.

No sooner were the mutual greetings interchanged, than Orlando and his friends led forward Rogero, and presented him to the Emperor. They vouch him son of Rogero, Duke of Risa, one of the most renowned of Christian warriors, by adverse fortune stolen in his infancy, and brought up by Saracens in the false faith, now by a kind Providence converted, and restored to fill the place his father once held among the foremost champions of the throne and Church.

Rogero had alighted from his horse, and stood respectfully before the Emperor. Charlemagne bade him remount and ride beside him; and omitted nothing which might do him honor in sight of his martial train. With pomp triumphal and with festive cheer the troop returned to the city; the streets were decorated with garlands, the houses hung with rich tapestry, and flowers fell like rain upon the conquering host from the hands of fair dames and damsels, from every balcony and window. So welcomed, the mighty Emperor passed on till he reached the royal palace, where many days he feasted, high in hall, with his lords, amid tourney, revel, dance, and song.

When Rinaldo told his father, Duke Aymon, how he had promised his sister to Rogero, his father heard him with indignation, having set his heart on seeing her united to the Grecian Emperor's son. The Lady Beatrice, her mother, also appealed to Bradamante herself to reject a knight who had neither title nor lands, and give the preference to one who would make her Empress of the wide Levant. But Bradamante, though respect forbade her to refuse her mother's entreaty, would not promise to do what her heart repelled, and answered only with a sigh, until she was alone, and then gave a loose to tears.

Meanwhile Rogero, indignant that a stranger should presume to rob him of his bride, determined to seek the Prince of Greece, and defy him to mortal combat. With this design he donned his armor, but exchanged his crest and emblazonment, and bore instead a white unicorn upon a crimson field. He chose a trusty squire, and, commanding him not to address him as Rogero, rode on his quest. Having crossed the Rhine and the Austrian countries into Hungary, he followed the course of the Danube till he reached Belgrade. There he saw the imperial ensigns spread, and white pavilions, thronged with troops, before the town. For the Emperor Constantine was laying siege to the city to recover it from the Bulgarians, who had taken it from him not long before.

A river flowed between the camp of the Emperor and the Bulgarians, and at the moment when Rogero approached, a skirmish had begun between the parties from either camp, who had approached the stream for the purpose of watering. The Greeks in that affray were four to one, and drove back the

Bulgarians in precipitate rout. Rogero, seeing this, and animated only by his hatred of the Grecian prince, dashed into the middle of the flying mass, calling aloud on the fugitives to turn. He encountered first a leader of the Grecian host in splendid armor, a nephew of the Emperor, as dear to him as a son. Rogero's lance pierced shield and armor, and stretched the warrior breathless on the plain. Another and another fell before him, and astonishment and terror arrested the advance of the Greeks, while the Bulgarians, catching courage from the cavalier, rally, change front, and chase the Grecian troops, who fly in their turn. Leo, the prince, was at a distance when this sudden skirmish rose, but not so far but that he could see distinctly, from an elevated position which he held, how the changed battle was all the work of one man, and could not choose but admire the bravery and prowess with which it was done. He knew by the blazonry displayed that the champion was not of the Bulgarian army, though he furnished aid to them. Although he suffered by his valor, the prince could not wish him ill, for his admiration surpassed his resentment. By this time the Greeks had regained the river, and crossing it by fording or swimming, some made their escape, leaving many more prisoners in the hands of the Bulgarians. Rogero, learning from some of the captives that Leo was at a point some distance down the river, rode thither with a view to meet him, but arrived not before the Greek prince had retired beyond the stream, and broken up the bridge. Day was spent, and Rogero, wearied, looked round for a shelter for the night. He found it in a cottage, where he soon yielded himself to repose. It so happened, a knight who had narrowly escaped Rogero's sword in the late battle also found shelter in the same cottage, and, recognizing the armor of the unknown knight, easily found means of securing him as he slept, and next morning carried him in chains and delivered him to the Emperor. By him he was in turn delivered to his sister Theodora, mother of the young knight, the first victim of Rogero's spear. By her he was cast into a dungeon, till her ingenuity could devise a death sufficiently painful to satiate her revenge.

Bradamante, meanwhile, to escape her father's and mother's importunity, had begged a boon of Charlemagne, which the monarch pledged his royal word to grant; it was that she should not be compelled to marry any one unless he should first vanquish her in single combat. The Emperor therefore proclaimed a tournament in these words: "He that would wed Duke Aymon's daughter must contend with the sword against that dame, from the sun's rise to his setting; and if, in that time, he is not overcome the lady shall be his."

Duke Aymon and the Lady Beatrice, though much incensed at the course things had taken, brought their daughter to court, to await the day appointed for the tournament. Bradamante, not finding there him whom her heart required, distressed herself with doubts what could be the cause of his absence. Of all fancies, the most painful one was that he had gone away to learn to forget her, knowing her father's and her mother's opposition to their union, and despairing to contend against them. But oh, how much worse would be the maiden's woe, if it were known to her what her betrothed was then enduring!

He was plunged in a dungeon where no ray of daylight ever penetrated, loaded with chains, and scantily supplied with the coarsest food. No wonder despair took possession of his heart, and he longed for death as a relief, when one night (or one day, for both were equally dark to him) he was roused with the glare of a torch and saw two men enter his cell. It was the Prince Leo, with an attendant, who had come as soon as he had learned the wretched fate of the brave knight whose valor he had seen and admired on the field of battle. "Cavalier," said he, "I am one whom thy valor hath so bound to thee, that I willingly peril my own safety to lend thee aid." "Infinite thanks I owe you," replied Rogero, "and the life you give me I promise faithfully to render back upon your call, and promptly to stake it at all times for your service." The prince then told Rogero his name and rank, at hearing which a tide of contending emotions almost overwhelmed

Rogero. He was set at liberty, and had his horse and arms restored to him.

Meanwhile, tidings arrived of King Charles' decree that whoever aspired to the hand of Bradamante must first encounter her with sword and lance. This news made the Grecian prince turn pale, for he knew he was no match for her in fight. Communing with himself, he sees how he may make his wit supply the place of valor, and employ the French knight, whose name was still unknown to him, to fight the battle for him. Rogero heard the proposal with extreme distress; yet it seemed worse than death to deny the first request of one to whom he owed his life. Hastily he gave his assent "to do in all things that which Leo should command." Afterward, bitter repentance came over him; yet, rather than confess his change of mind, death itself would be welcome. Death seems his only remedy; but how to die? Sometimes he thinks to make none but a feigned resistance, and allow her sword a ready access, for never can death come more happily than if her hand guide the weapon. Yet this will not avail, for, unless he wins the maid for the Greek prince, his debt remains unpaid. He had promised to maintain a real, not a feigned encounter. He will then keep his word, and banish every thought from his bosom except that which moved him to maintain his truth.

The young prince, richly attended, set out, and with him Rogero. They arrived at Paris, but Leo preferred not to enter the city, and pitched his tents without the walls, making known his arrival to Charlemagne by an embassy. The monarch was pleased, and testified his courtesy by visits and gifts. The prince set forth the purpose of his coming, and prayed the Emperor to dispatch his suit--"to send forth the damsel who refused ever to take in wedlock any lord inferior to herself in fight; for she should be his bride, or he would perish beneath her sword."

Rogero passed the night before the day assigned for the battle like that which the felon spends, condemned to pay the forfeit of his life on the ensuing day. He chose to fight with sword only, and on foot, for he would not let her see Frontino, knowing that she would recognize the steed. Nor would he use Balisarda, for against that enchanted blade all armor would be of no avail, and the sword that he did take he hammered well upon the edge to abate its sharpness. He wore the surcoat of Prince Leo, and his shield, emblazoned with a golden, double-headed eagle. The prince took care to let himself be seen by none.

Bradamante, meanwhile, prepared herself for the combat far differently. Instead of blunting the edge of her falchion she whets the steel, and would fain infuse into it her own acerbity. As the moment approached she seemed to have fire within her veins, and waited impatiently for the trumpet's sound. At the signal she drew her sword, and fell with fury upon her Rogero. But as a well-built wall or aged rock stands unmoved the fury of the storm, so Rogero, clad in those arms which Trojan Hector once wore, withstood the strokes which stormed about his head and breast and flank. Sparks flew from his shield, his helm, his cuirass; from direct and back strokes, aimed now high, now low, falling thick and fast, like hailstones on a cottage roof; but Rogero, with skilful ward, turns them aside, or receives them where his armor is a sure protection, careful only to protect himself, and with no thought of striking in return. Thus the hours passed away, and, as the sun approached the west, the damsel began to despair. But so much the more her anger increases, and she redoubles her efforts, like the craftsman who sees his work unfinished while the day is wellnigh spent. O miserable damsel! didst thou know whom thou wouldst kill,--if, in that cavalier matched against thee thou didst but know Rogero, on whom thy very life-threads hang, rather than kill him thou wouldst kill thyself, for he is dearer to thee than life.

King Charles and the peers, who thought the cavalier to be the Grecian prince, viewing such force and skill exhibited, and how without assaulting her the knight defended himself, were filled with admiration, and declared the champions well matched, and worthy of each other.

When the sun was set Charlemagne gave the signal for terminating the contest, and Bradamante was awarded to Prince Leo as a bride. Rogero, in deep distress, returned to his tent. There Leo unlaced his helmet, and kissed him on both cheeks. "Henceforth," said he, "do with me as you please, for you cannot exhaust my gratitude." Rogero replied little, laid aside the ensigns he had worn, and resumed the unicorn, then hasted to withdraw himself from all eyes. When it was midnight he rose, saddled Frontino, and sallied from his tent, taking that direction which pleased his steed. All night he rode absorbed in bitter woe, and called on Death as alone capable of relieving his sufferings. At last he entered a forest, and penetrated into its deepest recesses. There he unharnessed Frontino, and suffered him to wander where he would. Then he threw himself down on the ground, and poured forth such bitter wailings that the birds and beasts, for none else heard him, were moved to pity with his cries.

Not less was the distress of the lady Bradamante, who, rather than wed any one but Rogero, resolved to break her word, and defy kindred, court, and Charlemagne himself; and, if nothing else would do, to die. But relief came from an unexpected quarter. Marphisa, sister of Rogero, was a heroine of warlike prowess equal to Bradamante. She had been the confidante of their loves, and felt hardly less distress than themselves at seeing the perils which threatened their union. "They are already united by mutual vows," she said, "and in the sight of Heaven what more is necessary?" Full of this thought she presented herself before Charlemagne, and declared that she herself was witness that the maiden had spoken to Rogero those words which they who marry swear; and that the compact was so sealed between the pair that they were no longer free, nor could forsake the one the other to take another spouse. This her assertion she offered to prove, in single combat, against Prince Leo, or any one else.

Charlemagne, sadly perplexed at this, commanded Bradamante to be called, and told her what the bold Marphisa had declared. Bradamante neither denied nor confirmed the statement, but hung her head, and kept silence. Duke Aymon was enraged, and would fain have set aside the pretended contract on the ground that, if made at all, it must have been made before Rogero was baptized, and therefore void. But not so thought Rinaldo, nor the good Orlando, and Charlemagne knew not which way to decide, when Marphisa spoke thus:

"Since no one else can marry the maiden while my brother lives, let the prince meet Rogero in mortal combat, and let him who survives take her for his bride."

This saying pleased the Emperor, and was accepted by the prince, for he thought that, by the aid of his unknown champion, he should surely triumph in the fight. Proclamation was therefore made for Rogero to appear and defend his suit; and Leo, on his part, caused search to be made on all sides for the knight of the Unicorn.

Meanwhile Rogero, overwhelmed with despair, lay stretched on the ground in the forest night and day without food, courting death. Here he was discovered by one of Leo's people, who, finding him resist all attempts to remove him, hastened to his master, who was not far off, and brought him to the spot. As he approached he heard words which convinced him that love was the cause of the knight's despair; but no clew was given to guide him to the object of that love. Stooping down, the prince embraced the weeping warrior, and, in the tenderest accents, said: "Spare not, I entreat you, to disclose the cause of your distress, for few such desperate evils betide mankind as are wholly past cure. It grieves me much that you would hide your grief from me, for I am bound to you by ties that nothing can undo. Tell me, then, your grief, and leave me to try if wealth, art, cunning, force, or persuasion cannot relieve you. If not, it will be time enough after all has been tried in vain to die."

He spoke in such moving accents that Rogero could not choose but yield. It was some time before he could command utterance; at last he said, "My lord, when you shall know me for what I am, I doubt not you, like myself, will be content that I should die. Know, then, I am that Rogero whom you have so much cause to hate, and who so hated you that, intent on putting you to death, he went to seek you at your father's court. This I did because I could not submit to see my promised bride borne off by you. But, as man proposes and God disposes, your great courtesy, well tried in time of sore need, so moved my fixed resolve, that I not only laid aside the hate I bore, but purposed to be your friend forever. You then asked of me to win for you the lady Bradamante, which was all one as to demand of me my heart and soul. You know whether I served you faithfully or not. Yours is the lady; possess her in peace; but ask me not to live to see it. Be content rather that I die; for vows have passed between myself and her which forbid that while I live she can lawfully wive with another."

So filled was gentle Leo with astonishment at these words that for a while he stood silent, with lips unmoved and steadfast gaze, like a statue. And the discovery that the stranger was Rogero not only abated not the good will he bore him, but increased it, so that his distress for what Rogero suffered seemed equal to his own. For this, and because he would appear deservedly an Emperor's son, and, though in other things outdone, would not be surpassed in courtesy, he says: "Rogero, had I known that day when your matchless valor routed my troops that you were Rogero, your virtue would have made me your own, as then it made me while I knew not my foe, and I should have no less gladly rescued you from Theodora's dungeon. And if I would willingly have done so then, how much more gladly will I now restore the gift of which you would rob yourself to confer it upon me. The damsel is more due to you than to me, and though I know her worth, I would forego not only her, but life itself, rather than distress a knight like you."

This and much more he said to the same intent; till at last Rogero replied, "I yield, and am content to live, and thus a second time owe my life to you."

But several days elapsed before Rogero was so far restored as to return to the royal residence, where an embassy had arrived from the Bulgarian princes to seek the knight of the unicorn, and tender to him the crown of that country, in place of their king, fallen in battle.

Thus were things situated when Prince Leo, leading by the hand Rogero, clad in the battered armor in which he had sustained the conflict with Bradamante, presented himself before the king. "Behold," he said "the champion who maintained from dawn to setting sun the arduous contest; he comes to claim the guerdon of the fight." King Charlemagne, with all his peerage, stood amazed; for all believed that the Grecian prince himself had fought with Bradamante. Then stepped forth Marphisa, and said, "Since Rogero is not here to assert his rights, I, his sister, undertake his cause, and will maintain it against whoever shall dare dispute his claim." She said this with so much anger and disdain that the prince deemed it no longer wise to feign, and withdrew Rogero's helmet from his brow, saying, "Behold him here!" Who can describe the astonishment and joy of Marphisa! She ran and threw her arms about her brother's neck, nor would give way to let Charlemagne and Rinaldo, Orlando, Dudon, and the rest, who crowded round, embrace him, and press friendly kisses on his brow. The joyful tidings flew fast by many a messenger to Bradamante, who in her secret chamber lay lamenting. The blood that stagnated about her heart flowed at that notice so fast, that she had wellnigh died for joy. Duke Aymon and the Lady Beatrice no longer withheld their consent, and pledged their daughter to the brave Rogero before all that gallant company.

Now came the Bulgarian ambassadors, and, kneeling at the feet of Rogero, besought him to return with them to their country, where, in Adrianople, the crown and sceptre were awaiting his acceptance. Prince Leo united his persuasions to theirs, and promised, in his royal father's name, that peace should be restored on their part. Rogero gave his consent, and it was surmised that none of the virtues which shone so conspicuously in him so availed to recommend Rogero to the Lady Beatrice as the hearing her future son-in-law saluted as a sovereign prince.

THE BATTLE OF RONCESVALLES

After the expulsion of the Saracens from France Charlemagne led his army into Spain, to punish Marsilius, the king of that country, for having sided with the African Saracens in the late war. Charlemagne succeeded in all his attempts, and compelled Marsilius to submit, and pay tribute to France. Our readers will remember Gano, otherwise called Gan, or Ganelon, whom we mentioned in one of our early chapters as an old courtier of Charlemagne, and a deadly enemy of Orlando, Rinaldo, and all their friends. He had great influence over Charles, from equality of age and long intimacy; and he was not without good qualities: he was brave and sagacious, but envious, false, and treacherous. Gan prevailed on Charles to send him as ambassador to Marsilius, to arrange the tribute. He embraced Orlando over and over again at taking leave, using such pains to seem loving and sincere, that his hypocrisy was manifest to every one but the old monarch. He fastened with equal tenderness on Oliver, who smiled contemptuously in his face, and thought to himself, "You may make as many fair speeches as you choose, but you lie." All the other paladins who were present thought the same, and they said as much to the Emperor, adding that Gan should on no account be sent ambassador to the Spaniards. But Charles was infatuated.

Gan was received with great honor by Marsilius. The king, attended by his lords, came fifteen miles out of Saragossa to meet him, and then conducted him into the city with acclamations. There was nothing for several days but balls, games, and exhibitions of chivalry, the ladies throwing flowers on the heads of the French knights, and the people shouting, "France! Mountjoy and St. Denis!"

After the ceremonies of the first reception the king and the ambassador began to understand one another. One day they sat together in a garden on the border of a fountain. The water was so clear and smooth it reflected every object around, and the spot was encircled with fruit-trees which quivered with the fresh air. As they sat and talked, as if without restraint, Gan, without looking the king in the face, was enabled to see the expression of his countenance in the water, and governed his speech accordingly. Marsilius was equally adroit, and watched the face of Gan while he addressed him. Marsilius began by lamenting, not as to the ambassador, but as to the friend, the injuries which Charles had done him by invading his dominions, charging him with wishing to take his kingdom from him and give it to Orlando; till at length he plainly uttered his belief that if that ambitious paladin were but dead good men would get their rights.

Gan heaved a sigh, as if he was unwillingly compelled to allow the force of what the king said; but unable to contain himself long he lifted up his face, radiant with triumphant wickedness, and exclaimed: "Every word you utter is truth; die he must, and die also must Oliver, who struck me that foul blow at court. Is it treachery to punish affronts like these? I have planned everything,--I have settled everything already with their besotted master. Orlando will come to your borders--to Roncesvalles--for the purpose of receiving the tribute. Charles will await him at the foot of the mountains. Orlando will bring but a small band with him: you, when you meet him, will have secretly your whole army at your back. You surround him, and who receives tribute then?"

The new Judas had scarcely uttered these words when his exultation was interrupted by a change in the face of nature. The sky was suddenly overcast, there was thunder and lightning, a laurel was split in two from head to foot, and the Carob-tree under which Gan was sitting, which is said to be the species of tree on which Judas Iscariot hung himself, dropped one of its pods on his head.

Marsilius, as well as Gan, was appalled at this omen; but on assembling his soothsayers they came to the conclusion that the laurel-tree turned the omen against the Emperor, the successor of the Caesars, though one of them renewed the consternation of Gan by saying that he did not understand the meaning of the tree of Judas, and intimating that perhaps the ambassador could explain it. Gan relieved his vexation by anger; the habit of wickedness prevailed over all other considerations; and the king prepared to march to Roncesvalles at the head of all his forces.

Gan wrote to Charlemagne to say how humbly and submissively Marsilius was coming to pay the tribute into the hands of Orlando, and how handsome it would be of the Emperor to meet him half-way, and so be ready to receive him after the payment at his camp. He added a brilliant account of the tribute, and the accompanying presents. The good Emperor wrote in turn to say how pleased he was with the ambassador's diligence, and that matters were arranged precisely as he wished. His court, however, had its suspicion still, though they little thought Gan's object in bringing Charles into the neighborhood of Roncesvalles was to deliver him into the hands of Marsilius, after Orlando should have been destroyed by him.

Orlando, however, did as his lord and sovereign desired. He went to Roncesvalles, accompanied by a moderate train of warriors, not dreaming of the atrocity that awaited him. Gan, meanwhile, had hastened back to France, in order to show himself free and easy in the presence of Charles, and secure the success of his plot; while Marsilius, to make assurance doubly sure, brought into the passes of Roncesvalles no less than three armies, which were successively to fall on the paladin in case of the worst, and so extinguish him with numbers. He had also, by Gan's advice, brought heaps of wine and good cheer to be set before his victims in the first instance; "for that," said the traitor, "will render the onset the more effective, the feasters being unarmed. One thing, however, I must not forget," added he; "my son Baldwin is sure to be with Orlando; you must take care of his life for my sake."

"I give him this vesture off my own body," said the king; "let him wear it in the battle, and have no fear. My soldiers shall be directed not to touch him."

Gan went away rejoicing to France. He embraced the sovereign and the court all round with the air of a man who had brought them nothing but blessings, and the old king wept for very tenderness and delight.

"Something is going on wrong, and looks very black," thought Malagigi, the good wizard; "Rinaldo is not here, and it is indispensably necessary that he should be. I must find out where he is, and Ricciardetto too, and send for them with all speed."

Malagigi called up by his art a wise, terrible, and cruel spirit, named Ashtaroth. "Tell me, and tell me truly, of Rinaldo," said Malagigi to the spirit. The demon looked hard at the paladin, and said nothing. His aspect was clouded and violent.

The enchanter, with an aspect still cloudier, bade Ashtaroth lay down that look, and made signs as if he would resort to angrier compulsion; and the devil, alarmed, loosened his tongue, and said, "You have not told me what you desire to know of Rinaldo."

"I desire to know what he has been doing, and where he is."

"He has been conquering and baptizing the world, east and west," said the demon, "and is now in Egypt with Ricciardetto."

"And what has Gan been plotting with Marsilius?" inquired Malagigi; "and what is to come of it?"

"I know not," said the devil. "I was not attending to Gan at the time, and we fallen spirits know not the future. All I discern is that by the signs and comets in the heavens something dreadful is about to happen--something very strange, treacherous, and bloody; and that Gan has a seat ready prepared for him in hell."

"Within three days," cried the enchanter, loudly, "bring Rinaldo and Ricciardetto into the pass of Ronces-Valles. Do it, and I hereby undertake to summon thee no more."

"Suppose they will not trust themselves with me?" said the spirit.

"Enter Rinaldo's horse, and bring him, whether he trust thee or not."

"It shall be done," returned the demon.

There was an earthquake, and Ashtaroth disappeared.

Marsilius now made his first movement towards the destruction of Orlando, by sending before him his vassal, King Blanchardin, with his presents of wines and other luxuries. The temperate but courteous hero took them in good part, and distributed them as the traitor wished; and then Blanchardin, on pretence of going forward to salute Charlemagne, returned, and put himself at the head of the second army, which was the post assigned him by his liege-lord. King Falseron, whose son Orlando had slain in battle, headed the first army, and King Balugante the third. Marsilius made a speech to them, in which he let them into his design, and concluded by recommending to their good will the son of his friend Gan, whom they would know by the vest he had sent him, and who was the only soul amongst the Christian they were to spare.

This son of Gan, meanwhile, and several of the paladins, who distrusted the misbelievers, and were anxious at all events to be with Orlando, had joined the hero in the fatal valley; so that the little Christian host, considering the tremendous valor of their lord and his friends, were not to be sold for nothing. Rinaldo, alas! the second thunderbolt of Christendom, was destined not to be there in time to meet the issue. The paladins in vain begged Orlando to be on his guard against treachery, and send for a more numerous body of men. The great heart of the Champion of the Faith was unwilling to harbor suspicion as long as he could help it. He refused to summon aid which might be superfluous; neither would he do anything but what his liege-lord had directed. And yet he could not wholly repress a misgiving. A shadow had fallen on his heart, great and cheerful as it was. The anticipations of his friends disturbed him, in spite of the face with which he met them. Perhaps by a certain foresight he felt his death approaching; but he felt bound not to encourage the impression. Besides, time pressed; the moment of the looked-for tribute was at hand, and little combinations of circumstances determine often the greatest events.

King Marsilius was to arrive early next day with the tribute, and Oliver, with the morning sun, rode forth to reconnoitre, and see if he could discover the peaceful pomp of the Spanish court in the distance. He rode up the nearest height, and from the top of it beheld the first army of Marsilius already forming in the passes. "O devil Gan," he exclaimed, "this then is the consummation of thy labors!" Oliver put spurs to his horse, and galloped back down the mountain to Orlando.

"Well," cried the hero, "what news?"

"Bad news," said his cousin, "such as you would not hear of yesterday. Marsilius is here in arms, and all the world is with him."

The paladins pressed round Orlando, and entreated him to sound his horn, in token that he needed help. His only answer was to mount his horse, and ride up the mountain with Sansonetto.

As soon, however, as he cast forth his eyes, and beheld what was round about him, he turned in sorrow, and looked down into Roncesvalles, and said, "O miserable valley! the blood shed in thee this day will color thy name forever."

Orlando's little camp were furious against the Saracens. They armed themselves with the greatest impatience. There was nothing but lacing of helmets and mounting of horses, while good Archbishop Turpin went from rank to rank exhorting and encouraging the warriors of Christ. Orlando and his captains withdrew for a moment to consultation. He fairly groaned for sorrow, and at first had not a word to say, so wretched he felt at having brought his people to die in Roncesvalles. Then he said: "If it had entered into my heart to conceive the king of Spain to be such a villain never would you have seen this day. He has exchanged with me a thousand courtesies and good words; and I thought that the worse enemies we had been before, the better friends we had become now. I fancied every human being capable of this kind of virtue on a good opportunity, saving, indeed, such base-hearted wretches as can never forgive their very forgivers; and of these I did not suppose him to be one. Let us die, if die we must, like honest and gallant men, so that it shall be said of us it was only our bodies that died. The reason why I did not sound the horn was partly because I thought it did not become us, and partly because our liege lord could hardly save us, even if he heard it." And with these words Orlando sprang to his horse, crying, "Aways against the Saracens!" But he had no sooner turned his face than he wept bitterly, and said, "O Holy Virgin, think not of me, the sinner Orlando, but have pity on these thy servants!"

And now with a mighty dust, and an infinite sound of horns and tambours, which came filling the valley, the first army of the infidels made its appearance, horses neighing, and a thousand pennons flying in the air. King Falseron led them on, saying to his officers: "Let nobody dare to lay a finger on Orlando. He belongs to myself. The revenge of my son's death is mine. I will cut the man down that comes between us." "Now, friends," said Orlando, "every man for himself, and St. Michael for us all! There is not one here that is not a perfect knight." And he might well say it, for the flower of all France was there, except Rinaldo and Ricciardetto--every man a picked man, all friends and constant companions of Orlando.

So the captains of the little troop and of the great army sat looking at one another, and singling one another out as the latter came on, and then the knights put spear in rest, and ran for a while two and two in succession, one against the other.

Astolpho was the first to move. He ran against Arlotto of Sorio, and thrust his antagonist's body out of the saddle, and his soul into the other world. Oliver encountered Malprimo, and, though he received a thrust which hurt him, sent his lance right through the heart of Malprimo.

Falseron was daunted at this blow. "Truly," thought he, "this is a marvel." Oliver did not press on among the Saracens, his wound was too painful; but Orlando now put himself and his whole band in motion, and you may guess what an uproar ensued. The sound of the rattling of blows and helmets was as if the forge of

Vulcan had been thrown open. Falseron beheld Orlando coming so furiously, that he thought him a Lucifer who had burst his chain, and was quite of another mind than when he purposed to have him all to himself. On the contrary, he recommended himself to his gods, and turned away, meaning to wait for a more auspicious season of revenge. But Orlando hailed him with a terrible voice, saying, "O thou traitor! was this the end to which old quarrels were made up?" Then he dashed at Falseron with a fury so swift, and at the same time with a mastery of his lance so marvellous, that, though he plunged it in the man's body so as instantly to kill him, and then withdrew it, the body did not move in the saddle. The hero himself, as he rushed onwards, was fain to see the end of a stroke so perfect, and turning his horse back, touched the carcass with his sword, and it fell on the instant!

When the infidels beheld their leader dead such fear fell upon them that they were for leaving the field to the paladins, but they were unable. Marsilius had drawn the rest of his forces round the valley like a net, so that their shoulders were turned in vain. Orlando rode into the thick of them, and wherever he went thunderbolts fell upon helmets. Oliver was again in the fray, with Walter and Baldwin, Avino and Avolio, while Arch-bishop Turpin had changed his crosier for a lance, and chased a new flock before him to the mountains.

Yet what could be done against foes without number? Marsilius constantly pours them in. The paladins are as units to thousands. Why tarry the horses of Rinaldo and Ricciardetto?

The horses did not tarry, but fate had been quicker than enchantment. Ashtaroth had presented himself to Rinaldo in Egypt, and, after telling his errand, he and Foul-mouth, his servant, entered the horses of Rinaldo and Ricciardetto, which began to neigh, and snort, and leap with the fiends within them, till off they flew through the air over the pyramids and across the desert, and reached Spain and the scene of action just as Marsilius brought up his third army. The two paladins on their horses dropped right into the midst of the Saracens, and began making such havoc among them that Marsilius, who overlooked the fight from a mountain, thought his soldiers had turned against one another. Orlando beheld it, and guessed it could be no other but his cousins, and pressed to meet them. Oliver coming up at the same moment, the rapture of the whole party is not to be expressed. After a few hasty words of explanation they were forced to turn again upon the enemy, whose numbers seemed perfectly without limit.

Orlando, making a bloody passage towards Marsilius, struck a youth on the head, whose helmet was so strong as to resist the blow, but at the same time flew off, Orlando prepared to strike a second blow, when the youth exclaimed, "Hold! you loved my father; I am Bujaforte!" The paladin had never seen Bujaforte, but he saw the likeness to the good old man, his father, and he dropped his sword. "O Bujaforte," said he, "I loved him indeed; but what does his son do here fighting against his friends?"

Bujaforte could not at once speak for weeping. At length he said: "I am forced to be here by my lord and master, Marsilius; and I have made a show of fighting, but have not hurt a single Christian. Treachery is on every side of you. Baldwin himself has a vest given him by Marsilius, that everybody may know the son of his friend Gan, and do him no harm."

"Put your helmet on again," said Orlando, "and behave just as you have done. Never will your father's friend be an enemy to the son."

The hero then turned in fury to look for Baldwin, who was hastening towards him at that moment, with friendliness in his looks.

"'Tis strange," said Baldwin, "I have done my duty as well as I could, yet nobody will come against me. I have slain right and left, and cannot comprehend what it is that makes the stoutest infidels avoid me."

"Take off your vest," said Orlando, contemptuously, "and you will soon discover the secret, if you wish to know it. Your father has sold us to Marsilius, all but his honorable son."

"If my father," said Baldwin, impetuously tearing off the vest, "has been such a villain, and I escape dying, I will plunge this sword through his heart. But I am no traitor, Orlando, and you do me wrong to say it. Think not I can live with dishonor."

Baldwin spurred off into the fight, not waiting to hear another word from Orlando, who was very sorry for what he had said, for he perceived that the youth was in despair.

And now the fight raged beyond all it had done before; twenty pagans went down for one paladin, but still the paladins fell. Sansonetto was beaten to earth by the club of Grandonio, Walter d'Amulion had his shoulder broken, Berlinghieri and Ottone were slain, and at last Astolpho fell, in revenge of whose death Orlando turned the spot where he died into a lake of Saracen blood. The luckless Bujaforte met Rinaldo, and before he could explain how he seemed to be fighting on the Saracen side received such a blow upon the head that he fell, unable to utter a word. Orlando, cutting his way to a spot where there was a great struggle and uproar, found the poor youth Baldwin, the son of Gan, with two spears in his breast. "I am no traitor now," said Baldwin, and those were the last words he said. Orlando was bitterly sorry to have been the cause of his death, and tears streamed from his eyes. At length down went Oliver himself. He had become blinded with his own blood, and smitten Orlando without knowing him. "How now, cousin," cried Orlando, "have you too gone over to the enemy?" "O my lord and master," cried the other, "I ask your pardon. I can see nothing; I am dying. Some traitor has stabbed me in the back. If you love me, lead my horse into the thick of them, so that I may not die unavenged."

"I shall die myself before long," said Orlando, "out of very toil and grief; so we will go together."

Orlando led his cousin's horse where the press was thickest, and dreadful was the strength of the dying man and his tired companion. They made a street through which they passed out of the battle, and Orlando led his cousin away to his tent, and said, "Wait a little till I return, for I will go and sound the horn on the hill yonder."

"'Tis of no use," said Oliver, "my spirit is fast going and desires to be with its Lord and Saviour."

He would have said more, but his words came from him imperfectly, like those of a man in a dream, and so he expired.

When Orlando saw him dead he felt as if he was alone on the earth, and he was quite willing to leave it, only he wished that King Charles, at the foot of the mountains, should know how the case stood before he went. So he took up the horn and blew it three times, with such force that the blood burst out of his nose and mouth. Turpin says that at the third blast the horn broke in two.

In spite of all the noise of the battle, the sound of the horn broke over it like a voice out of the other world. They say that birds fell dead at it, and that the whole Saracen army drew back in terror. Charlemagne was sitting in the midst of his court when the sound reached him, and Gan was there. The Emperor was the first to hear it.

"Do you hear that?" said he to his nobles. "Did you hear the horn as I heard it?"

Upon this they all listened, and Gan felt his heart misgive him. The horn sounded a second time.

"What is the meaning of this?" said Charles.

"Orlando is hunting," observed Gan, "and the stag is killed."

But when the horn sounded yet a third time, and the blast was one of so dreadful a vehemence, everybody looked at the other, and then they all looked at Gan in a fury. Charles rose from his seat.

"This is no hunting of the stag," said he. "The sound goes to my very heart. O Gan! O Gan! Not for thee do I blush, but for myself. O foul and monstrous villain! Take him, gentleman, and keep him in close prison. Would to God I had not lived to see this day!"

But it was no time for words. They put the traitor in prison and then Charles, with all his court, took his way to Roncesvalles, grieving and praying.

It was afternoon when the horn sounded, and half an hour after it when the Emperor set out; and meantime Orlando had returned to the fight that he might do his duty, however hopeless, as long as he could sit his horse. At length he found his end approaching, for toil and fever, and rode all alone to a fountain where he had before quenched his thirst. His horse was wearier than he, and no sooner had his master alighted than the beast, kneeling down as if to take leave, and to say, "I have brought you to a place of rest," fell dead at his feet. Orlando cast water on him from the fountain, not wishing to believe him dead; but when he found it to no purpose, he grieved for him as if he had been a human being, and addressed him by name with tears, and asked forgiveness if he had ever done him wrong. They say that the horse, at these words, opened his eyes a little, and looked kindly at his master, and then stirred never more. They say also that Orlando then summoning all his strength, smote a rock near him with his beautiful sword Durindana, thinking to shiver the steel in pieces, and so prevent its falling into the hands of the enemy, but though the rock split like a slate, and a great cleft remained ever after to astonish the eyes of pilgrims, the sword remained uninjured.

And now Rinaldo and Ricciardetto came up, with Turpin, having driven back the Saracens, and told Orlando that the battle was won. Then Orlando knelt before Turpin and begged remission of his sins, and Turpin gave him absolution. Orlando fixed his eyes on the hilt of his sword as on a crucifix, and embraced it, and he raised his eyes and appeared like a creature seraphical and transfigured, and bowing his head, he breathed out his pure soul.

And now King Charles and his nobles came up. The Emperor, at sight of the dead Orlando, threw himself, as if he had been a reckless youth, from his horse, and embraced and kissed the body, and said: "I bless thee, Orlando; I bless thy whole life, and all that thou wast, and all that thou ever didst, and the father that begat thee; and I ask pardon of thee for believing those who brought thee to thine end. They shall have their reward, O thou beloved one! But indeed it is thou that livest, and I who am worse than dead."

Horrible to the Emperor's eyes was the sight of the field of Roncesvalles. The Saracens indeed had fled, conquered; but all his paladins but two were left on it dead, and the whole valley looked like a great slaughter-house, trampled into blood and dirt, and reeking to the heat. Charles trembled to his heart's core for wonder and agony. After gazing dumbly on the place he cursed it with a solemn curse, and wished that never grass might grow in it again, nor seed of any kind, neither within it nor on any of its mountains around, but the anger of Heaven abide over it forever.

Charles and his warriors went after the Saracens into Spain. They took and fired Saragossa, and Marsilius was hung to the carob-tree under which he had planned his villainy with Gan; and Gan was hung and drawn and quartered in Roncesvalles, amidst the execrations of the country.

RINALDO AND BAYARD

CHARLEMAGNE was overwhelmed with grief at the loss of so many of his bravest warriors at the disaster of Roncesvalles, and bitterly reproached himself for his credulity in resigning himself so completely to the counsels of the treacherous Count Gan. Yet he soon fell into a similar snare when he suffered his unworthy son, Charlot, to acquire such an influence over him, that he constantly led him into acts of cruelty and injustice that in his right mind he would have scorned to commit. Rinaldo and his brothers, for some slight offence to the imperious young prince, were forced to fly from Paris, and to take shelter in their castle of Montalban; for Charles had publicly said, if he could take them he would hang them all. He sent numbers of his bravest knights to arrest them, but all without success. Either Rinaldo foiled their efforts and sent them back, stripped of their armor and of their glory, or, after meeting and conferring with him, they came back and told the king they could not be his instruments for such a work.

At last Charles himself raised a great army, and went in person to compel the paladin to submit. He ravaged all the country round about Montalban, so that supplies of food should be cut off, and he threatened death to any who should attempt to issue forth, hoping to compel the garrison to submit for want of food.

Rinaldo's resources had been brought so low that it seemed useless to contend any longer. His brothers had been taken prisoners in a skirmish, and his only hope of saving their lives was in making terms with the king.

So he sent a messenger, offering to yield himself and his castle if the king would spare his and his brothers' lives. While the messenger was gone Rinaldo, impatient to learn what tidings he might bring, rode out to meet him. When he had ridden as far as he thought prudent he stopped in a wood, and alighting, tied Bayard to a tree. Then he sat down, and, as he waited, he fell asleep. Bayard meanwhile got loose, and strayed away where the grass tempted him. Just then came along some country people, who said to one another, "Look, is not that the great horse Bayard that Rinaldo rides? Let us take him, and carry him to King Charles, who will pay us well for our trouble." They did so, and the king was delighted with his prize, and gave them a present that made them rich to their dying day.

When Rinaldo woke he looked round for his horse, and, finding him not, he groaned, and said, "O unlucky hour that I was born! how fortune persecutes me!" So desperate was he that he took off his armor and his spurs, saying, "What need have I of these, since Bayard is lost?" While he stood thus lamenting, a man came from the thicket, seemingly bent with age. He had a long beard hanging over his breast, and eyebrows that almost covered his eyes. He bade Rinaldo good day. Rinaldo thanked him, and said, "A good day I have hardly had since I was born." Then said the old man, "Signor Rinaldo, you must not despair, for God will make all things turn to the best." Rinaldo answered, "My trouble is too heavy for me to hope relief. The king has taken my brothers, and means to put them to death. I thought to rescue them by means of my horse Bayard, but while I slept some thief has stolen him." The old man replied, "I will remember you and your brothers in my prayers. I am a poor man, have you not something to give me?" Rinaldo said, "I have nothing to give," but then he recollected his spurs. He gave them to the beggar, and said, "Here, take my spurs. They are the first present my mother gave me when my father, Count Aymon, dubbed me knight. They ought to bring you ten pounds."

The old man took the spurs, and put them into his sack, and said, "Noble sir, have you nothing else you can give me?" Rinaldo replied, "Are you making sport of me? I tell you truly if it were not for shame to beat one so helpless, I would teach you better manners." The old man said, "Of a truth, sir, if you did so you would do a great sin. If all had beaten me of whom I have begged I should have been killed long ago, for I ask alms in churches and convents, and wherever I can." "You say true," replied Rinaldo, "if you did not ask, none would relieve you." The old man said, "True, noble sir, therefore I pray if you have anything more to spare, give it me." Rinaldo gave him his mantle, and said, "Take it, pilgrim. I give it you for the love of Christ, that God would save my brothers from a shameful death, and help me to escape out of King Charles's power."

The pilgrim took the mantle, folded it up, and put it into his bag. Then a third time he said to Rinaldo, "Sir, have you nothing left to give me that I may remember you in my prayers?" "Wretch!" exclaimed Rinaldo, "do you make me your sport?" and he drew his sword, and struck at him; but the old man warded off the blow with his staff, and said, "Rinaldo, would you slay your cousin, Malagigi?" When Rinaldo heard that he stayed his hand, and gazed doubtingly on the old man, who now threw aside his disguise, and appeared to be indeed Malagigi. "Dear cousin," said Rinaldo, "pray forgive me. I did not know you. Next to God, my trust is in you. Help my brothers to escape out of prison, I entreat you. I have lost my horse, and therefore cannot render them any assistance." Malagigi answered, "Cousin Rinaldo, I will enable you to recover your horse. Meanwhile, you must do as I say."

Then Malagigi took from his sack a gown, and gave it to Rinaldo to put on over his armor, and a hat that was full of holes, and an old pair of shoes to put on. They looked like two pilgrims, very old and poor. Then they went forth from the wood, and after a little while saw four monks riding along the road. Malagigi said to Rinaldo, "I will go meet the monks, and see what news I can learn."

Malagigi learned from the monks that on the approaching festival there would be a great crowd of people at court, for the prince was going to show the ladies the famous horse Bayard that used to belong to Rinaldo. "What!" said the pilgrim; "is Bayard there?" "Yes," answered the monks; "the king has given him to Charlot, and, after the prince has ridden him the king means to pass sentence on the brothers of Rinaldo, and have them hanged." Then Malagigi asked alms of the monks, but they would give him none, till he threw aside his pilgrim garb, and let them see his armor, when, partly for charity and partly for terror, they gave him a golden cup, adorned with precious stones that sparkled in the sunshine.

Malagigi then hastened back to Rinaldo, and told him what he had learned.

The morning of the feast-day Rinaldo and Malagigi came to the place where the sports were to be held. Malagigi gave Rinaldo his spurs back again, and said, "Cousin, put on your spurs, for you will need them." "How shall I need them," said Rinaldo, "since I have lost my horse?" Yet he did as Malagigi directed him.

When the two had taken their stand on the border of the field among the crowd the princes and ladies of the court began to assemble. When they were all assembled the king came also, and Charlot with him, near whom the horse Bayard was led, in the charge of grooms, who were expressly enjoined to guard him safely. The king, looking round on the circle of spectators, saw

Malagigi and Rinaldo, and observed the splendid cup that they had, and said to Charlot, "See, my son, what a brilliant cup those two pilgrims have got. It seems to be worth a hundred ducats." "That is true," said Charlot; "Let us go and ask where they got it." So they rode to the place where the pilgrims stood, and Charlot stopped Bayard close to them.

The horse snuffed at the pilgrims, knew Rinaldo, and caressed his master. The king said to Malagigi, "Friend, where did you get that beautiful cup?" Malagigi replied, "Honorable sir, I paid for it all the money I have saved from eleven years' begging in churches and convents. The Pope himself has blessed it, and given it the power that whosoever eats or drinks out of it shall be pardoned of all his sins." Then said the king to Charlot, "My son, these are right holy men; see how the dumb beast worships them."

Then the king said to Malagigi, "Give me a morsel from your cup, that I may be cleared of my sins." Malagigi answered, "Illustrious lord, I dare not do it, unless you will forgive all who have at any time offended you. You know that Christ forgave all those who had betrayed and crucified him." The king replied, "Friend, that is true; but Rinaldo has so grievously offended me, that I cannot forgive him, nor that other man, Malagigi, the magician. These two shall never live in my kingdom again. If I catch them I will certainly have them hanged. But tell me, pilgrim, who is that man who stands beside you?" "He is deaf, dumb, and blind," said Malagigi. Then the king said again, "Give me to drink of your cup, to take away my sins." Malagigi answered, "My lord king, here is my poor brother, who for fifty days has not heard, spoken, nor seen. This misfortune befell him in a house where we found shelter, and the day before yesterday we met with a wise woman, who told him the only hope of a cure for him was to come to some place where Bayard was to be ridden, and to mount and ride him; that would do him more good than anything else." Then said the king, "Friend, you have come to the right place, for Bayard is to be ridden here to-day. Give me a draught from your cup, and your companion shall ride upon Bayard." Malagigi, hearing these words, said, "Be it so." Then the king, with great devotion, took a spoon, and dipped a portion from the pilgrim's cup, believing that his sins should be thereby forgiven.

When this was done, the king said to Charlot, "Son, I request that you will let this sick pilgrim sit on your horse, and ride if he can, for by so doing he will be healed of all his infirmities." Charlot replied, "That will I gladly do." So saying, he dismounted, and the servants took the pilgrim in their arms, and helped him on the horse.

Wher Rinaldo was mounted, he put his feet in the stirrups, and said, "I would like to ride a little." Malagigi, hearing him speak, seemed delighted, and asked him whether he could see and hear also. "Yes," said Rinaldo, "I am healed of all my infirmities." When the king heard it he said to Bishop Turpin, "My lord bishop, we must celebrate this with a procession, with crosses and banners, for it is a great miracle."

When Rinaldo remarked that he was not carefully watched, he spoke to the horse, and touched him with the spurs. Bayard knew that his master was upon him, and he started off upon a rapid pace, and in a few moments was a good way off. Malagigi pretended to be in great alarm. "O noble king and master," he cried, "my poor companion is run away with; he will fall and break his neck." The king ordered his knights to ride after the pilgrim, and bring him back, or help him if need were. They did so, but it was in vain. Rinaldo left them all behind him, and kept on his way till he reached Montalban. Malagigi was suffered to depart, unsuspected, and he went his way, making sad lamentation for the fate of his comrade, who he pretended to think must surely be dashed to pieces.

Malagigi did not go far, but having changed his disguise, returned to where the king was, and employed his best art in getting the brothers of Rinaldo out of prison. He succeeded; and all three got safely to Montalban, where Rinaldo's joy at the rescue of his brothers and the recovery of Bayard was more than tongue can tell.

DEATH OF RINALDO

THE distress in Rinaldo's castle for want of food grew more severe every day, under the pressure of the siege. The garrison were forced to kill their horses, both to save the provision they would consume, and to make food of their flesh. At last all the horses were killed except Bayard, and Rinaldo said to his brothers, "Bayard must die, for we have nothing else to eat." So they went to the stable and brought out Bayard to kill him. But Alardo said, "Brother, let Bayard live a little longer; who knows what God may do for us?"

Bayard heard these words, and understood them as if he was a man, and fell on his knees, as if he would beg for mercy. When Rinaldo saw the distress of his horse his heart failed him, and he let him live.

Just at this time Aya, Rinaldo's mother, who was the sister of the Emperor, came to the camp, attended by knights and ladies, to intercede for her sons. She fell on her knees before the king, and besought him that he would pardon Rinaldo and his brothers: and all the peers and knights took her side, and entreated the king to grant her prayer. Then said the king, "Dear sister, you act the part of a good mother, and I respect your tender heart, and yield to your entreaties. I will spare your sons their lives if they submit implicitly to my will."

When Charlot heard this he approached the king and whispered in his ear. And the king turned to his sister and said, "Charlot must have Bayard, because I have given the horse to him. Now go, my sister, and tell Rinaldo what I have said."

When the Lady Aya heard these words she was delighted, thanked God in her heart, and said, "Worthy king and brother, I will do as you bid me." So she went into the castle, where her sons received her most joyfully and affectionately, and she told them the king's offer. Then Alardo said, "Brother, I would rather have the king's enmity than give Bayard to Charlot, for I believe he will kill him." Likewise said all the brothers. When Rinaldo heard them he said, "Dear brothers, if we may win our forgiveness by giving up the horse, so be it. Let us make our peace, for we cannot stand against the king's power." Then he went to his mother, and told her they would give the horse to Charlot, and more, too, if the king would pardon them, and forgive all that they had done against his crown and dignity. The lady returned to Charles and told him the answer of her sons.

When the peace was thus made between the king and the sons of Aymon, the brothers came forth from the castle, bringing Bayard with them, and, falling at the king's feet, begged his forgiveness. The king bade them rise, and received them into favor in the sight of all his noble knights and counsellors, to the great joy of all, especially of the Lady Aya, their mother. Then Rinaldo took the horse Bayard, gave him to Charlot, and said, "My lord and prince, this horse I give to you; do with him as to you seems good." Charlot took him, as had been agreed on. Then he made the servants take him to the bridge, and throw him into the water. Bayard sank to the bottom, but soon came to the surface again and swam, saw Rinaldo looking at him, came to land, ran to his old master, and stood by him as proudly as if he had understanding, and would say, "Why did you treat me so?" When the prince saw that he said, "Rinaldo, give me the horse again, for he must die." Rinaldo replied, "My lord and prince, he is yours without dispute," and gave him to him. The prince then had a millstone tied to each foot, and two to his neck, and made them throw him again into the water. Bayard struggled in the water, looked up to his master, threw off the stones, and came back to Rinaldo.

When Alardo saw that, he said, "Now must thou be disgraced forever, brother, if thou give up the horse again." But Rinaldo answered, "Brother, be still. Shall I for the horse's life provoke the anger of the king again?" Then Alardo said, "Ah, Bayard! what a return do we make for all thy true love and service!" Rinaldo gave the horse to the prince again, and said, "My lord, if the horse comes out again I cannot return him to you any more, for it wrings my heart too much." Then Charlot had Bayard loaded with the stones as before, and thrown into the water; and commanded Rinaldo that he should not stand where the horse would see him. When Bayard rose to the surface he stretched his neck out of the water and looked round for his master, but saw him not. Then he sunk to the bottom.

Rinaldo was so distressed for the loss of Bayard that he made a vow to ride no horse again all his life long, nor to bind a sword to his side, but to become a hermit. He resolved to betake himself to some wild wood, but first to return to his castle, to see his children, and to appoint to each his share of his estate.

So he took leave of the king and of his brothers, and returned to Montalban, and his brothers remained with the king. Rinaldo called his children to him, and he made his eldest born, Aymeric, a knight, and made him lord of his castle and of his land. He gave to the rest what other goods he had, and kissed and embraced them all, commended them to God, and then departed from them with a heavy heart.

He had not travelled far when he entered a wood, and there met with a hermit, who had long been retired from the world. Rinaldo greeted him, and the hermit replied courteously, and asked him who he was and what was his purpose. Rinaldo replied, "Sir, I have led a sinful life; many deeds of violence have I done, and many men have I slain, not always in a good cause, but often under the impulse of my own headstrong passions. I have also been the cause of the death of many of my friends, who took my part, not because they thought me in the right, but only for love of me. And now I come to make confession of all my sins, and to do penance for the rest of my life, if perhaps the mercy of God will forgive me." The hermit said, "Friend, I perceive you have fallen into great sins, and have broken the commandments of God, but his mercy is greater than your sins; and if you repent from your heart, and lead a new life, there is yet hope for you that he will forgive you what is past." So Rinaldo was comforted, and said, "Master, I will stay with you, and what you bid ane I will do." The hermit replied, "Roots and vegetables will be your food; shirt or shoes you may not wear; your lot must be poverty and want if you stay with me." Rinaldo replied, "I will cheerfully bear all this, and more." So he remained three whole years with the hermit, and after that his strength failed, and it seemed as if he was like to die.

One night the hermit had a dream, and heard a voice from heaven, which commanded him to say to his companion that he must without delay go to the Holy Land, and fight against the heathen. The hermit, when he heard that voice, was glad, and calling Rinaldo, he said, "Friend, God's angel has commanded me to say to you that you must without delay go to Jerusalem, and help our fellow-Christians in their struggle with the Infidels." Then said Rinaldo, "Ah! master, how can I do that? It is over three years since I made a vow no more to ride a horse, nor take a sword or spear in my hand." The hermit answered, "Dear friend, obey God, and do what the angel commanded." "I will do so," said Rinaldo, "and pray for me, my master, that God may guide me right." Then he departed, and went to the seaside, and took ship and came to Tripoli in Syria.

And as he went on his way his strength returned to him, till it was equal to what it was in his best days. And though he never mounted a horse, nor took a sword in his hand, yet with his pilgrim's staff he did good service in the armies of the Christians; and it pleased God that he escaped unhurt, though he was present in many battles, and his courage inspired the men with the same. At last a truce was made with the Saracens, and Rinaldo, now old and infirm, wishing to see his native land again before he died, took ship and sailed for France. When he arrived he shunned to go to the resorts of the great, and preferred to live among the humble folk, where he was unknown. He did country work, and lived on milk and bread, drank water, and was therewith content. While he so lived he heard that the city of Cologne was the holiest and best of cities, on account of the relics and bodies of saints who had there poured out their blood for the faith. This induced him to betake himself thither. When the pious hero arrived at Cologne he went to the monastery of St. Peter, and lived a holy life, occupied night and day in devotion. It so happened that at that time in the next town to Cologne there raged a dreadful pestilence. Many people came to Rinaldo, to beg him to pray for them, that the plague might be stayed. The holy man prayed fervently, and besought the Lord to take away the plague from the people, and his prayer was heard. The stroke of the pestilence was arrested, and all the people thanked the holy man and praised God.

Now there was at this time at Cologne a bishop, called Agilolphus, who was a wise and understanding man, who led a pure and secluded life, and set a good example to others. This bishop undertook to build the Church of St. Peter, and gave notice to all stonemasons and other workmen round about to come to Cologne, where they should find work and wages. Among others came Rinaldo; and he worked among the laborers and did more than four or five common workmen. When they went to dinner he brought stone and mortar so that they had enough for the whole day. When the others went to bed he stretched himself out on the stones. He ate bread only, and drank nothing but water; and had for his wages but a penny a day. The head workman asked him his name, and where he belonged. He would not tell, but said nothing and pursued his work. They called him St. Peter's workman, because he was so devoted to his work.

When the overseer saw the diligence of this holy man he chid the laziness of the other workmen, and said, "You receive more pay than this good man, but do not do half as much work." For this reason the other workmen hated Rinaldo, and made a secret agreement to kill him. They knew that he made it a practice to go every night to a certain church to pray and give alms. So they agreed to lay wait for him, with the purpose to kill him. When he came to the spot, they seized him, and beat him over the head till he was dead. Then they put his body into a sack, and stones with it, and cast it into the Rhine, in the hope the sack would sink to the bottom, and be there concealed. But God willed not that it should be so, but caused the sack to float on the surface, and be thrown upon the bank. And the soul of the holy martyr was carried by angels, with songs of praise, up to the heavens.

Now at that time the people of Dortmund had become converted to the Christian faith; and they sent to the Bishop of Cologne, and desired him to give them some of the holy relics that are in such abundance in that city. So the Bishop called together his clergy to deliberate what answer they should give to this request. And it was determined to give to the people of Dortmund the body of the holy man who had just suffered martyrdom.

When now the body with the coffin was put on the cart, the cart began to move toward Dortmund without horses or help of men, and stopped not till it reached the place where the church of St. Rinaldo now stands. The Bishop and his clergy followed the holy man to do him honor, with singing of hymns, for a space of three miles. And St. Rinaldo has ever since been the patron of that place, and many wonderful works has God done through him, as may be seen in the legends.

HUON OF BORDEAUX

WHEN Charlemagne grew old he felt the burden of government become heavier year by year, till at last he called together his high barons and peers to propose to abdicate the empire and the throne of France in favor of his sons, Charlot and Lewis.

The Emperor was unreasonably partial to his eldest son; he would have been glad to have had the barons and peers demand Charlot for their only sovereign; but that prince was so infamous, for his falsehood and cruelty, that the council strenuously opposed the Emperor's proposal of abdicating, and implored him to continue to hold a sceptre which he wielded with so much glory.

Amaury of Hauteville, cousin of Ganelon, and now head of the wicked branch of the house of Maganza, was the secret partisan of Charlot, whom he resembled in his loose morals and bad dispositions. Amaury nourished the most bitter resentment against the house of Guienne, of which the former Duke, Sevinus, had often rebuked his misdeeds. He took advantage of this occasion to do an injury to the two young children whom the Duke Sevinus had left under the charge of the Duchess Alice, their mother; and at the same time, to advance his interest with Charlot by increasing his wealth and power. With this view he suggested to the prince a new idea.

He pretended to agree with the opinion of the barons; he said that it would be best to try Charlot's capacity for government by giving him some rich provinces before placing him upon the throne; and that the Emperor, without depriving himself of any part of his realm, might give Charlot the investiture of Guienne. For although seven years had passed since the death of Sevinus, the young Duke, his son, had not yet repaired to the court of Charlemagne to render the homage due to his lawful sovereign.

We have often had occasion to admire the justice and wisdom of the advice which on all occasions the Duke Namo of Bavaria gave to Charlemagne, and he now discountenanced, with indignation, the selfish advice of Amaury. He represented to the Emperor the early age of the children of Sevinus, and the useful and glorious services of their late father, and proposed to Charlemagne to send two knights to the Duchess at Bordeaux, to summon her two sons to the court of the Emperor, to pay their respects and render homage.

Charlemagne approved this advice, and sent two chevaliers to demand the two young princes of their mother. No sooner had the Duchess learned the approach of the two knights, than she sent distinguished persons to receive them; and as soon as they entered the palace she presented herself before them, with her elder and younger sons, Huon and Girard.

The deputies, delighted with the honors and caresses they received, accompanied with rich presents, left Bordeaux with regret and on their return represented to Charlemagne that the young Duke Huon seemed born to tread in the footsteps of his brave father, informing him that in three months the young princes of Guienne would present themselves at his court.

The Duchess employed the short interval in giving her sons her last instructions. Huon received them in his heart, and Girard gave as much heed to them as could be expected from one so young.

The preparations for their departure having been made, the Duchess embraced them tenderly, commending them to the care of Heaven, and charged them to call, on their way, at the celebrated monastery of Cluny, to visit the Abbot, the brother of their father. This Abbot, worthy of his high dignity, had never lost an opportunity of doing good, setting an example of every excellence, and making virtue attractive by his example.

He received his nephews with the greatest magnificence; and, aware how useful his presence might be to them with Charlemagne, whose valued counsellor he was, he took with them the road to Paris.

When Amaury learned what reception the two deputies of Charlemagne had received at Bordeaux, and the arrangements made for the visit of the young princes to the Emperor's court, he suggested to Charlot to give him a troop of his guards, with which he proposed to lay wait for the young men in the wood of Montlery, put them to death, and thereby give the prince Charlot possession of the duchy of Guienne.

A plan of treachery and violence agreed but too well with Charlot's disposition. He not only adopted the suggestion of Amaury, but insisted upon taking a part in it. They went out secretly, by night, followed by a great number of attendants, all armed in black, to lie in ambuscade in the wood where the brothers were to pass.

Girard, the younger of the two, having amused himself as he rode by flying his hawk at such game as presented itself, had ridden in advance of his brother and the Abbot of Cluny. Charlot, who saw him coming, alone and unarmed, went forth to meet him, sought a quarrel with him, and threw him from his horse with a stroke of his lance. Girard uttered a cry as he fell; Huon heard it, and flew to his defence, with no other weapon than his sword. He came up with him, and saw the blood flowing from his wound. "What has this child done to you, wretch!" he exclaimed to Charlot. "How cowardly to attack him when unprepared to defend himself!" "By my faith," said Charlot, "I mean to do the same by you. Know that I am the son of Duke Thierry of Ardennes, from whom your father, Sevinus, took three castles; I have sworn to avenge him, and I defy you." "Coward," answered Huon, "I know well the baseness that dwells in your race; worthy son of Thierry, use the advantage that your armor gives you; but know that I fear you not." At these words Charlot had the wickedness to put his lance in rest, and to run upon Huon, who had barely time to wrap his arm in his mantle. With this feeble buckler he received the thrust of the lance. It penetrated the mantle, but missed his body. Then, rising upon his stirrups, Sir Huon struck Charlot so terrible a blow with his sword that the helmet was cleft asunder, and his head too. The dastardly prince fell dead upon the ground.

Huon now perceived that the wood was full of armed men. He called the men of his suite, and they hastily put themselves in order, but nobody issued from the wood to attack him. Amaury, who saw Charlot's fall, had no desire to compromise himself; and, feeling sure that Charlemagne would avenge the death of his son, he saw no occasion for his doing anything more at present. He left Huon and the Abbot of Cluny to bind up the wound of Girard, and, having seen them depart and resume their way to Paris, he took up the body of Charlot, and, placing it across a horse, had it carried to Paris, where he arrived four hours after Huon.

The Abbot of Cluny presented his nephew to Charlemagne, but Huon refrained from paying his obeisance, complaining grievously of the ambush which had been set for him, which he said could not have been without the Emperor's permission. Charlemagne, surprised at a charge which his magnanimous soul was incapable of meriting, asked eagerly of the Abbot what were the grounds of the complaints of his nephew. The Abbot told him faithfully all that had happened, informing him that a coward knight, who called himself the son of Thierry of Ardennes, had wounded Girard, and run upon Huon, who was unarmed; but by his force and valor he had overcome the traitor, and left him dead upon the plain.

Charlemagne indignantly disavowed any connection with the action of the infamous Thierry, congratulated the young Duke upon his victory, himself conducted the two brothers to a rich apartment, stayed to see the first dressing applied to the wound of Girard, and left the brothers in charge of Duke Namo of Bavaria, who, having been a companion in arms of the Duke Sevinus, regarded the young men almost as if they were his own sons.

Charlemagne had hardly quitted them when, returning to his chamber, he heard cries, and saw through the window a party of armed men just arrived. He recognized Amaury, who bore a dead knight stretched across a horse; and the name of Charlot was heard among the exclamations of the people assembled in the court-yard.

Charles's partiality for this unworthy son was one of his weaknesses. He descended in trepidation to the court-yard, ran to Amaury, and uttered a cry of grief on recognizing Charlot. "It is Huon of Bordeaux," said the traitor Amaury, "who has massacred your son before it was in my power to defend him." Charlemagne, furious at these words, seized a sword, and flew to the apartment of the two brothers to plunge it into the heart of the murderer of his son. Duke Namo stopped his hand for an instant, while Charles told him the crime of which Huon was accused. "He is a peer of the realm," said Namo, "and if he is guilty, is he not here in your power, and are not we peers the proper judges to condemn him to death? Let not your hand be stained with his blood." The Emperor, calmed by the wisdom of Duke Namo, summoned Amaury to his presence. The peers assembled to hear his testimony, and the traitor accused Huon of Bordeaux of having struck the fatal blow without allowing Charlot an opportunity to defend himself, and though he knew that his opponent was the Emperor's eldest son.

The Abbot of Cluny, indignant at the false accusation of Amaury, advanced, and said, "By Saint Benedict, sire, the traitor lies in his throat. If my nephew has slain Charlot it was in his own defence, and after having seen his brother wounded by him, and also in ignorance that his adversary was the prince. Though I am a son of the Church," added the good Abbot, "I forget not that I am a knight by birth. I offer to prove with my body the lie upon Amaury, if he dares sustain it, and I shall feel that I am doing a better work to punish a disloyal traitor, than to sing lauds and matins."

Huon to this time had kept silent, amazed at the black calumny of Amaury; but now he stepped forth, and, addressing Amaury, said: "Traitor! darest thou maintain in arms the lie thou hast uttered?" Amaury, a knight of great prowess, despising the youth and slight figure of Huon, hesitated not to offer his glove, which Huon seized; then, turning again to the peers, he said: "I pray you let the combat be allowed me, for never was there a more legitimate cause." The Duke Namo and the rest, deciding that the question should be remitted to the judgment of Heaven, the combat was ordained, to which Charlemagne unwillingly consented. The young Duke was restored to the charge of Duke Namo, who the next morning invested him with the honors of knighthood, and gave him armor of proof, with a white shield. The Abbot of Cluny, delighted to find in his nephew sentiments worthy of his birth, embraced him, gave him his blessing, and hastened to the church of St. Germains to pray for him, while the officers of the king prepared the lists for the combat.

The battle was long and obstinate. The address and agility of Huon enabled him to avoid the terrible blows which the ferocious Amaury aimed at him. But Huon had more than once drawn blood from his antagonist. The effect began to be perceived in the failing strength of the traitor; at last he threw himself from his horse, and kneeling, begged for mercy. "Spare me," he said, "and I will confess all. Aid me to rise, and lead me to Charlemagne." The brave and loyal Huon, at these words, put his sword under his left arm, and stretched out his right to raise the prostrate man, who seized the opportunity to give him a thrust in the side. The hauberk of Huon resisted the blow, and he was wounded but slightly. Transported with rage at this act of baseness, he forgot how necessary for his complete acquittal the confession of Amaury was, and without delay dealt him the fatal blow.

Duke Namo and the other peers approached, had the body of Amaury dragged forth from the lists, and conducted Huon to Charlemagne. The Emperor, however, listening to nothing but his resentment and grief for the death of his son, refused to be satisfied; and under the plea that Huon had not succeeded in making his accuser retract his charge seemed resolved to confiscate his estates and to banish him forever from France. It was not till after long entreaties on the part of Duke Namo and the rest that he consented to grant Huon his pardon, under conditions which he should impose.

Huon approached, and knelt before the Emperor, rendered his homage, and cried him mercy for the involuntary killing of his son. Charlemagne would not receive the hands of Huon in his own, but touched him with his sceptre, saying, "I receive thy homage, and pardon thee the death of my son, but only on one condition. You shall go immediately to the court of the Sultan Gaudisso; you shall present yourself before him as he sits at meat; you shall cut off the head of the most illustrious guest whom you shall find sitting nearest to him; you shall kiss three times on the mouth the fair princess, his daughter, and you shall demand of the Sultan, as token of tribute to me, a handful of the white hair of his beard, and four grinders from his mouth."

These conditions caused a murmur from all the assembly. "What!" said the Abbot of Cluny; "slaughter a Saracen prince without first offering him baptism?" "The second condition is not so hard," said the young peers, "but the demand that Huon is bound to make of the old Sultan is very uncivil, and will be hard to obtain."

The Emperor's obstinacy when he had once resolved upon a thing is well known. To the courage of Huon nothing seemed impossible. "I accept the conditions," said he, silencing the intercessions of the old Duke of Bavaria; "my liege, I accept my pardon at this price. I go to execute your commands, as your vassal and a peer of France."

The Duke Namo and Abbot of Cluny, being unable to obtain any relaxation of the sentence passed by Charlemagne, led forth the young Duke, who determined to set out at once on his expedition. All that the good Abbot could obtain of him was, that he should prepare for this perilous undertaking by going first to Rome, to pay his homage to the Pope, who was the brother of the Duchess Alice, Huon's mother, and from him demand absolution and his blessing. Huon promised it, and forthwith set out on his way to Rome.

HUON OF BORDEAUX (Continued)

HUON, having traversed the Apennines and Italy, arrived at the environs of Rome, where, laying aside his armor, he assumed the dress of a pilgrim. In this attire he presented himself before the Pope, and not till after he had made a full confession of his sins did he announce himself as his nephew. "Ah! my dear nephew," exclaimed the Holy Father, "what harder penance could I impose than the Emperor has already done? Go in peace, my son," he added, absolving him, "I go to intercede for you with the Most High." Then he led his nephew into his palace, and introduced him to all the Cardinals and Princes of Rome as the Duke of Guienne, son of the Duchess Alice, his sister.

Huon, at setting out, had made a vow not to stop more than three days in a place. The Holy Father took advantage of this time to inspire him with zeal for the glory of Christianity, and with confidence in the protection of the Most High. He advised him to embark for Palestine, to visit the Holy Sepulchre, and to depart thence for the interior of Asia.

Loaded with the blessings of the Holy Father, Huon, obeying his counsels, embarked for Palestine, arrived, and visited with the greatest reverence the holy places. He then departed, and took his way toward the east.

But, ignorant of the country and of the language, he lost himself in a forest, and remained three days without seeing a human creature, living on honey and wild fruits which he found on the trees. The third day, seeking a passage through a rocky defile, he beheld a man in tattered clothing, whose beard and hair covered his breast and shoulders. This man stopped on seeing him, observed him, and recognized the arms and bearing of a French knight. He immediately approached, and exclaimed, in the language of the South of France, "God be praised! Do I indeed behold a chevalier of my own country, after fifteen years passed in this desert without seeing the face of a fellow-countryman?"

Huon, to gratify him still more, unlaced his helmet, and came towards him with a smiling countenance. The other regarded him with more surprise than at first. "Good Heaven!" he exclaimed, "was there ever such a resemblance? Ah, noble sir," he added, "tell me, I beseech you, of what country and race you come?" "I require," replied Huon, "before telling you mine, that you first reveal your own; let it suffice you at present to know that I am a Christian, and that in Guienne I was born." "Ah! Heaven grant that my eyes and my heart do not deceive me," exclaimed the unknown; "my name is Sherasmin; I am brother to Guire, the Mayor of Bordeaux. I was taken prisoner in the battle where my dear and illustrious master, Sevinus, lost his life. For three years I endured the miseries of slavery; at length I broke my chains and escaped to this desert, where I have sustained myself in solitude ever since. Your features recall to me my beloved sovereign, in whose service I was from my infancy till his death." Huon made no reply but by embracing the old man, with tears in his eyes. Then Sherasmin learned that his arms enfolded the son of the Duke Sevinus. He led him to his cabin, and spread before him the dry fruits and honey which formed his only aliment.

Huon recounted his adventures to Sherasmin, who was moved to tears at the recital. He then consulted him on means of conducting his enterprise. Sherasmin hesitated not to confess that success seemed impossible; nevertheless he swore a solemn oath never to abandon him. The Saracen language, which he was master of, would be serviceable to them when they should leave the desert, and mingle with men.

They took the route of the Red Sea, and entered Arabia. Their way lay through a region which Sherasmin described as full of terrors. It was inhabited by Oberon, King of the Fairies, who made captive such knights as were rash enough to penetrate into it, and transformed them into Hobgoblins. It was possible to avoid this district at the expense of somewhat lengthening their route; but no dangers could deter Huon of Bordeaux; and the brave Sherasmin, who had now resumed the armor of a knight, reluctantly consented to share with him the dangers of the shorter route.

They entered a wood, and arrived at a spot whence alleys branched off in various directions. One of them seemed to be terminated by a superb palace, whose gilded roofs were adorned with brilliant weathercocks covered with diamonds. A superb chariot issued from the gate of the palace, and drove toward Huon and his companion, as if to meet them half-way. The prince saw no one in the chariot but a child apparently about five years old, very beautiful, and clad in a robe which glittered with precious stones. At the sight of him, Sherasmin's terror was extreme. He seized the reins of Huon's horse, and turned him about, hurrying the prince away, and assuring him that they were lost if they stopped to parley with the mischievous dwarf, who, though he appeared a child, was full of years and of treachery. Huon was sorry to lose sight of the beautiful dwarf, whose aspect had nothing in it to alarm; yet he followed his friend, who urged on his horse with all possible speed. Presently a storm began to roar through the forest, the daylight grew dim, and they found their way with difficulty. From time to time they seemed to hear an infantine voice, which said, "Stop, Duke Huon; listen to me: it is in vain you fly me!"

Sherasmin only fled the faster, and stopped not until he had reached the gate of a monastery of monks and nuns, the two communities of which were assembled at that time in a religious procession. Sherasmin, feeling safe from the malice of the dwarf in the presence of so many holy persons and the sacred banners, stopped to ask an asylum, and made Huon dismount also. But at that moment they were joined by the dwarf, who blew a blast upon an ivory horn which hung from his neck. Immediately the good Sherasmin, in spite of himself, began to dance like a young collegian, and seizing the hand of an aged nun, who felt as if it would be her death, they footed it briskly over the grass, and were imitated by all the other monks and nuns, mingled together, forming the strangest dancing-party ever beheld. Huron alone felt no disposition to dance; but he came near dying of laughter at seeing the ridiculous postures and leaps of the others.

The dwarf, approaching Huon, said, in a sweet voice, and in Huon's own language, "Duke of Guienne, why do you shun me? I conjure you, in Heaven's name, speak to me." Huon, hearing himself addressed in this serious manner, and knowing that no evil spirit would dare to use the holy name in aid of his schemes, replied, "Sir, whoever you are, I am ready to hear and answer you." "Huon, my friend," continued the dwarf, "I always loved your race, and you have been dear to me ever since your birth. The gracious state of conscience in which you were when you entered my wood has protected you from all enchantments, even if I had intended to practise any upon you. If these monks, these nuns, and even your friend Sherasmin, had had a conscience as pure as yours, my horn would not have set them dancing; but where is the monk or the nun who can always be deaf to the voice of the tempter, and Sherasmin in the desert has often doubted the power of Providence."

At these words Huon saw the dancers overcome with exertion. He begged mercy for them, the dwarf granted it, and the effect of the horn ceased at once; the nuns got rid of their partners, smoothed their dresses, and hastened to resume their places in the procession. Sherasmin, overcome with heat, panting, and unable to stand on his legs, threw himself upon the grass, and began, "Did not I tell you"--He was going on in an angry tone, but the dwarf, approaching, said, "Sherasmin, why have you murmured against Providence? Why have you thought evil of me? You deserved this light punishment; but I know you to be good and loyal; I mean to show myself your friend, as you shall soon see." At these words he presented him a rich goblet. "Make the sign of the cross on this cup," said he, "and then believe that I hold my power from the God you adore, whose faithful servant I am, as well as you." Sherasmin obeyed, and on the instant the cup was filled with delicious wine, a draught of which restored vigor to his limbs, and made him feel young again. Overcome with gratitude, he threw himself on his knees, but the dwarf raised him, and bade him sit beside him, and thus commenced his history:

"Julius Caesar, going by sea to join his army, was driven by a storm to take shelter in the island of Celea, where dwelt the fairy Glorianda. From this renowned pair I draw my birth. I am the inheritor of that which was most admirable in each of my parents: my father's heroic qualities, and my mother's beauty and magic art. But a malicious sister of my mother's, in revenge for some slight offence, touched me with her wand when I was only five years old, and forbade me to grow any bigger; and my mother, with all her power, was unable to annul the sentence. I have thus continued infantile in appearance, though full of years and experience. The power which I derive from my mother I use sometimes for my own diversion, but always to promote justice and to reward virtue. I am able and willing to assist you, Duke of Guienne, for I know the errand on which you come hither. I presage for you, if you follow my counsels, complete success; and the beautiful Clarimunda for a wife."

When he had thus spoken he presented to Huon the precious and useful cup, which had the faculty of filling itself when a good man took it in his hand. He gave him also his beautiful horn of ivory, saying to him, "Huon, when you sound this gently, you will make the hearers dance, as you have seen; but if you sound it forcibly, fear not that I shall hear it, though at a hundred leagues' distance, and will fly to your relief; but be careful not to sound it in that way, unless upon the most urgent occasion."

Oberon directed Huon what course he should take to reach the country of the Sultan Gaudisso. "You will encounter great perils," said he, "before arriving there, and I fear me," he added, with tears in his eyes, "that you will not in everything obey my directions, and in that case you will suffer much calamity." Then he embraced Huon and Sherasmin, and left them.

Huon and his follower travelled many days through the desert before they reached any inhabited place, and all this while the wonderful cup sustained them, furnishing them not only wine, but food also. At last they came to a great city. As day was declining, they entered its suburbs, and Sherasmin, who spoke the Saracen language perfectly, inquired for an inn where they could pass the night. A person who appeared to be one of the principal inhabitants, seeing two strangers of respectable appearance making this inquiry, stepped forward and begged them to accept the shelter of his mansion. They entered, and their host did the honors of his abode with a politeness which they were astonished to see in a Saracen. He had them served with coffee and sherbet, and all was conducted with great decorum, till one of the servants awkwardly overturned a cup of hot coffee on the host's legs, when he started up, exclaiming in very good Gascon, "Blood and thunder! you blockhead, you deserve to be thrown over the mosque!"

Huon could not help laughing to see the vivacity and the language of his country thus break out unawares. The host, who had no idea that his guests understood his words, was astonished when Huon addressed him in the dialect of his country. Immediately confidence was established between them; especially when the domestics had retired. The host, seeing that he was discovered, and that the two pretended Saracens were from the borders of the Garonne, embraced them, and disclosed that he was a Christian. Huon, who had learned prudence from the advice of Oberon, to test his host's sincerity, drew from his robe the cup which the Fairy-king had given him, and presented it empty to the host. "A fair cup," said he, "but I should like it better if it was full." Immediately it was so. The host, astonished, dared not put it to his lips. "Drink boldly, my dear fellow-countryman," said Huon; "your truth is proved by this cup, which only fills itself in the hands of an honest man." The host did not hesitate longer; the cup passed freely from hand to hand; their mutual cordiality increased as it passed, and each recounted his adventures. Those of Huon redoubled his host's respect; for he recognized in him his legitimate sovereign: while the host's narrative was in these words:

"My name is Floriac; this great and strong city, you will hear with surprise and grief, is governed by a brother of Duke Sevinus, and your uncle. You have no doubt heard that a young brother of the Duke of Guienne was stolen away from the sea-shore, with his companions, by some corsairs. I was then his page, and we were carried by those corsairs to Barbary, where we were sold for slaves. The Barbary prince sent us as part of the tribute which he yearly paid to his sovereign, the Sultan Gaudisso. Your uncle, who had been somewhat puffed up by the flattery of his attendants, thought to increase his importance with his new master by telling him his rank. The Sultan, who, like a true Mussulman, detested all Christian princes, exerted himself from that moment to bring him over to the Saracen faith. He succeeded but too well. Your uncle, seduced by the arts of the Santons, and by the pleasures and indulgences which the Sultan allowed him, committed the horrid crime of apostasy; he renounced his baptism, and embraced Mahometanism. Gaudisso then loaded him with honors, made him espouse one of his nieces, and sent him to reign over this city and adjoining country. Your uncle preserved for me the same friendship which he had had when a boy; but all his caresses and efforts could not make me renounce my faith. Perhaps he respected me in his heart for my resistance to his persuasions, perhaps he had hopes of inducing me in time to imitate him. He made me accompany him to this city, of which he was master, he gave me his confidence, and permits me to keep in my service some Christians, whom I protect for the sake of their faith."

"Ah!" exclaimed Huon, "take me to this guilty uncle. A prince of the house of Guienne, must he not blush at the cowardly abandonment of the faith of his fathers?"

"Alas!" replied Floriac, "I fear he will neither be sensible of shame at your reproaches, nor of pleasure at the sight of a nephew so worthy of his lineage. Brutified by sensuality, jealous of his power, which he often exercises with cruelty, he will more probably restrain you by force or put you to death."

"Be it so," said the brave and fervent Huon, "I could not die in a better cause; and I demand of you to conduct me to him tomorrow, after having told him of my arrival and my birth." Floriac still objected, but Huon would take no denial, and he promised obedience.

Next morning Floriac waited upon the Governor and told him of the arrival of his nephew, Huon of Bordeaux; and of the intention of the prince to present himself at his court that very day. The Governor, surprised, did not immediately answer; though he at once made up his mind what to do. He knew that Floriac loved Christians and the princes of his native land too well to aid in any treason to one of them; he therefore feigned great pleasure at hearing of the arrival of the eldest born of his family at his court. He immediately sent Floriac to find him; he caused his palace to be put in festal array, his divan to be assembled, and after giving some secret orders, went himself to meet his nephew, whom he introduced under his proper name and title to all the great officers of his court.

Huon burned with indignation at seeing his uncle with forehead encircled with a rich turban, surmounted with a crescent of precious stones. His natural candor made him receive with pain the embraces which the treacherous Governor lavished upon him. Meanwhile the hope of finding a suitable moment to reproach him for his apostasy made him submit to those honors which his uncle caused to be rendered to him. The Governor evaded with address the chance of being alone with Huon and spent all the morning in taking him through his gardens and palace. At last, when the hour of dinner approached, and the Governor took him by the hand to lead him into the dining-hall, Huon seized the opportunity and said to him in a low voice, "O my uncle! O Prince, brother of the Duke Sevinus! in what condition have I the grief and shame of seeing you!" The Governor pretended to be moved, pressed his hand, and whispered in his ear, "Silence! my dear nephew; to-morrow morning I will hear you fully."

Huon, comforted a little by these words, took his seat at the table by the side of the Governor. The Mufti, some Cadis, Agas, and Santons, filled the other places. Sherasmin sat down with them; but Floriac, who would not lose sight of his guests, remained standing, and passed in and out to observe what was going on within the palace. He soon perceived a number of armed men gliding through the passages and antechambers connected with the dining-hall. He was about to enter to give his guests notice of what he had seen when he heard a violent noise and commotion in the hall. The cause was this.

Huon and Sherasmin were well enough suited with the first course and ate with good appetite; but the people of their country not being accustomed to drink only water at their meals, Huon and Sherasmin looked at one another, not very well pleased at such a regimen. Huon laughed outright at the impatience of Sherasmin, but soon, experiencing the same want himself, he drew forth Oberon's cup and made the sign of the cross. The cup filled and he drank it off, and handed it to Sherasmin, who followed his example. The Governor and his officers, seeing this abhorred sign, contracted their brows and sat in silent consternation. Huon pretended not to observe it, and having filled the cup again handed it to his uncle, saying, "Pray, join us, dear uncle; it is excellent Bordeaux wine, the drink that will be to you like mother's milk." The Governor, who often drank in secret with his own favorite Sultanas the wines of Greece and Shiraz, never in public drank anything but water. He had not for a long time tasted the excellent wines of his native land; he was sorely tempted to drink what was now handed to him, it looked so bright in the cup, outshining the gold itself. He stretched forth his hand, took the brimming goblet, and raised it to his lips, when immediately it dried up and disappeared. Huon and Sherasmin, like Gascons as they were, laughed at his astonishment. "Christian dogs!" he exclaimed, "do you dare to insult me at my own table? But I will soon be revenged." At these words he threw the cup at the head of his nephew, who caught it with his left hand, while with the other he snatched the turban, with its crescent, from the Governor's head and threw it on the floor. All the Saracens started up from table, with loud outcries, and prepared to avenge the insult. Huon and Sherasmin put themselves on their defence, and met with their swords the scimitars directed against them. At this moment the doors of the hall opened and a crowd of soldiers and armed eunuchs rushed in, who joined in the attack upon Huon and Sherasmin. The Prince and his followers took refuge on a broad shelf or side-board, where they kept at bay the crowd of assailants, making the most forward of them smart for their audacity. But more troops came pressing in and the brave Huon, inspired by the wine of Bordeaux, and not angry enough to lose his relish for a joke, blew a gentle note on his horn, and no sooner was it heard than it quelled the rage of the combatants and set them to dancing. Huon and Sherasmin, no longer attacked, looked down from their elevated position on a scene the most singular and amusing. Very soon the Sultanas, hearing the sound of the dance and finding their guards withdrawn, came into the hall and mixed with the dancers. The favorite Sultana seized upon a young Santon, who performed jumps two feet high; but soon the long dresses of this couple got intermingled and threw them down. The Santon's beard was caught in the Sultana's necklace, and they could not disentangle them. The Governor by no means approved this familiarity, and took two steps forward to get at the Santon, but he stumbled over a prostrate Dervise and measured his length on the floor. The dancing continued till the strength of the performers was exhausted, and they fell, one after the other, and lay helpless. The Governor at length made signs to Huon that he would yield everything if he would but allow him to rest. The bargain was ratified; the Governor allowed Huon and Sherasmin to depart on their way, and even gave them a ring which would procure them safe passage through his country and access to the Sultan Gaudisso. The two friends hastened to avail themselves of this favorable turn, and taking leave of Floriac, pursued their journey.

HUON OF BORDEAUX (Continued)

HUON had seen many beauties at his mother's court, but his heart had never been touched with love. Honor had been his mistress, and in pursuit of that he had never found time to give a thought to softer cares. Strange that a heart so insensible should first be touched by something so unsubstantial as a dream; but so it was.

The day after the adventure with his uncle night overtook the travellers as they passed through a forest. A grotto offered them shelter from the night dews. The magic cup supplied their evening meal; for such was its virtue that it afforded not only wine, but more solid fare when desired. Fatigue soon threw them into profound repose. Lulled by the murmur of the foliage, and breathing the fragrance of the flowers, Huon dreamed that a lady more beautiful than he had ever before seen hung over him and imprinted a kiss upon his lips. As he stretched out his arms to embrace her a sudden gust of wind swept her away.

Huon awoke in an agony of regret. A few moments sufficed to afford some consolation in showing him that what had passed was but a dream; but his perplexity and sadness could not escape the notice of Sherasmin. Huon hesitated not to inform his faithful follower of the reason of his pensiveness; and got nothing in return but his rallyings for allowing himself to be disturbed by such a cause. He recommended a draught from the fairy goblet, and Huon tried it with good effect.

At early dawn they resumed their way. They travelled till high noon, but said little to one another. Huon was musing on his dream, and Sherasmin's thoughts flew back to his early days on the banks of the flowery Garonne.

On a sudden they were startled by the cry of distress, and turning an angle of the wood, came where a knight hard pressed was fighting with a furious lion. The knight's horse lay dead, and it seemed as if another moment would end the combat, for terror and fatigue had quite disabled the knight for further resistance. He fell, and the lion's paw was raised over him, when a blow from Huon's sword turned the monster's rage upon a new enemy. His roar shook the forest, and he crouched in act to spring, when, with the rapidity of lightning, Huon plunged his sword into his side. He rolled over on the plain in the agonies of death.

They raised the knight from the ground, and Sherasmin hastened to offer him a draught from the fairy cup. The wine sparkled to the brim, and the warrior put forth his lips to quaff it, but it shrunk away, and did not even wet his lips. He dashed the goblet angrily on the ground, with an exclamation of resentment. This incident did not tend to make either party more acceptable to the other; and what followed was worse. For when Huon said, "Sir knight, thank God for your deliverance,"--"Thank Mahomet, rather, yourself," said he, "for he has led you this day to render service to no less a personage than the Prince of Hyrcania."

At the sound of this blasphemy Huon drew his sword and turned upon the miscreant, who, little disposed to encounter the prowess of which he had so lately seen proof, betook himself to flight. He ran to Huon's horse, and lightly vaulting on his back, clapped spurs to his side, and galloped out of sight.

The adventure was vexatious, yet there was no remedy. The prince and Sherasmin continued their journey with the aid of the remaining horse as they best might. At length, as evening set in, they descried the pinnacles and towers of a great city full before them, which they knew to be the famous city of Bagdad.

They were well-nigh exhausted with fatigue when they arrived at its precincts, and in the darkness, not knowing what course to take, were glad to meet an aged woman, who, in reply to their inquiries, offered them such accommodations as her cottage could supply. They thankfully accepted the offer, and entered the low door. The good dame busily prepared the best fare her stores supplied,--milk, figs, and peaches,--deeply regretting that the bleak winds had nipped her almond-trees.

Sir Huon thought he had never in his life tasted any fare so good. The old lady talked while her guests ate. She doubted not, she said, they had come to be present at the great feast in honor of the marriage of the Sultan's daughter, which was to take place on the morrow. They asked who the bridegroom was to be, and the old lady answered, "The Prince of Hyrcania," but added, "Our princess hates him, and would rather wed a dragon than him." "How know you that?" asked Huon; and the dame informed him that she had it from the princess herself, who was her foster-child. Huon inquired the reason of the princess's aversion; and the woman pleased to find her chat excite so much interest, replied that it was all in consequence of a dream. "A dream!" exclaimed Huon. "Yes! a dream. She dreamed that she was a hind, and that the Prince, as a hunter, was pursuing her, and had almost overtaken her, when a beautiful dwarf appeared in view, drawn in a golden car, having by his side a young man of yellow hair and fair complexion, like one from a foreign land. She dreamed that the car stopped where she stood, and that, having resumed her own form, she was about to ascend it, when suddenly it faded from her view, and with it the dwarf and the fair-haired youth. But from her heart that vision did not fade, and from that time her affianced bridegroom, the Hyrcanian prince, had become odious to her sight. Yet the Sultan, her father, by no means regarding such a cause as sufficient to prevent the marriage, had named the morrow as the time when it should be solemnized, in presence of his court and many princes of the neighboring countries, whom the fame of the princess's beauty and the bridegroom's splendor had brought to the scene."

We may suppose this conversation woke a tumult of thoughts in the breast of Huon. Was it not clear that Providence led him on, and cleared the way for his happy success? Sleep did not early visit the eyes of Huon that night; but, with the sanguine temper of youth, he indulged his fancy in imagining the sequel of his strange experience.

The next day, which he could not but regard as the decisive day of his fate, he prepared to deliver the message of Charlemagne. Clad in his armor, fortified with his ivory horn and his ring, he reached the palace of Gaudisso when the guests were assembled at the banquet. As he approached the gate a voice called on all true believers to enter; and Huon, the brave and faithful Huon, in his impatience passed in under that false pretention. He had no sooner passed the barrier than he felt ashamed of his baseness, and was overwhelmed with regret. To make amends for his fault he ran forward to the second gate, and cried to the porter, "Dog of a misbeliever, I command you in the name of Him who died on the cross, open to me!" The points of a hundred weapons immediately opposed his passage. Huon then remembered for the first time the ring he had received from his uncle, the Governor. He produced it, and demanded to be led to the Sultan's presence. The officer of the guard recognized the ring, made a respectful obeisance, and allowed him free entrance. In the same way he passed the other doors to the rich saloon where the great Sultan was at dinner with his tributary princes. At sight of the ring the chief attendant led Huon to the head of the hall, and introduced him to the Sultan and his princes as the ambassador of Charlemagne. A seat was provided for him near the royal party.

The Prince of Hyrcania, the same whom Huon had rescued from the lion, and who was the destined bridegroom of the beautiful Clarimunda, sat on the Sultan's right hand, and the princess herself on his left. It chanced that Huon found himself near the seat of the princess, and hardly were the ceremonies of reception over before he made haste to fulfill the commands of Charlemagne by imprinting a kiss upon her rosy lips, and after that a second, not by command, but by good will. The Prince of Hyrcania cried out, "Audacious infidel! take the reward of thy insolence!" and aimed a blow at Huon, which, if it had reached him, would have brought his embassy to a speedy termination. But the ingrate failed of his aim, and Huon punished his blasphemy and ingratitude at once by a blow which severed his head from his body.

So suddenly had all this happened that no hand had been raised to arrest it; but now Gaudisso cried out, "Seize the murderer!" Huon was hemmed in on all sides, but his redoubtable sword kept the crowd of courtiers at bay. But he saw new combatants enter, and could not hope to maintain his ground against so many. He recollected his horn, and raising it to his lips, blew a blast almost as loud as that of Roland at Roncesvalles. It was in vain. Oberon heard it; but the sin of which Huon had been guilty in bearing, though but for a moment, the character of a believer in the false prophet, had put it out of Oberon's power to help him. Huon, finding himself deserted, and conscious of the cause, lost his strength and energy, was seized, loaded with chains, and plunged into a dungeon.

His life was spared for the time, merely that he might be reserved for a more painful death. The Sultan meant that, after being made to feel all the torments of hunger and despair, he should be flayed alive.

But an enchanter more ancient and more powerful than Oberon himself interested himself for the brave Huon. The enchanter was Love. The Princess Clarimunda learned with horror the fate to which the young prince was destined. By the aid of her governante she gained over the keeper of the prison, and went herself to lighten the chains of her beloved. It was her hand that removed his fetters, from her he received supplies of food to sustain a life which he devoted from thenceforth wholly to her. After the most tender explanations the princess departed, promising to repeat her visit on the morrow.

The next day she came according to promise, and again brought supplies of food. These visits were continued during a whole month. Huon was too good a son of the Church to forget that the amiable princess was a Saracen, and he availed himself of these interviews to instruct her in the true faith. How easy it is to believe the truth when uttered by the lips of those we love! Clarimunda ere long professed her entire belief in the Christian doctrines, and desired to be baptized.

Meanwhile the Sultan had repeatedly inquired of the jailer how his prisoner bore the pains of famine, and learned to his surprise that he was not yet much reduced thereby. On his repeating the inquiry, after a short interval, the keeper replied that the prisoner had died suddenly, and had been buried in the cavern. The Sultan could only regret that he had not sooner ordered the execution of the sentence.

While these things were going on the faithful Sherasmin, who had not accompanied Huon in his last adventure, but had learned by common rumor the result of it, came to the court in hopes of doing something for the rescue of his master. He presented himself to the Sultan as Solario, his nephew. Guadisso received him with kindness, and all the courtiers loaded him with attentions. He soon found means to inform himself how the Princess regarded the brave but unfortunate Huon, and having made himself known to her, confidence was soon established between them. Clarimunda readily consented to assist in the escape of Huon, and to quit with him her father's court to repair to that of Charlemagne. Their united efforts had nearly perfected their arrangement, a vessel was secretly prepared, and all things in forwardness for the flight, when an unlooked-for obstacle presented itself. Huon himself positively refused to go leaving the orders of Charlemagne unexecuted.

Sherasmin was in despair. Bitterly he complained of the fickleness and cruelty of Oberon in withdrawing his aid at the very crisis when it was most necessary. Earnestly he urged every argument to satisfy the prince that he had done enough for honor, and could not be held bound to achieve impossibilities. But all was of no avail, and he knew not which way to turn, when one of those events occurred which are so frequent under Turkish despotisms. A courier arrived at the court of the Sultan, bearing the ring of his sovereign, the mighty Agrapard, Caliph of Arabia, and bringing the bow-string for the neck of Gaudisso. No reason was assigned; none but the pleasure of the Caliph is ever required in such cases; but it was suspected that the bearer of the bow-string had persuaded the Caliph that Gaudisso, whose rapacity was well known, had accumulated immense treasures, which he had not duly shared with his sovereign, and thus had obtained an order to supersede him in his Emirship.

The body of Gaudisso would have been cast out a prey to dogs and vultures, had not Sherasmin, under the character of nephew of the deceased, been permitted to receive it, and give it decent burial, which he did, but not till he had taken possession of the beard and grinders, agreeably to the orders of Charlemagne.

No obstacle now stood in the way of the lovers and their faithful follower in returning to France. They sailed, taking Rome in their way, where the Holy Father himself blessed the union of his nephew, Duke Huon of Bordeaux, with the Princess Clarimunda.

Soon afterward they arrived in France, where Huon laid his trophies at the feet of Charlemagne, and, being restored to the favor of the Emperor, hastened to present himself and his bride to the Duchess, his mother, and to the faithful liegemen of his province of Guienne and his city of Bordeaux, where the pair were received with transports of joy.

OGIER, THE DANE

OGIER, the Dane, was the son of Geoffrey, who wrested Denmark from the Pagans, and reigned the first Christian king of that country. When Ogier was born, and before he was baptized, six ladies of ravishing beauty appeared all at once in the chamber of the infant. They encircled him, and she who appeared the eldest took him in her arms, kissed him, and laid her hand upon his heart. "I give you," said she, "to be the bravest warrior of your times." She delivered the infant to her sister, who said, "I give you abundant opportunities to display your valor." "Sister," said the third lady, "you have given him a dangerous boon; I give him that he shall never be vanquished." The fourth sister added, as she laid her hand upon his eyes and his mouth, "I give you the gift of pleasing." The fifth said, "Lest all these gifts serve only to betray, I give you sensibility to return the love you inspire." Then spoke Morgana, the youngest and handsomest of the group. "Charming creature, I claim you for my own; and I give you not to die till you shall have come to pay me a visit in my isle of Avalon." Then she kissed the child and departed with her sisters.

After this the king had the child carried to the font and baptized with the name of Ogier.

In his education nothing was neglected to elevate him to the standard of a perfect knight, and render him accomplished in all the arts necessary to make him a hero.

He had hardly reached the age of sixteen years when Charlemagne, whose power was established over all the sovereigns of his time, recollected that Geoffroy, Ogier's father, had omitted to render the homage due to him as Emperor, and sovereign lord of Denmark, one of the grand fiefs of the empire. He accordingly sent an embassy to demand of the king of Denmark this homage, and on receiving a refusal, couched in haughty terms, sent an army to enforce the demand. Geoffroy, after an unsuccessful resistance, was forced to comply, and as a pledge of his sincerity delivered Ogier, his eldest son, a hostage to Charles, to be brought up at his court. He was placed in charge of the Duke Namo of Bavaria, the friend of his father, who treated him like his own son.

Ogier grew up more and more handsome and amiable every day. He surpassed in form, strength, and address all the noble youths his companions; he failed not to be present at all tourneys; he was attentive to the elder knights, and burned with impatience to imitate them. Yet his heart rose sometimes in secret against his condition as a hostage, and as one apparently forgotten by his father.

The King of Denmark, in fact, was at this time occupied with new loves. Ogier's mother having died, he had married a second wife, and had a son named Guyon. The new queen had absolute power over her husband, and fearing that, if he should see Ogier again, he would give him the preference over Guyon, she had adroitly persuaded him to delay rendering his homage to Charlemagne, till now four years had passed away since the last renewal of that ceremony. Charlemagne, irritated at this delinquency, drew closer the bonds of Ogier's captivity until he should receive a response from the king of Denmark to a fresh summons which he caused to be sent to him.

The answer of Geoffroy was insulting and defiant, and the rage of Charlemagne was roused in the highest degree. He was at first disposed to wreak his vengeance upon Ogier, his hostage; but at the entreaties of Duke Namo, who felt towards his pupil like a father, consented to spare his life, if Ogier would swear fidelity to him as his liege-lord, and promise not to quit his court without his permission. Ogier accepted these terms, and was allowed to retain all the freedom he had before enjoyed.

The Emperor would have immediately taken arms to reduce his disobedient vassal, if he had not been called off in another direction by a message from Pope Leo, imploring his assistance. The Saracens had landed in the neighborhood of Rome, occupied Mount Janiculum, and prepared to pass the Tiber and carry fire and sword to the capital of the Christian world. Charlemagne hesitated not to yield to the entreaties of the Pope. He speedily assembled an army, crossed the Alps, traversed Italy, and arrived at Spoleto, a strong place to which the Pope had retired. Leo, at the head of his Cardinals, advanced to meet him, and rendered him homage, as to the son of Pepin, the illustrious protector of the Holy See, coming, as his father had done, to defend it in the hour of need.

Charlemagne stopped but two days at Spoleto, and learning that the Infidels, having rendered themselves masters of Rome, were besieging the Capitol, which could not long hold out against them, marched promptly to attack them.

The advanced posts of the army were commanded by Duke Namo, on whom Ogier waited as his squire. He did not yet bear arms, not having received the order of knighthood. The Oriflamme, the royal standard, was borne by a knight named Alory, who showed himself unworthy of the honor.

Duke Namo, seeing a strong body of the Infidels advancing to attack him, gave the word to charge them. Ogier remained in the rear, with the other youths, grieving much that he was not permitted to fight. Very soon he saw Alory lower the Oriflamme, and turn his horse in flight. Ogier pointed him out to the young men, and seizing a club, rushed upon Alory and struck him from his horse. Then, with his companions, he disarmed him, clothed himself in his armor, raised the Oriflamme, and mounting the horse of the unworthy knight, flew to the front rank, where he joined Duke Namo, drove back the Infidels, and carried the Oriflamme quite through their broken ranks. The Duke, thinking it was Alory, whom he had not held in high esteem, was astonished at his strength and valor. Ogier's young companions imitated him, supplying themselves with armor from the bodies of the slain; they followed Ogier and carried death into the ranks of the Saracens, who fell back in confusion upon their main body.

Duke Namo now ordered a retreat, and Ogier obeyed with reluctance, when they perceived Charlemagne advancing to their assistance. The combat now became general, and was more terrible than ever. Charlemagne had overthrown Corsuble, the commander of the Saracens, and had drawn his famous sword, Joyeuse, to cut off his head, when two Saracen knights set upon him at once, one of whom slew his horse, and the other overthrew the Emperor on the sand. Perceiving by the eagle on his casque who he was, they dismounted in haste to give him his deathblow. Never was the life of the Emperor in such peril. But Ogier, who saw him fall, flew to his rescue. Though embarrassed with the Oriflamme, he pushed his horse against one of the Saracens and knocked him down; and with his sword dealt the other so vigorous a blow that he fell stunned to the earth. Then helping the Emperor to rise, he remounted him on the horse of one of the fallen knights. "Brave and generous Alory!" Charles exclaimed, "I owe to you my honor and my life!" Ogier made no answer; but, leaving Charlemagne surrounded by a great many of the knights who had flown to his succor, he plunged into the thickest ranks of the enemy, and carried the Oriflamme, followed by a gallant train of youthful warriors, till the standard of Mahomet turned in retreat, and the Infidels sought safety in their intrenchments.

Then the good Archbishop Turpin laid aside his helmet and his bloody sword (for he always felt that he was clearly in the line of his duty while slaying Infidels), took his mitre and his crosier, and intoned Te Deum.

At this moment Ogier, covered with blood and dust, came to lay the Oriflamme at the feet of the Emperor. He was followed by a train of warriors of short stature, who walked ill at ease loaded with armor too heavy for them. Ogier knelt at the feet of Charlemagne, who embraced him, calling him Alory, while Turpin from the height of the altar, blessed him with all his might. Then young Orlando, son of the Count Milone, and nephew of Charlemagne, no longer able to endure this misapprehension, threw down his helmet, and ran to unlace Ogier's, while the other young men laid aside theirs. Our author says he cannot express the surprise, the admiration, and the tenderness of the Emperor and his peers. Charles folded Ogier in his arms, and the happy fathers of those brave youths embraced them with tears of joy. The good Duke Namo stepped forward, and Charlemagne yielded Ogier to his embrace. "How much do I owe you," he said, "good and wise friend, for having restrained my anger! My dear Ogier! I owe you my life! My sword leaps to touch your shoulder, yours and those of your brave young friends." At these words he drew that famous sword, Joyeuse, and while Ogier and the rest knelt before him, gave them the accolade conferring on them the order of knighthood. The young Orlando and his cousin Oliver could not refrain, even in the presence of the Emperor, from falling upon Ogier's neck, and pledging with him that brotherhood in arms, so dear and so sacred to the knights of old times; but Charlot, the Emperor's son, at the sight of the glory with which Ogier had covered himself, conceived the blackest jealousy and hate.

The rest of the day and the next were spent in the rejoicings of the army. Turpin in a solemn service implored the favor of Heaven upon the youthful knights, and blessed the white armor which was prepared for them. Duke Namo presented them with golden spurs, Charles himself girded on their swords. But what was his astonishment when he examined that intended for Ogier! The loving Fairy, Morgana, had had the art to change it, and to substitute one of her own procuring, and when Charles drew it out of the scabbard, these words appeared written on the steel: "My name is Cortana, of the same steel and temper as Joyeuse and Durindana." Charles saw that a superior power watched over the destinies of Ogier; he vowed to love him as a father would, and Ogier promised him the devotion of a son. Happy had it been for both if they had always continued mindful of their promises.

The Saracen army had hardly recovered from its dismay when Carahue, King of Mauritania, who was one of the knights overthrown by Ogier at the time of the rescue of Charlemagne, determined to challenge him to single combat. With that view he assumed the dress of a herald, resolved to carry his own message. The French knights admired his air, and said to one another that he seemed more fit to be a knight than a bearer of messages.

Carahue began by passing the warmest eulogium upon the knight who bore the Oriflamme on the day of the battle, and concluded by saying that Carahue, King of Mauritania, respected that knight so much that he challenged him to the combat.

Ogier had risen to reply, when he was interrupted by Charlot, who said that the gage of the King of Mauritania could not fitly be received by a vassal, living in captivity; by which he meant Ogier, who was at that time serving as hostage for his father. Fire flashed from the eyes of Ogier, but the presence of the Emperor restrained his speech, and he was calmed by the kind looks of Charlemagne, who said, with an angry voice, "Silence, Charlot! By the life of Bertha, my queen, he who has saved my life is as dear to me as yourself. Ogier," he continued, "you are no longer a hostage. Herald! report my answer to your master, that never does knight of my court refuse a challenge on equal terms. Ogier, the Dane, accepts of his, and I myself am his security."

Carahue, profoundly bowing, replied, "My lord, I was sure that the sentiments of so great a sovereign as yourself would be worthy of your high and brilliant fame; I shall report your answer to my master, who I know admires you, and unwillingly takes arms against you." Then, turning to Charlot, whom he did not know as the son of the Emperor, he continued, "As for you, Sir Knight, if the desire of battle inflames you, I have it in charge from Sadon, cousin of the King of Mauritania, to give the like defiance to any French knights who will grant him the honor of the combat."

Charlot, inflamed with rage and vexation at the public reproof which he had just received, hesitated not to deliver his gage. Carahue received it with Ogier's, and it was agreed that the combat should be on the next day in a meadow environed by woods and equally distant from both armies.

The perfidious Charlot meditated the blackest treason. During the night he collected some knights unworthy of the name, and like himself in their ferocious manners; he made them swear to avenge his injuries, armed them in black armor, and sent them to lie in ambush in the wood, with orders to make a pretended attack upon the whole party, but in fact, to lay heavy hands upon Ogier and the two Saracens.

At the dawn of day Sadon and Carahue, attended only by two pages to carry their spears, took their way to the appointed meadow; and Charlot and Ogier repaired thither also, but by different paths. Ogier advanced with a calm air, saluted courteously the two Saracen knights, and joined them in arranging the terms of combat.

While this was going on the perfidious Charlot remained behind and gave his men the signal to advance. That cowardly troop issued from the wood and encompassed the three knights. All three were equally surprised at the attack, but neither of them suspected the other to have any hand in the treason. Seeing the attack made equally upon them all, they united their efforts to resist it, and made the most forward of the assailants bite the dust. Cortana fell on no one without inflicting a mortal wound, but the sword of Carahue was not of equal temper and broke in his hands. At the same instant his horse was slain, and Carahue fell, without a weapon, and entangled with his prostrate horse. Ogier, who saw it, ran to his defence, and leaping to the ground covered the prince with his shield, supplied him with the sword of one of the fallen ruffians, and would have him mount his own horse. At that moment Charlot, inflamed with rage, pushed his horse upon Ogier, knocked him down, and would have run him through with his lance if Sadon, who saw the treason, had not sprung upon him and thrust him back. Carahue leapt lightly upon the horse which Ogier presented him, and had time only to exclaim, "Brave Ogier, I am no longer your enemy, I pledge to you an eternal friendship," when numerous Saracen knights were seen approaching, having discovered the treachery, and Charlot with his followers took refuge in the wood.

The troop which advanced was commanded by Dannemont, the exiled king of Denmark, whom Geoffroy, Ogier's father, had driven from his throne and compelled to take refuge with the Saracens. Learning who Ogier was, he instantly declared him his prisoner, in spite of the urgent remonstrances and even threats of Carahue and Sadon, and carried him under a strong guard to the Saracen camp. Here he was at first subjected to the most rigorous captivity, but Carahue and Sadon insisted so vehemently on his release, threatening to turn their arms against their own party if it was not granted, while Dannemont as eagerly opposed the measure, that Corsuble, the Saracen commander, consented to a middle course, and allowed Ogier the freedom of his camp, upon his promise not to leave it without permission.

Carahue was not satisfied with this partial concession. He left the city next morning, proceeded to the camp of Charlemagne, and demanded to be led to the Emperor. When he reached his presence he dismounted from his horse, took off his helmet, drew his sword, and holding it by the blade presented it to Charlemagne as he knelt before him.

"Illustrious prince," he said, "behold before you the herald who brought the challenge to your knights from the King of Mauritania. The cowardly old King Dannemont has made the brave Ogier prisoner, and has prevailed on our general to refuse to give him up. I come to make amends for this ungenerous conduct by yielding myself, Carahue, King of Mauritania, your prisoner."

Charlemagne, with all his peers, admired the magnanimity of Carahue; he raised him, embraced him, and restored to him his sword. "Prince," said he, "your presence and the bright example you afford my knights consoles me for the loss of Ogier. Would to God you might receive our holy faith, and be wholly united with us." All the lords of the court, led by Duke Namo, paid their respects to the King of Mauritania. Charlot only failed to appear, fearing to be recognized as a traitor; but the heart of Carahue was too noble to pierce that of Charlemagne by telling him the treachery of his son.

Meanwhile the Saracen army was rent by discord. The troops of Carahue clamored against the commander-in-chief because their king was left in captivity. They even threatened to desert the cause and turn their arms against their allies. Charlemagne pressed the siege vigorously, till at length the Saracen leaders found themselves compelled to abandon the city and betake themselves to their ships. A truce was made; Ogier was exchanged for Carahue, and the two friends embraced one another with vows of perpetual brotherhood. The Pope was reestablished in his dominions, and Italy being tranquil, Charlemagne returned with his peers and their followers to France.

OGIER, THE DANE (Continued)

CHARLEMAGNE had not forgotten the offence of Geoffroy, the King of Denmark, in withholding homage, and now prepared to enforce submission. But at this crisis he was waited upon by an embassy from Geoffroy, acknowledging his fault, and craving assistance against an army of invaders who had attacked his states with a force which he was unable to repel. The soul of Charlemagne was too great to be implacable, and he took this opportunity to test that of Ogier, who had felt acutely the unkindness of his father, in leaving him, without regard or notice, fifteen years in captivity. Charles asked Ogier whether, in spite of his father's neglect, he was disposed to lead an army to his assistance. He replied, "A son can never be excused from helping his father by any cause short of death." Charlemagne placed an army of a thousand knights under the command of Ogier, and great numbers more volunteered to march under so distinguished a leader. He flew to the succor of his father, repelled the invaders, and drove them in confusion to their vessels. Ogier then hastened to the capital, but as he drew near the city he heard all the bells sounding a knell. He soon learned the cause; it was the obsequies of Geoffroy, the King. Ogier felt keenly the grief of not having been permitted to embrace his father once more, and to learn his latest commands; but he found that his father had declared him heir to his throne. He hastened to the church where the body lay; he knelt and bathed the lifeless form with his tears. At that moment a celestial light beamed all around, and a voice of an angel said, "Ogier, leave thy crown to Guyon, thy brother, and bear no other title than that of 'The Dane.' Thy destiny is glorious, and other kingdoms are reserved for thee." Ogier obeyed the divine behest. He saluted his stepmother respectfully, and embracing his brother, told him that he was content with his lot in being reckoned among the paladins of Charlemagne, and resigned all claims to the crown of Denmark.

Ogier returned covered with glory to the court of Charlemagne, and the Emperor, touched with this proof of his attachment, loaded him with caresses, and treated him almost as an equal.

We pass in silence the adventures of Ogier for several ensuing years, in which the fairy-gifts of his infancy showed their force in making him successful in all enterprises, both of love and war. He married the charming Belicene, and became the father of young Baldwin, a youth who seemed to inherit in full measure the strength and courage of his father and the beauty of his mother. When the lad was old enough to be separated from his mother, Ogier took him to court and presented him to Charlemagne, who embraced him and took him into his service. It seemed to Duke

Namo, and all the elder knights, as if they saw in him Ogier himself, as he was when a youth; and this resemblance won for the lad their kind regards. Even Charlot at first seemed to be fond of him, though after a while the resemblance to Ogier which he noticed had the effect to excite his hatred.

Baldwin was attentive to Charlot, and lost no occasion to be serviceable. The Prince loved to play chess, and Baldwin, who played well, often made a party with him.

One day Charlot was nettled at losing two pieces in succession; he thought he could, by taking a piece from Baldwin, get some amends for his loss; but Baldwin, seeing him fall into a trap which he had set for him, could not help a slight laugh, as he said, "Check-mate." Charlot rose in a fury, seized the rich and heavy chess-board, and dashed it with all his strength on the head of Baldwin, who fell, and died where he fell.

Frightened at his own crime, and fearing the vengeance of the terrible Ogier, Charlot concealed himself in the interior of the palace. A young companion of Baldwin hastened and informed Ogier of the event. He ran to the chamber, and beheld the body of his child bathed in blood, and it could not be concealed from him that Charlot gave the blow. Transported with rage, Ogier sought Charlot through the palace, and Charlot, feeling safe nowhere else, took refuge in the hall of Charlemagne, where he seated himself at table with Duke Namo and Salomon, Duke of Brittany. Ogier, with sword drawn, followed him to the very table of the Emperor. When a cupbearer attempted to bar his way he struck the cup from his hand and dashed the contents in the Emperor's face. Charles rose in a passion, seized a knife, and would have plunged it into his breast, had not Salomon and another baron thrown themselves between, while Namo, who had retained his ancient influence over Ogier, drew him out of the room. Foreseeing the consequence of this violence, pitying Ogier, and in his heart excusing him, Namo hurried him away before the guards of the palace could arrest him, made him mount his horse, and leave Paris.

Charlemagne called together his peers, and made them take an oath to do all in their power to arrest Ogier, and bring him to condign punishment. Ogier on his part sent messages to the Emperor, offering to give himself up on condition that Charlot should be punished for his atrocious crime. The Emperor would listen to no conditions, and went in pursuit of Ogier at the head of a large body of soldiers. Ogier, on the other hand, was warmly supported by many knights, who pledged themselves in his defence. The contest raged long, with no decisive results. Ogier more than once had the Emperor in his power, but declined to avail himself of his advantage, and released him without conditions. He even implored pardon for himself, but demanded at the same time the punishment of Charlot. But Charlemagne was too blindly fond of his unworthy son to subject him to punishment for the sake of conciliating one who had been so deeply injured.

At length, distressed at the blood which his friends had lost in his cause, Ogier dismissed his little army, and slipping away from those who wished to attend him, took his course to rejoin the Duke Guyon, his brother. On his way, having reached the forest of Ardennes, weary with long travel, the freshness of a retired valley tempted him to lie down to take some repose. He unsaddled Beiffror, relieved himself of his helmet, lay down on the turf, rested his head on his shield, and slept.

It so happened that Turpin, who occasionally recalled to mind that he was Archbishop of Rheins, was at that time in the vicinity, making a pastoral visit to the churches under his jurisdiction. But his dignity of peer of France, and his martial spirit, which caused him to be reckoned among the "preux chevaliers" of his time, forbade him to travel without as large a retinue of knights as he had of clergymen. One of these was thirsty, and knowing the fountain on the borders of which Ogier was reposing, he rode to it, and was struck by the sight of a knight stretched on the ground. He hastened back, and let the Archbishop know, who approached the fountain, and recognized Ogier.

The first impulse of the good and generous Turpin was to save his friend, for whom he felt the warmest attachment; but his archdeacons and knights, who also recognized Ogier, reminded the Archbishop of the oath which the Emperor had exacted of them all. Turpin could not be false to his oath; but it was not without a groan that he permitted his followers to bind the sleeping knight. The Archbishop's attendants secured the horse and arms of Ogier, and conducted their prisoner to the Emperor at Soissons.

The Emperor had become so much embittered by Ogier's obstinate resistance, added to his original fault, that he was disposed to order him to instant death. But Turpin, seconded by the good Dukes Namo and Salomon, prayed so hard for him that Charlemagne consented to remit a violent death, but sentenced him to close imprisonment, under the charge of the Archbishop, strictly limiting his food to one quarter of a loaf of bread per day, with one piece of meat, and a quarter of a cup of wine. In this way he hoped to quickly put an end to his life without bringing on himself the hostility of the King of Denmark, and other powerful friends of Ogier. He exacted a new oath of Turpin to obey his order strictly.

The good Archbishop loved Ogier too well not to cast about for some means of saving his life, which he foresaw he would soon lose if subjected to such scanty fare, for Ogier was seven feet tall, and had an appetite in proportion. Turpin remembered, moreover, that Ogier was a true son of the Church, always zealous to propagate the faith and subdue unbelievers; so he felt justified in practising on this occasion what in later times has been entitled "mental reservation," without swerving from the letter of the oath which he had taken. This is the method he hit upon.

Every morning he had his prisoner supplied with a quarter of a loaf of bread, made of two bushels of flour, to this he added a quarter of a sheep or a fat calf, and he had a cup made which held forty pints of wine, and allowed Ogier a quarter of it daily.

Ogier's imprisonment lasted long; Charlemagne was astonished to hear, from time to time, that he still held out; and when he inquired more particularly of Turpin, the good Archbishop, relying on his own understanding of the words, did not hesitate to affirm positively that he allowed his prisoner no more than the permitted ration.

We forgot to say that, when Ogier was led prisoner to Soissons, the Abbot of Saint Faron, observing the fine horse Beiffror, and not having at the time any other favor to ask of Charlemagne, begged the Emperor to give him the horse, and had him taken to his abbey. He was impatient to try his new acquisition, and when he had arrived in his litter at the foot of the mountain where the horse had been brought to meet him mounted him and rode onward. The horse, accustomed to bear the enormous weight of Ogier in his armor, when he perceived nothing on his back but the light weight of the Abbot, whose long robes fluttered against his sides, ran away, making prodigious leaps over the steep acclivities of the mountain till he reached the convent of Jouaire, where, in sight of the Abbess and her nuns, he threw the Abbot, already half dead with fright, to the ground. The Abbot, bruised and mortified, revenged himself on poor Beiffror, whom he condemned, in his wrath, to be given to the workmen to drag stones for a chapel that he was building near the abbey. Thus, ill-fed, hard-worked, and often beaten, the noble horse Beiffror passed the time while his master's imprisonment lasted.

That imprisonment would have been as long as his life if it had not been for some important events which forced the Emperor to set Ogier at liberty.

The Emperor learned at the same time that Carahue, King of Mauritania, was assembling an army to come and demand the liberation of Ogier; that Guyon, King of Denmark, was prepared to second the enterprise with all his forces; and, worse than all, that the Saracens, under Bruhier, Sultan of Arabia, had landed in Gascony, taken Bordeaux, and were marching with all speed for Paris.

Charlemagne now felt how necessary the aid of Ogier was to him. But, in spite of the representations of Turpin, Namo, and Salomon, he could not bring himself to consent to surrender Charlot to such punishment as Ogier should see fit to impose. Besides, he believed that Ogier was without strength and vigor, weakened by imprisonment and long abstinence.

At this crisis he received a message from Bruhier, proposing to put the issue upon the result of a combat between himself and the Emperor or his champion; promising, if defeated, to withdraw his army. Charlemagne would willingly have accepted the challenge, but his counsellors all opposed it. The herald was therefore told that the Emperor would take time to consider his proposition, and give his answer the next day.

It was during this interval that the three Dukes succeeded in prevailing upon Charlemagne to pardon Ogier, and to send for him to combat the puissant enemy who now defied him; but it was no easy task to persuade Ogier. The idea of his long imprisonment and the recollection of his son, bleeding and dying in his arms by the blow of the ferocious Charlot, made him long resist the urgency of his friends. Though glory called him to encounter Bruhier, and the safety of Christendom demanded the destruction of this proud enemy of the faith, Ogier only yielded at last on condition that Charlot should be delivered into his hands to be dealt with as he should see fit.

The terms were hard, but the danger was pressing, and Charlemagne, with a returning sense of justice, and a strong confidence in the generous though passionate soul of Ogier, at last consented to them.

Ogier was led into the presence of Charlemagne by the three peers. The Emperor, faithful to his word, had caused Charlot to be brought into the hall where the high barons were assembled, his hands tied, and his head uncovered. When the Emperor saw Ogier approach he took Charlot by the arm, led him towards Ogier, and said these words: "I surrender the criminal; do with him as you think fit." Ogier, without replying, seized Charlot by the hair, forced him on his knees, and lifted with the other hand his irresistible sword. Charlemagne, who expected to see the head of his son rolling at his feet, shut his eyes and uttered a cry of horror.

Ogier had done enough. The next moment he raised Charlot, cut his bonds, kissed him on the mouth, and hastened to throw himself at the feet of the Emperor.

Nothing can exceed the surprise and joy of Charlemagne at seeing his son unharmed and Ogier kneeling at his feet. He folded him in his arms, bathed him with tears, and exclaimed to his barons, "I feel at this moment that Ogier is greater than I." As for Charlot, his base soul felt nothing but the joy of having escaped death; he remained such as he had been, and it was not till some years afterwards he received the punishment he deserved, from the hands of Huon of Bordeaux, as we have seen in a former chapter.

OGIER, THE DANE (Continued)

WHEN Charlemagne had somewhat recovered his composure he was surprised to observe that Ogier appeared in good case, and had a healthy color in his cheeks. He turned to the Archbishop, who could not help blushing as he met his eye. "By the head of Bertha, my queen," said Charlemagne, "Ogier has had good quarters in your castle, my Lord Archbishop; but so much the more am I indebted to you." All the barons laughed and jested with Turpin, who only said, "Laugh as much as you please, my lords; but for my part I am not sorry to see the arm in full vigor that is to avenge us on the proud Saracen."

Charlemagne immediately despatched his herald, accepting the challenge, and appointing the next day but one for the encounter. The proud and crafty Bruhier laughed scornfully when he heard the reply accepting his challenge, for he had a reliance on certain resources besides his natural strength and skill. However, he swore by Mahomet to observe the conditions as proposed and agreed upon.

Ogier now demanded his armor, and it was brought to him in excellent condition, for the good Turpin had kept it faithfully; but it was not easy to provide a horse for the occasion. Charlemagne had the best horses of his stables brought out, except Blanchard, his own charger; but all in vain, the weight of Ogier bent their backs to the ground. In this embarrassment the Archbishop remembered that the Emperor had given Beiffror to the Abbot of St. Faron, and sent off a courier in haste to re-demand him.

Monks are hard masters, and the one who directed the laborers at the abbey had but too faithfully obeyed the orders of the Abbot. Poor Beiffror was brought back, lean, spiritless, and chafed with the harness of the vile cart that he had had to draw so long. He carried his head down, and trod heavily before Charlemagne; but when he heard the voice of Ogier he raised his head, he neighed, his eyes flashed, his former ardor showed itself by the force with which he pawed the ground. Ogier caressed him, and the good steed seemed to return his caresses; Ogier mounted him, and Beiffror, proud of carrying his master again, leapt and curvetted with all his youthful vigor.

Nothing being now wanted, Charlemagne, at the head of his army, marched forth from the city of Paris, and occupied the hill of Montmartre, whence the view extended over the plain of St. Denis, where the battle was to be fought.

When the appointed day came the Dukes Namo and Salomon, as seconds of Ogier, accompanied him to the place marked out for the lists, and Bruhier, with two distinguished Emirs, presented himself on the other side.

Bruhier was in high spirits, and jested with his friends, as he advanced, upon the appearance of Beiffror. "Is that the horse they presume to match with Marchevallee, the best steed that ever fed in the vales of Mount Atlas?" But now the combatants, having met and saluted each other, ride apart to come together in full career. Beiffror flew over the plain, and met the adversary more than half-way. The lances of the two combatants were shivered at the shock, and Bruhier was astonished to see almost at the same instant the sword of Ogier gleaming above his head. He parried it with his buckler, and gave Ogier a blow on his helmet, who returned it with another, better aimed or better seconded by the temper of his blade, for it cut away part of Bruhier's helmet, and with it his ear and part of his cheek. Ogier, seeing the blood, did not immediately repeat his blow, and Bruhier seized the moment to gallop off at one side. As he rode he took a vase of gold which hung at his saddle-bow, and bathed with its contents the wounded part. The blood instantly ceased to flow, the ear and the flesh were restored quite whole, and the Dane was astonished to see his antagonist return to the ground as sound as ever.

Bruhier laughed at his amazement. "Know," said he, "that I possess the precious balm that Joseph of Arimathea used upon the body of the crucified one, whom you worship. If I should lose an arm I could restore it with a few drops of this. It is useless for you to contend with me. Yield yourself, and, as you appear to be a strong fellow, I will make you first oarsman in one of my galleys."

Ogier, though boiling with rage, forgot not to implore the assistance of Heaven. "O Lord!" he exclaimed, "suffer not the enemy of thy name to profit by the powerful help of that which owes all its virtue to thy divine blood." At these words he attacked Bruhier again with more vigor than ever; both struck terrible blows, and made grievous wounds; but the blood flowed from those of Ogier, while Bruhier stanched his by the application of his balm. Ogier, desperate at the unequal contest, grasped Cortana with both hands, and struck his enemy such a blow that it cleft his buckler, and cut off his arm with it; but Bruhier at the same time launched one at Ogier, which, missing him, struck the head of Beiffror, and the good horse fell, and drew down his master in his fall.

Bruhier had time to leap to the ground, to pick up his arm and apply his balsam; then, before Ogier had recovered his footing, he rushed forward with sword uplifted to complete his destruction.

Charlemagne, from the height of Montmartre, seeing the brave Ogier in this situation, groaned, and was ready to murmur against Providence; but the good Turpin, raising his arms, with a faith like that of Moses, drew down upon the Christian warrior the favor of Heaven.

Ogier, promptly disengaging himself, pressed Bruhier with so much impetuosity that he drove him to a distance from his horse, to whose saddle-bow the precious balm was suspended; and very soon Charlemagne saw Ogier, now completely in the advantage, bring his enemy to his knees, tear off his helmet, and, with a sweep of his sword, strike his head from his body.

After the victory, Ogier seized Marchevallee, leaped upon his back, and became possessed of the precious flask, a few drops from which closed his wounds and restored his strength. The French knights who had been Bruhier's captives, now released, pressed round Ogier to thank him for their deliverance.

Charlemagne and his nobles, as soon as their attention was relieved from the single combat, perceived from their elevated position an unusual agitation in the enemy's camp. They attributed it at first to the death of their general, but soon the noise of arms, the cries of combatants, and new standards which advanced, disclosed to them the fact that Bruhier's army was attacked by a new enemy.

The Emperor was right; it was the brave Carahue of Mauritania, who, with an army, had arrived in France, resolved to attempt the liberation of Ogier, his brother in arms. Learning on his arrival the changed aspect of affairs, he hesitated not to render a signal service to the Emperor, by attacking the army of Bruhier in the midst of the consternation occasioned by the loss of its commander.

Ogier recognized the standard of his friend, and leaping upon Marchevallee, flew to aid his attack. Charlemagne followed with his army; and the Saracen host, after an obstinate conflict, was forced to surrender unconditionally.

The interview of Ogier and Carahue was such as might be anticipated of two such attached friends and accomplished knights. Charlemagne went to meet them, embraced them, and putting the King of Mauritania on his right and Ogier on his left, returned with triumph to Paris. There the Empress Bertha and the ladies of her court crowned them with laurels, and the sage and gallant Eginhard, chamberlain and secretary of the Emperor, wrote all these great events in his history.

A few days after Guyon, King of Denmark, arrived in France with a chosen band of knights, and sent an ambassador to Charlemagne, to say that he came, not as an enemy, but to render homage to him as the best knight of the time and the head of the Christian world. Charlemagne gave the ambassador a cordial reception, and mounting his horse, rode forward to meet the King of Denmark.

These great princes, being assembled at the court of Charles, held council together, and the ancient and sage barons were called to join it.

It was decided that the united Danish and Mauritanian armies should cross the sea and carry the war to the country of the Saracens, and that a thousand French knights should range themselves under the banner of Ogier, the Dane, who, though not a king, should have equal rank with the two others.

We have not space to record all the illustrious actions performed by Ogier and his allies in this war. Suffice it to say, they subdued the Saracens of Ptolemais and Judaea, and, erecting those regions into a kingdom, placed the crown upon the head of Ogier. Guyon and Carahue then left him, to return to their respective dominions. Ogier adopted Walter, the son of Guyon of Denmark, to be his successor in his kingdom. He superintended his education, and saw the young prince grow up worthy of his cares. But Ogier, in spite of all the honors of his rank, often regretted the court of Charlemagne, the Duke Namo, and Salomon of Brittany, for whom he had the respect and attachment of a son. At last, finding Walter old enough to sustain the weight of government, Ogier caused a vessel to be prepared secretly, and, attended only by one squire, left his palace by night, and embarked to return to France.

The vessel, driven by a fair wind, cut the sea with the swiftness of a bird; but on a sudden it deviated from its course, no longer obeyed the helm, and sped fast towards a black promontory which stretched into the sea. This was a mountain of loadstone, and, its attractive power increasing as the distance diminished, the vessel at last flew with the swiftness of an arrow towards it, and was dashed to pieces on its rocky base. Ogier alone saved himself, and reached the shore on a fragment of the wreck.

Ogier advanced into the country, looking for some marks of inhabitancy, but found none. On a sudden he encountered two monstrous animals, covered with glittering scales, accompanied by a horse breathing fire. Ogier drew his sword and prepared to defend himself; but the monsters, terrific as they appeared, made no attempt to assail him, and the horse, Papillon, knelt down, and appeared to court Ogier to mount upon his back. Ogier hesitated not to see the adventure through; he mounted Papillon, who ran with speed, and soon cleared the rocks and precipices which hemmed in and concealed a beautiful landscape. He continued his course till he reached a magnificent palace, and, without allowing Ogier time to admire it, crossed a grand court-yard adorned with colonnades, and entered a garden, where, making his way through alleys of myrtle, he checked his course, and knelt down on the enamelled turf of a fountain.

Ogier dismounted and took some steps along the margin of the stream, but was soon stopped by meeting a young beauty, such as they paint the Graces, and almost as lightly attired as they. At the same moment, to his amazement, his armor fell off of its own accord. The young beauty advanced with a tender air, and placed upon his head a crown of flowers. At that instant the Danish hero lost his memory; his combats, his glory, Charlemagne and his court, all vanished from his mind; he saw only Morgana, he desired nothing but to sigh forever at her feet.

We abridge the narrative of all the delights which Ogier enjoyed for more than a hundred years. Time flew by, leaving no impression of its flight. Morgana's youthful charms did not decay, and Ogier had none of those warnings of increasing years which less favored mortals never fail to receive. There is no knowing how long this blissful state might have lasted, if it had not been for an accident, by which Morgana one day, in a sportive moment, snatched the crown from his head. That moment Ogier regained his memory, and lost his contentment. The recollection of Charlemagne, and of his own relatives and friends, saddened the hours which he passed with Morgana. The fairy saw with grief the changed looks of her lover. At last she drew from him the acknowledgment that he wished to go, at least for a time, to revisit Charles's court. She consented with reluctance, and with her own hands helped to reinvest him with his armor. Papillon was led forth, Ogier mounted him, and, taking a tender adieu of the tearful Morgana, crossed at rapid speed the rocky belt which separated Morgana's palace from the borders of the sea. The sea-goblins which had received him at his coming awaited him on the shore. One of them took Ogier on his back, and the other placing himself under Papillon, they spread their broad fins, and in a short time traversed the wide space that separates the isle of Avalon from France. They landed Ogier on the coast of Languedoc, and then plunged into the sea and disappeared.

Ogier remounted on Papillon, who carried him across the kingdom almost as fast as he had passed the sea. He arrived under the walls of Paris, which he would scarcely have recognized if the high towers of St. Genevieve had not caught his eye. He went straight to the palace of Charlemagne, which seemed to him to have been entirely rebuilt. His surprise was extreme, and increased still more on finding that he understood with difficulty the language of the guards and attendants in replying to his questions; and seeing them smile as they tried to explain to one another the language in which he addressed them. Presently the attention of some of the barons who were going to court was attracted to the scene, and Ogier, who recognized the badges of their rank, addressed them, and inquired if the Dukes Namo and Salomon were still residing at the Emperor's court. At this question the barons looked at one another in amazement; and one of the eldest said to the rest, "How much this knight resembles the portrait of my grand-uncle, Ogier the Dane." "Ah! my dear nephew, I am Ogier the Dane," said he; and he remembered that Morgana had told him that he was little aware of the flight of time during his abode with her.

The barons, more astonished than ever, concluded to conduct him to the monarch who then reigned, the great Hugh Capet.

The brave Ogier entered the palace without hesitation; but when, on reaching the royal hall, the barons directed him to make his obeisance to the King of France, he was astonished to see a man of short stature and large head, whose air, nevertheless, was noble and martial, seated upon the throne on which he had so often seen Charlemagne, the tallest and handsomest sovereign of his time.

Ogier recounted his adventures with simplicity and affectedness. Hugh Capet was slow to believe him; but Ogier recalled so many proofs and circumstances, that at last he was forced to recognize the aged warrior to be the famous Ogier the Dane.

The king informed Ogier of the events which had taken place during his long absence; that the line of Charlemagne was extinct; that a new dynasty had commenced; that the old enemies of the kingdom, the Saracens, were still troublesome; and that at that very time an army of those miscreants was besieging the city of Chartres, to which he was about to repair in a few days to its relief. Ogier, always inflamed with the love of glory, offered the service of his arm, which the illustrious monarch accepted graciously, and conducted him to the queen. The astonishment of Ogier was redoubled when he saw the new ornaments and head-dresses of the ladies; still, the beautiful hair which they built up on their foreheads, and the feathers interwoven, which waved with so much grace, gave them a noble air that delighted him. His admiration increased when, instead of the old Empress Bertha, he saw a young queen who combined a majestic mien with the graces of her time of life, and manners candid and charming, suited to attach all hearts. Ogier saluted the youthful queen with a respect so profound that many of the courtiers took him for a foreigner, or at least for some nobleman brought up at a distance from Paris, who retained the manners of what they called the old court.

When the queen was informed by her husband that it was the celebrated Ogier the Dane whom he presented to her, whose memorable exploits she had often read in the chronicles of antiquity, her surprise was extreme, which was increased when she remarked the dignity of his address, the animation and even the youthfulness of his countenance. This queen had too much intelligence to believe hastily; proof alone could compel her assent; and she asked him many questions about the old court of Charlemagne, and received such instructive and appropriate answers as removed every doubt. It is to the corrections which Ogier was at that time enabled to make to the popular narratives of his exploits that we are indebted for the perfect accuracy and trustworthiness of all the details of our own history.

King Hugh Capet, having received that same evening couriers from the inhabitants of Chartres, informing him that they were hard pressed by the besiegers, resolved to hasten with Ogier to their relief.

Ogier terminated this affair as expeditiously as he had so often done others. The Saracens having dared to offer battle, he bore the Oriflamme through the thickest of their ranks; Papillon, breathing fire from his nostrils, threw them into disorder, and Cortana, wielded by his invincible arm, soon finished their overthrow.

The king, victorious over the Saracens, led back the Danish hero to Paris, where the deliverer of France received the honors due to his valor. Ogier continued some time at the court, detained by the favor of the king and queen; but erelong he had the pain to witness the death of the king. Then it was that, impressed with all the perfections which he had discerned in the queen, he could not withhold the tender homage of the offer of his hand. The queen would perhaps have accepted it, she had even called a meeting of her great barons to deliberate on the proposition, when, the day before the meeting was to be held, at the moment when Ogier was kneeling at her feet, she perceived a crown of gold which an invisible hand had placed on his brow, and in an instant a cloud enveloped Ogier, and he disappeared forever from her sight. It was Morgana, the fairy, whose jealousy was awakened at what she beheld, who now resumed her power, and took him away to dwell with her in the island of Avalon. There, in company with the great King Arthur of Britain, he still lives, and when his illustrious friend shall return to resume his ancient reign he will doubtless return with him, and share his triumph.

GLOSSARY

Abdalrahman, founder of the independent Ommiad (Saracenic) power in Spain, conquered at Tours by Charles Martel.

Aberfraw, scene of nuptials of Branwen and Matholch.

Absyrtus, younger brother of Medea.

Abydos, a town on the Hellespont, nearly opposite to Sestos.

Abyla, Mount, or Columna, a mountain in Morocco, near Ceuta, now called Jebel Musa or Ape's Hill, forming the Northwestern extremity of the African coast opposite Gibraltar (See Pillars of Hercules).

Acestes, son of a Trojan woman who was sent by her father to Sicily, that she might not be devoured by the monsters which infested the territory of Troy.

Acetes, Bacchanal captured by Pentheus.

Achates, faithful friend and companion of Aeneas.

Achelous, river-god of the largest river in Greece--his Horn of Plenty.

Achilles, the hero of the Iliad, son of Peleus and of the Nereid Thetis, slain by Paris.

Acis, youth loved by Galatea and slain by Polyphemus.

Acontius, a beautiful youth, who fell in love with Cydippe, the daughter of a noble Athenian.

Acrisius, son of Abas, king of Argos, grandson of Lynceus, the great-grandson of Danaus.

Actaeon, a celebrated huntsman, son of Aristaeus and Autonoe, who, having seen Diana bathing, was changed by her to a stag and killed by his own dogs.

Admeta, daughter of Eurystheus, covets Hippolyta's girdle.

Admetus, king of Thessaly, saved from death by Alcestis.

Adonis, a youth beloved by Aphrodite (Venus), and Proserpine; killed by a boar.

Adrastus, a king of Argos.

Aeacus, son of Zeus (Jupiter) and Aegina, renowned in all Greece for his justice and piety.

Aeaea, Circe's island, visited by Ulysses.

Aeetes, or Aeeta, son of Helios (the Sun) and Perseis, and father of Medea and Absyrtus.

Aegeus, king of Athens.

Aegina, a rocky island in the middle of the Saronic gulf.

Aegis, shield or breastplate of Jupiter and Minerva.

Aegisthus, murderer of Agamemnon, slain by Orestes.

Aeneas, Trojan hero, son of Anchises and Aphrodite (Venus), and born on Mount Ida, reputed first settler of Rome.

Aeneid, poem by Virgil, relating the wanderings of Aeneas from Troy to Italy.

Ae'olus, son of Hellen and the nymph Orseis, represented in Homer as the happy ruler of the Aeolian Islands, to whom Zeus had given dominion over the winds.

Aesculapius, god of the medical art.

Aeson, father of Jason, made young again by Medea.

Aethiopians, inhabitants of the country south of Egypt.

Aethra, mother of Theseus by Aegeus.

Aetna, volcano in Sicily.

Agamedes, brother of Trophonius, distinguished as an architect.

Agamemnon, son of Plisthenis and grandson of Atreus, king of Mycenae, although the chief commander of the Greeks, is not the hero of the Iliad, and in chivalrous spirit altogether inferior to Achilles.

Agave, daughter of Cadmus, wife of Echion, and mother of Pentheus.

Agenor, father of Europa, Cadmus, Cilix, and Phoenix.

Aglaia, one of the Graces.

Agni, Hindu god of fire.

Agramant, a king in Africa.

Agrican, fabled king of Tartary, pursuing Angelica, finally killed by Orlando.

Agrivain, one of Arthur's knights.

Ahriman, the Evil Spirit in the dual system of Zoroaster, See Ormuzd

Ajax, son of Telamon, king of Salamis, and grandson of Aeacus, represented in the Iliad as second only to Achilles in bravery.

Alba, the river where King Arthur fought the Romans.

Alba Longa, city in Italy founded by son of Aeneas.

Alberich, dwarf guardian of Rhine gold treasure of the Nibelungs

Albracca, siege of.

Alcestis, wife of Admetus, offered herself as sacrifice to spare her husband, but rescued by Hercules.

Alcides (Hercules).

Alcina, enchantress.

Alcinous, Phaeacian king.

Alcippe, daughter of Mars, carried off by Halirrhothrus.

Alcmena, wife of Jupiter, and mother of Hercules.

Alcuin, English prelate and scholar.

Aldrovandus, dwarf guardian of treasure.

Alecto, one of the Furies.

Alexander the Great, king of Macedonia, conqueror of Greece, Egypt, Persia, Babylonia, and India.

Alfadur, a name for Odin.

Alfheim, abode of the elves of light.

Alice, mother of Huon and Girard, sons of Duke Sevinus.

Alphenor, son of Niobe.

Alpheus, river god pursuing Arethusa, who escaped by being changed to a fountain.

Althaea, mother of Meleager, whom she slew because he had in a quarrel killed her brothers, thus disgracing "the house of Thestius," her father.

Amalthea, nurse of the infant Jupiter in Crete.

Amata, wife of Latinus, driven mad by Alecto.

Amaury of Hauteville, false hearted Knight of Charlemagne.

Amazons, mythical race of warlike women.

Ambrosia, celestial food used by the gods.

Ammon, Egyptian god of life identified by Romans with phases of Jupiter, the father of gods.

Amphiaraus, a great prophet and hero at Argos.

Amphion, a musician, son of Jupiter and Antiope (See Dirce).

Amphitrite, wife of Neptune.

Amphyrsos, a small river in Thessaly.

Ampyx, assailant of Perseus, turned to stone by seeing Gorgon's head.

Amrita, nectar giving immortality.

Amun, See Ammon

Amymone, one of the fifty daughters of Danaus, and mother by Poseidon (Neptune) of Nauplius, the father of Palamedes.

Anaxarete, a maiden of Cyprus, who treated her lover Iphis with such haughtiness that he hanged himself at her door.

Anbessa, Saracenic governor of Spain (725 AD).

Anceus, one of the Argonauts.

Anchises, beloved by Aphrodite (Venus), by whom he became the father of Aeneas.

Andraemon, husband of Dryope, saw her changed into a tree.

Andret, a cowardly knight, spy upon Tristram.

Andromache, wife of Hector

Andromeda, daughter of King Cephas, delivered from monster by Perseus

Aneurin, Welsh bard

Angelica, Princess of Cathay

Anemone, short lived wind flower, created by Venus from the blood of the slain Adonis

Angerbode, giant prophetess, mother of Fenris, Hela and the Midgard Serpent

Anglesey, a Northern British island, refuge of Druids fleeing from Romans

Antaeus, giant wrestler of Libya, killed by Hercules, who, finding him stronger when thrown to the earth, lifted him into the air and strangled him

Antea, wife of jealous Proetus

Antenor, descendants of, in Italy

Anteros, deity avenging unrequited love, brother of Eros (Cupid)

Anthor, a Greek

Antigone, daughter of Aedipus, Greek ideal of filial and sisterly fidelity

Antilochus, son of Nestor

Antiope, Amazonian queen. See Dirce

Anubis, Egyptian god, conductor of the dead to judgment

Apennines

Aphrodite See Venus, Dione, etc.

Apis, Egyptian bull god of Memphis

Apollo, god of music and song

Apollo Belvedere, famous antique statue in Vatican at Rome

Apples of the Hesperides, wedding gifts to Juno, guarded by daughters of Atlas and Hesperis, stolen by Atlas for Hercules.

Aquilo, or Boreas, the North Wind.

Aquitaine, ancient province of Southwestern France.

Arachne, a maiden skilled in weaving, changed to a spider by Minerva for daring to compete with her.

Arcadia, a country in the middle of Peloponnesus, surrounded on all sides by mountains.

Arcady, star of, the Pole star.

Arcas, son of Jupiter and Callisto.

Archer, constellation of the.

Areopagus, court of the, at Athens.

Ares, called Mars by the Romans, the Greek god of war, and one of the great Olympian gods.

Arethusa, nymph of Diana, changed to a fountain.

Argius king of Ireland, father of Isoude the Fair.

Argo, builder of the vessel of Jason for the Argonautic expedition.

Argolis, city of the Nemean games.

Argonauts, Jason's crew seeking the Golden Fleece.

Argos, a kingdom in Greece.

Argus, of the hundred eyes, guardian of Io.

Ariadne, daughter of King Minos, who helped Theseus slay the Minotaur.

Arimanes SEE Ahriman.

Arimaspians, one-eyed people of Syria.

Arion, famous musician, whom sailors cast into the sea to rob him, but whose lyric song charmed the dolphins, one of which bore him safely to land.

Aristaeus, the bee keeper, in love with Eurydice.

Armorica, another name for Britain.

Arridano, a magical ruffian, slain by Orlando.

Artemis SEE Diana

Arthgallo, brother of Elidure, British king.

Arthur, king in Britain about the 6th century.

Aruns, an Etruscan who killed Camilla.

Asgard, home of the Northern gods.

Ashtaroth, a cruel spirit, called by enchantment to bring Rinaldo to death.

Aske, the first man, made from an ash tree.

Astolpho of England, one of Charlemagne's knights.

Astraea, goddess of justice, daughter of Astraeus and Eos.

Astyages, an assailant of Perseus.

Astyanax, son of Hector of Troy, established kingdom of Messina in Italy.

Asuias, opponents of the Braminical gods.

Atalanta, beautiful daughter of King of Icaria, loved and won in a foot race by Hippomenes.

Ate, the goddess of infatuation, mischief and guilt.

Athamas, son of Aeolus and Enarete, and king of Orchomenus, in Boeotia, SEE Ino

Athene, tutelary goddess of Athens, the same as Minerva.

Athens, the capital of Attica, about four miles from the sea, between the small rivers Cephissus and Ilissus.

Athor, Egyptian deity, progenitor of Isis and Osiris.

Athos, the mountainous peninsula, also called Acte, which projects from Chalcidice in Macedonia.

Atlantes, foster father of Rogero, a powerful magician.

Atlantis, according to an ancient tradition, a great island west of the Pillars of Hercules, in the ocean, opposite Mount Atlas.

Atlas, a Titan, who bore the heavens on his shoulders, as punishment for opposing the gods, one of the sons of Iapetus.

Atlas, Mount, general name for range in northern Africa.

Atropos, one of the Fates

Attica, a state in ancient Greece.

Audhumbla, the cow from which the giant Ymir was nursed. Her milk was frost melted into raindrops.

Augean stables, cleansed by Hercules.

Augeas, king of Elis.

Augustan age, reign of Roman Emperor Augustus Caesar, famed for many great authors.

Augustus, the first imperial Caesar, who ruled the Roman Empire 31 BC--14 AD.

Aulis, port in Boeotia, meeting place of Greek expedition against Troy.

Aurora, identical with Eos, goddess of the dawn.

Aurora Borealis, splendid nocturnal luminosity in northern sky, called Northern Lights, probably electrical.

Autumn, attendant of Phoebus, the Sun.

Avalon, land of the Blessed, an earthly paradise in the Western Seas, burial place of King Arthur.

Avatar, name for any of the earthly incarnations of Vishnu, the Preserver (Hindu god).

Aventine, Mount, one of the Seven Hills of Rome.

Avernus, a miasmatic lake close to the promontory between Cumae and Puteoli, filling the crater of an extinct volcano, by the ancients thought to be the entrance to the infernal regions.

Avicenna, celebrated Arabian physician and philosopher.

Aya, mother of Rinaldo.

Aymon, Duke, father of Rinaldo and Bradamante.

B

Baal, king of Tyre.

Babylonian River, dried up when Phaeton drove the sun chariot.

Bacchanali a, a feast to Bacchus that was permitted to occur but once in three years, attended by most shameless orgies.

Bacchanals, devotees and festal dancers of Bacchus.

Bacchus (Dionysus), god of wine and revelry.

Badon, battle of, Arthur's final victory over the Saxons

Bagdemagus, King, a knight of Arthur's time.

Baldur, son of Odin, and representing in Norse mythology the sun god.

Balisardo, Orlando's sword.

Ban, King of Brittany, ally of Arthur, father of Launcelot.

Bards, minstrels of Welsh Druids.

Basilisk SEE Cockatrice

Baucis, wife of Philemon, visited by Jupiter and Mercury.

Bayard, wild horse subdued by Rinaldo.

Beal, Druids' god of life.

Bedivere, Arthur's knight.

Bedver, King Arthur's butler, made governor of Normandy.

Bedwyr, knightly comrade of Geraint.

Belisarda, Rogero's sword.

Bellerophon, demigod, conqueror of the Chimaera.

Bellona, the Roman goddess of war, represented as the sister or wife of Mars.

Beltane, Druidical fire festival.

Belus, son of Poseidon (Neptune) and Libya or Eurynome, twin brother of Agenor.

Bendigeid Vran, King of Britain.

Beowulf, hero and king of the Swedish Geats.

Beroe, nurse of Semele.

Bertha, mother of Orlando.

Bifrost, rainbow bridge between the earth and Asgard

Bladud, inventor, builder of the city of Bath.

Blamor, a knight of Arthur.

Bleoberis, a knight of Arthur.

Boeotia, state in ancient Greece, capital city Thebes.

Bohort, King, a knight of Arthur.

Bona Dea, a Roman divinity of fertility.

Bootes, also called Areas, son of Jupiter and Calisto, changed to constellation of Ursa Major.

Boreas, North wind, son of Aeolus and Aurora.

Bosporus (Bosphorus), the Cow-ford, named for Io, when as a heifer she crossed that strait.

Bradamante, sister to Rinaldo, a female warrior.

Brademagus, King, father of Sir Maleagans.

Bragi, Norse god of poetry.

Brahma, the Creator, chief god of Hindu religion.

Branwen, daughter of Llyr, King of Britain, wife of Mathclch.

Breciliande, forest of, where Vivian enticed Merlin.

Brengwain, maid of Isoude the Fair

Brennus, son of Molmutius, went to Gaul, became King of the Allobroges.

Breuse, the Pitiless, a caitiff knight.

Briareus, hundred armed giant.

Brice, Bishop, sustainer of Arthur when elected king.

Brigliadoro, Orlando's horse.

Briseis, captive maid belonging to Achilles.

Britto, reputed ancestor of British people.

Bruhier, Sultan of Arabia.

Brunello, dwarf, thief, and king

Brunhild, leader of the Valkyrie.

Brutus, great grandson of Aeneas, and founder of city of New Troy (London), SEE Pandrasus

Bryan, Sir, a knight of Arthur.

Buddha, called The Enlightened, reformer of Brahmanism, deified teacher of self abnegation, virtue, reincarnation, Karma (inevitable sequence of every act), and Nirvana (beatific absorption into the Divine), lived about

Byblos, in Egypt.

Byrsa, original site of Carthage.

C

Cacus, gigantic son of Vulcan, slain by Hercules, whose captured cattle he stole.

Cadmus, son of Agenor, king of Phoenicia, and of Telephassa, and brother of Europa, who, seeking his sister, carried off by Jupiter, had strange adventures--sowing in the ground teeth of a dragon he had killed, which sprang up armed men who slew each other, all but five, who helped Cadmus to found the city of Thebes.

Caduceus, Mercury's staff.

Cadwallo, King of Venedotia (North Wales).

Caerleon, traditional seat of Arthur's court.

Caesar, Julius, Roman lawyer, general, statesman and author, conquered and consolidated Roman territory, making possible the Empire.

Caicus, a Greek river.

Cairns, Druidical store piles.

Calais, French town facing England.

Calchas, wisest soothsayer among the Greeks at Troy.

Caliburn, a sword of Arthur.

Calliope, one of the nine Muses

Callisto, an Arcadian nymph, mother of Arcas (SEE Bootes), changed by Jupiter to constellation Ursa Minor.

Calpe, a mountain in the south of Spain, on the strait between the Atlantic and Mediterranean, now Rock of Gibraltar.

Calydon, home of Meleager.

Calypso, queen of Island of Ogyia, where Ulysses was wrecked and held seven years.

Camber, son of Brutus, governor of West Albion (Wales).

Camelot, legendary place in England where Arthur's court and palace were located.

Camenae, prophetic nymphs, belonging to the religion of ancient Italy.

Camilla, Volscian maiden, huntress and Amazonian warrior, favorite of Diana.

Camlan, battle of, where Arthur was mortally wounded.

Canterbury, English city.

Capaneus, husband of Evadne, slain by Jupiter for disobedience.

Capet, Hugh, King of France (987-996 AD).

Caradoc Briefbras, Sir, great nephew of King Arthur.

Carahue, King of Mauretania.

Carthage, African city, home of Dido

Cassandra, daughter of Priam and Hecuba, and twin sister of Helenus, a prophetess, who foretold the coming of the Greeks but was not believed.

Cassibellaunus, British chieftain, fought but not conquered by Caesar.

Cassiopeia, mother of Andromeda.

Castalia, fountain of Parnassus, giving inspiration to Oracular priestess named Pythia.

Castalian Cave, oracle of Apollo.

Castes (India).

Castor and Pollux--the Dioscuri, sons of Jupiter and Leda,--Castor a horseman, Pollux a boxer (SEE Gemini).

Caucasus, Mount

Cavall, Arthur's favorite dog.

Cayster, ancient river.

Cebriones, Hector's charioteer.

Cecrops, first king of Athens.

Celestials, gods of classic mythology.

Celeus, shepherd who sheltered Ceres, seeking Proserpine, and whose infant son Triptolemus was in gratitude made great by Ceres.

Cellini, Benvenuto, famous Italian sculptor and artificer in metals.

Celtic nations, ancient Gauls and Britons, modern Bretons, Welsh, Irish and Gaelic Scotch.

Centaurs, originally an ancient race, inhabiting Mount Pelion in Thessaly, in later accounts represented as half horses and half men, and said to have been the offspring of Ixion and a cloud.

Cephalus, husband of beautiful but jealous Procris.

Cephe us, King of Ethiopians, father of Andromeda.

Cephisus, a Grecian stream.

Cerberus, three-headed dog that guarded the entrance to Hades, called a son of Typhaon and Echidna

CERES (See Demeter)

CESTUS, the girdle of Venus

CEYX, King of Thessaly (See Halcyone)

CHAOS, original Confusion, personified by Greeks as most ancient of the gods

CHARLEMAGNE, king of the Franks and emperor of the Romans

CHARLES MARTEL', king of the Franks, grandfather of Charlemagne, called Martel (the Hammer) from his defeat of the Saracens at Tours

CHARLOT, son of Charlemagne

CHARON, son of Erebos, conveyed in his boat the shades of the dead across the rivers of the lower world

CHARYB'DIS, whirlpool near the coast of Sicily, See Scylla

CHIMAERA, a fire breathing monster, the fore part of whose body was that of a lion, the hind part that of a dragon, and the middle that of a goat, slain by Bellerophon

CHINA, Lamas (priests) of

CHOS, island in the Grecian archipelago

CHIRON, wisest of all the Centaurs, son of Cronos (Saturn) and Philyra, lived on Mount Pelion, instructor of Grecian heroes

CHRYSEIS, Trojan maid, taken by Agamemnon

CHRYSES, priest of Apollo, father of Chryseis

CICONIANS, inhabitants of Ismarus, visited by Ulysses

CIMBRI, an ancient people of Central Europe

Cimmeria, a land of darkness

Cimon, Athenian general

Circe, sorceress, sister of Aeetes

Cithaeron, Mount, scene of Bacchic worship

Clarimunda, wife of Huon

Clio, one of the Muses

Cloridan, a Moor

Clotho, one of the Fates

Clymene, an ocean nymph

Clytemnestra, wife of Agamemnon, killed by Orestes

Clytie, a water nymph, in love with Apollo

Cnidos, ancient city of Asia Minor, seat of worship of Aphrodite (Venus)

Cockatrice (or Basilisk), called King of Serpents, supposed to kill with its look

Cocytus, a river of Hades

Colchis, a kingdom east of the Black Sea

Colophon, one of the seven cities claiming the birth of Homer

Columba, St, an Irish Christian missionary to Druidical parts of Scotland

Conan, Welsh king

Constantine, Greek emperor

Cordeilla, daughter of the mythical King Leir

Corineus, a Trojan warrior in Albion

Cornwall, southwest part of Britain

Cortana, Ogier's sword

Corybantes, priests of Cybele, or Rhea, in Phrygia, who celebrated her worship with dances, to the sound of the drum and the cymbal, 143

Crab, constellation

Cranes and their enemies, the Pygmies, of Ibycus

Creon, king of Thebes

Crete, one of the largest islands of the Mediterranean Sea, lying south of the Cyclades

Creusa, daughter of Priam, wife of Aeneas

Crocale, a nymph of Diana

Cromlech, Druidical altar

Cronos, See Saturn

Crotona, city of Italy

Cuchulain, Irish hero, called the "Hound of Ireland,"

Culdees', followers of St. Columba, Cumaean Sibyl, seeress of Cumae, consulted by Aeneas, sold Sibylline books to Tarquin

Cupid, child of Venus and god of love

Curoi of Kerry, wise man

Cyane, river, opposed Pluto's passage to Hades

Cybele (Rhea)

Cyclopes, creatures with circular eyes, of whom Homer speaks as a gigantic and lawless race of shepherds in Sicily, who devoured human beings, they helped Vulcan to forge the thunderbolts of Zeus under Aetna

Cymbeline, king of ancient Britain

Cynosure (Dog's tail), the Pole star, at tail of Constellation Ursa Minor

Cynthian mountain top, birthplace of Artemis (Diana) and Apollo

Cyprus, island off the coast of Syria, sacred to Aphrodite

Cyrene, a nymph, mother of Aristaeus

D

Daedalus, architect of the Cretan Labyrinth, inventor of sails

Daguenet, King Arthur's fool

Dalai Lama, chief pontiff of Thibet

Danae, mother of Perseus by Jupiter

Danaides, the fifty daughters of Danaus, king of Argos, who were betrothed to the fifty sons of Aegyptus, but were commanded by their father to slay each her own husband on the marriage night

Danaus (See Danaides)

Daphne, maiden loved by Apollo, and changed into a laurel tree

Dardanelles, ancient Hellespont

Dardanus, progenitor of the Trojan kings

Dardinel, prince of Zumara

Dawn, See Aurora

Day, an attendant on Phoebus, the Sun

Day star (Hesperus)

Death, See Hela

Deiphobus, son of Priam and Hecuba, the bravest brother of Paris

Dejanira, wife of Hercules

Delos, floating island, birthplace of Apollo and Diana

Delphi, shrine of Apollo, famed for its oracles

Demeter, Greek goddess of marriage and human fertility, identified by Romans with Ceres

Demeha, South Wales

Demodocus, bard of Alomous, king of the Phaeaeians

Deucalion, king of Thessaly, who with his wife Pyrrha were the only pair surviving a deluge sent by Zeus

Dia, island of

Diana (Artemis), goddess of the moon and of the chase, daughter of Jupiter and Latona

Diana of the Hind, antique sculpture in the Louvre, Paris

Diana, temple of

Dictys, a sailor

Didier, king of the Lombards

Dido, queen of Tyre and Carthage, entertained the shipwrecked Aeneas

Diomede, Greek hero during Trojan War

Dione, female Titan, mother of Zeus, of Aphrodite (Venus)

Dionysus See Bacchus

Dioscuri, the Twins (See Castor and Pollux)

Dirce, wife of Lycus, king of Thebes, who ordered Amphion and Zethus to tie Antiope to a wild bull, but they, learning Antiope to be their mother, so treated Dirce herself

Dis See Pluto

Discord, apple of, See Eris.

Discordia, See Eris.

Dodona, site of an oracle of Zeus (Jupiter)

Dorceus, a dog of Diana

Doris, wife of Nereus

Dragon's teeth sown by Cadmus

Druids, ancient Celtic priests

Dryades (or Dryads), See Wood nymphs

Dryope, changed to a lotus plant, for plucking a lotus--enchanted form of the nymph Lotis

Dubricius, bishop of Caerleon.

Dudon, a knight, comrade of Astolpho.

Dunwallo Molmu'tius, British king and lawgiver

Durindana, sword of Orlando or Rinaldo

Dwarfs in Wagner's Nibelungen Ring

E

Earth (Gaea); goddess of the

Ebudians, the

Echo, nymph of Diana, shunned by Narcissus, faded to nothing but a voice

Ecklenlied, the

Eddas, Norse mythological records.

Ederyn, son of Nudd

Egena, nymph of the Fountain

Eisteddfod, session of Welsh bards and minstrels

Electra, the lost one of the Pleiades, also, sister of Orestes

Eleusian Mysteries, instituted by Ceres, and calculated to awaken feelings of piety and a cheerful hope of better life in the future

Eleusis, Grecian city

Elgin Marbles, Greek sculptures from the Parthenon of Athens, now in British Museum, London, placed there by Lord Elgin

Eliaures, enchanter

Elidure, a king of Britain

Elis, ancient Greek city

Elli, old age; the one successful wrestler against Thor

Elphin, son of Gwyddiro

Elves, spiritual beings, of many powers and dispositions--some evil, some good

Elvidnir, the ball of Hela

Elysian Fields, the land of the blest

Elysian Plain, whither the favored of the gods were taken without death

Elysium, a happy land, where there is neither snow, nor cold, nor rain. Hither favored heroes, like Menelaus, pass without dying, and live happy under the rule of Rhadamanthus. In the Latin poets Elysium is part of the lower world, and the residence of the shades of the blessed

Embla, the first woman

Enseladus, giant defeated by Jupiter

Endymion, a beautiful youth beloved by Diana

Enid, wife of Geraint

Enna, vale of home of Proserpine

Enoch, the patriarch

Epidaurus, a town in Argolis, on the Saronic gulf, chief seat of the worship of Aeculapius, whose temple was situated near the town

Epimetheus, son of Iapetus, husband of Pandora, with his brother Prometheus took part in creation of man

Epirus, country to the west of Thessaly, lying along the Adriatic Sea

Epopeus, a sailor

Erato, one of the Muses

Erbin of Cornwall, father of Geraint

Erebus, son of Chaos, region of darkness, entrance to Hades

Eridanus, river

Erinys, one of the Furies

Eriphyle, sister of Polynices, bribed to decide on war, in which her husband was slain

Eris (Discordia), goddess of discord. At the wedding of Peleus and Thetis, Eris being uninvited threw into the gathering an apple "For the Fairest," which was claimed by Hera (Juno), Aphrodite (Venus) and Athena (Minerva) Paris, being called upon for judgment, awarded it to Aphrodite

Erisichthon, an unbeliever, punished by famine

Eros See Cupid

Erytheia, island

Eryx, a mount, haunt of Venus

Esepus, river in Paphlagonia

Estrildis, wife of Locrine, supplanting divorced Guendolen

Eteocles, son of Oeipus and Jocasta

Etruscans, ancient people of Italy.

Etzel, king of the Huns

Euboic Sea, where Hercules threw Lichas, who brought him the poisoned shirt of Nessus

Eude, king of Aquitaine, ally of Charles Martel

Eumaeus, swineherd of Aeeas

Eumenides, also called Erinnyes, and by the Romans Furiae or Diraae, the Avenging Deities, See Furies

Euphorbus, a Trojan, killed by Menelaus

Euphros'yne, one of the Graces

Europa, daughter of the Phoenician king Agenor, by Zeus the mother of Minos, Rhadamanthus, and Sarpedon

Eurus, the East wind

Euyalus, a gallant Trojan soldier, who with Nisus entered the Grecian camp, both being slain.

Eurydice, wife of Orpheus, who, fleeing from an admirer, was killed by a snake and borne to Tartarus, where Orpheus sought her and was permitted to bring her to earth if he would not look back at her following him, but he did, and she returned to the Shades.

Eurylochus, a companion of Ulysses.

Eurynome, female Titan, wife of Ophlon

Eurystheus, taskmaster of Hercules.

Eurytion, a Centaur (See Hippodamia).

Euterpe, Muse who presided over music.

Evadne, wife of Capaneus, who flung herself upon his funeral pile and perished with him

Evander, Arcadian chief, befriending Aeneas in Italy.

Evnissyen, quarrelsome brother of Branwen.

Excalibar, sword of King Arthur.

F

Fafner, a giant turned dragon, treasure stealer, by the Solar Theory simply the Darkness who steals the day.

Falerina, an enchantress.

Fasolt, a giant, brother of Fafner, and killed by him.

"Fasti," Ovid's, a mythological poetic calendar.

FATA MORGANA, a mirage

FATES, the three, described as daughters of Night--to indicate the darkness and obscurity of human destiny--or of Zeus and Themis, that is, "daughters of the just heavens" they were Clo'tho, who spun the thread of life, Lach'esis, who held the thread and fixed its length and At'ropos, who cut it off

FAUNS, cheerful sylvan deities, represented in human form, with small horns, pointed ears, and sometimes goat's tail

FAUNUS, son of Picus, grandson of Saturnus, and father of Latinus, worshipped as the protecting deity of agriculture and of shepherds, and also as a giver of oracles

FAVONIUS, the West wind

FEAR

FENRIS, a wolf, the son of Loki the Evil Principle of Scandinavia, supposed to have personated the element of fire, destructive except when chained

FENSALIR, Freya's palace, called the Hall of the Sea, where were brought together lovers, husbands, and wives who had been separated by death

FERRAGUS, a giant, opponent of Orlando

FERRAU, one of Charlemagne's knights

FERREX. brother of Porrex, the two sons of Leir

FIRE WORSHIPPERS, of ancient Persia, See Parsees
FLOLLO, Roman tribune in Gaul

FLORA, Roman goddess of flowers and spring

FLORDELIS, fair maiden beloved by Florismart

FLORISMART, Sir, a brave knight.

FLOSSHILDA, one of the Rhine daughters

FORTUNATE FIELDS

FORTUNATE ISLANDS (See Elysian Plain)

FORUM, market place and open square for public meetings in Rome, surrounded by court houses, palaces, temples. etc

FRANCUS, son of Histion, grandson of Japhet, great grandson of Noah, legendary ancestor of the Franks, or French

FREKI, one of Odin's two wolves

FREY, or Freyr, god of the sun

FREYA, Norse goddess of music, spring, and flowers

FRICKA, goddess of marriage

FRIGGA, goddess who presided over smiling nature, sending sunshine, rain, and harvest

FROH, one of the Norse gods

FRONTI'NO, Rogero's horse

FURIES (Erinnyes), the three retributive spirits who punished crime, represented as snaky haired old woman, named Alecto, Megaeira, and Tisiphone

FUSBERTA, Rinaldo's sword

G

GAEA, or Ge, called Tellus by the Romans, the personification of the earth, described as the first being that sprang fiom Chaos, and gave birth to Uranus (Heaven) and Pontus (Sea)

GAHARIET, knight of Arthur's court

GAHERIS, knight

GALAFRON, King of Cathay, father of Angelica

GALAHAD, Sir, the pure knight of Arthur's Round Table, who safely took the Siege Perilous (which See)

GALATEA, a Nereid or sea nymph

GALATEA, statue carved and beloved by Pygmalion

GALEN, Greek physician and philosophical writer

GALLEHANT, King of the Marches

GAMES, national athletic contests in Greece--Olympian, at Olympia, Pythian, near Delphi, seat of Apollo's oracle, Isthmian, on the Corinthian Isthmus, Nemean, at Nemea in Argolis

GAN, treacherous Duke of Maganza

GANELON of Mayence, one of Charlemagne's knights

GANGES, river in India

GANO, a peer of Charlemagne

GANYMEDE, the most beautiful of all mortals, carried off to Olympus that he might fill the cup of Zeus and live among the immortal gods

GARETH, Arthur's knight

GAUDISSO, Sultan

GAUL, ancient France

GAUTAMA, Prince, the Buddha

GAWAIN, Arthur's knight

GAWL, son of Clud, suitor for Rhiannon

GEMINI (See Castor), constellation created by Jupiter from the twin brothers after death, 158

GENGHIS Khan, Tartar conqueror

GENIUS, in Roman belief, the protective Spirit of each individual man, See Juno

GEOFFREY OF MON'MOUTH, translator into Latin of the Welsh History of the Kings of Britain (1150)

GERAINT, a knight of King Arthur

GERDA, wife of Frey

GERI, one of Odin's two wolves

GERYON, a three bodied monster

GESNES, navigator sent for Isoude the Fair

GIALLAR HORN, the trumpet that Heimdal will blow at the judgment day

GIANTS, beings of monstrous size and of fearful countenances, represented as in constant opposition to the gods, in Wagner's Nibelungen Ring

GIBICHUNG RACE, ancestors of Alberich

GIBRALTAR, great rock and town at southwest corner of Spain (See Pillars of Hercules)

GILDAS, a scholar of Arthur's court

GIRARD, son of Duke Sevinus

GLASTONBURY, where Arthur died

GLAUCUS, a fisherman, loving Scylla

GLEIPNIR, magical chain on the wolf Fenris

GLEWLWYD, Arthur's porter

GOLDEN FLEECE, of ram used for escape of children of Athamas, named Helle and Phryxus (which See), after sacrifice of ram to Jupiter, fleece was guarded by sleepless dragon and gained by Jason and Argonauts (which See, also Helle)

GONERIL, daughter of Leir

GORDIAN KNOT, tying up in temple the wagon of Gordius, he who could untie it being destined to be lord of Asia, it was cut by Alexander the Great, 48

Gordius, a countryman who, arriving in Phrygia in a wagon, was made king by the people, thus interpreting an oracle, 48

Gorgons, three monstrous females, with huge teeth, brazen claws and snakes for hair, sight of whom turned beholders to stone, Medusa, the most famous, slain by Perseus

Gorlois, Duke of Tintadel

Gouvernail, squire of Isabella, queen of Lionesse, protector of her son Tristram while young, and his squire in knighthood

Graal, the Holy, cup from which the Saviour drank at Last Supper, taken by Joseph of Arimathea to Europe, and lost, its recovery becoming a sacred quest for Arthur's knights

Graces, three goddesses who enhanced the enjoyments of life by refinement and gentleness; they were Aglaia (brilliance), Euphrosyne (joy), and Thalia (bloom)

Gradas'so, king of Sericane

Graeae, three gray haired female watchers for the Gorgons, with one movable eye and one tooth between the three

Grand Lama, Buddhist pontiff in Thibet

Grendel, monster slain by Beowulf

Gryphon (griffin), a fabulous animal, with the body of a lion and the head and wings of an eagle, dwelling in the Rhipaean mountains, between the Hyperboreans and the one eyed Arimaspians, and guarding the gold of the North.

Guebers, Persian fire worshippers.

Guendolen, wife of Locrine.

Guenevere, wife of King Arthur, beloved by Launcelot.

Guerin, lord of Vienne, father of Oliver.

Guiderius, son of Cymbeline.

Guillamurius, king in Ireland.

Guimier, betrothed of Caradoc.

Gullinbursti, the boar drawing Frey's car.

Gulltopp, Heimdell's horse.

Gunfasius, King of the Orkneys.

Ganther, Burgundian king, brother of Kriemhild.

Gutrune, half sister to Hagen.

Gwern son of Matholch and Branwen.

Gwernach the Giant.

Gwiffert Petit, ally of Geraint.

Gwyddno, Garanhir, King of Gwaelod.

Gwyr, judge in the court of Arthur.

Gyoll, river.

H

Hades, originally the god of the nether world--the name later used to designate the gloomy subterranean land of the dead.

Haemon, son of Creon of Thebes, and lover of Antigone.

Haemonian city.

Haemus, Mount, northern boundary of Thrace.

Hagan, a principal character in the Nibelungen Lied, slayer of Siegfried.

HALCYONE, daughter of Aeneas, and the beloved wife of Ceyx, who, when he was drowned, flew to his floating body, and the pitying gods changed them both to birds (kingfishers), who nest at sea during a certain calm week in winter ("halcyon weather")

HAMADRYADS, tree-nymphs or wood-nymphs, See Nymphs

HARMONIA, daughter of Mars and Venus, wife of Cadmus

HAROUN AL RASCHID, Caliph of Arabia, contemporary of Charlemagne

HARPIES, monsters, with head and bust of woman, but wings, legs and tail of birds, seizing souls of the wicked, or punishing evildoers by greedily snatching or defiling their food

HARPOCRATES, Egyptian god, Horus

HEBE, daughter of Juno, cupbearer to the gods

HEBRUS, ancient name of river Maritzka

HECATE, a mighty and formidable divinity, supposed to send at night all kinds of demons and terrible phantoms from the lower world

HECTOR, son of Priam and champion of Troy

HECTOR, one of Arthur's knights

HECTOR DE MARYS', a knight

HECUBA, wife of Priam, king of Troy, to whom she bore Hector, Paris, and many other children

HEGIRA, flight of Mahomet from Mecca to Medina (622 AD), era from which Mahometans reckon time, as we do from the birth of Christ

HEIDRUN, she goat, furnishing mead for slain heroes in Valhalla

HEIMDALL, watchman of the gods

HEL, the lower world of Scandinavia, to which were consigned those who had not died in battle

HELA (Death), the daughter of Loki and the mistress of the Scandinavian Hel

HELEN, daughter of Jupiter and Leda, wife of Menelaus, carried off by Paris and cause of the Trojan War

HELENUS, son of Priam and Hecuba, celebrated for his prophetic powers

HELIADES, sisters of Phaeton

HELICON, Mount, in Greece, residence of Apollo and the Muses, with fountains of poetic inspiration, Aganippe and Hippocrene

HELIOOPOLIS, city of the Sun, in Egypt

HELLAS, Gieece

HELLE, daughter of Thessalian King Athamas, who, escaping from cruel father with her brother Phryxus, on ram with golden fleece, fell into the sea strait since named for her (See Golden Fleece)

HELLESPONt, narrow strait between Europe and Asia Minor, named for Helle

HENGIST, Saxon invader of Britain, 449 AD

HEPHAESTOS, See VULCAN

HERA, called Juno by the Romans, a daughter of Cronos (Saturn) and Rhea, and sister and wife of Jupiter, See JUNO

HERCULES, athletic hero, son of Jupiter and Alcmena, achieved twelve vast labors and many famous deeds

HEREWARD THE WAKE, hero of the Saxons

HERMES (Mercury), messenger of the gods, deity of commerce, science, eloquence, trickery, theft, and skill generally

HERMIONE, daughter of Menelaus and Helen

HERMOD, the nimble, son of Odin

HERO, a priestess of Venus, beloved of Leander

HERODOTUS, Greek historian

HESIOD, Greek poet

HESPERIA, ancient name for Italy

HESPERIDES (See Apples of the Hesperides)

HESPERUS, the evening star (also called Day Star)

HESTIA, cilled Vesta by the Romans, the goddess of the hearth

HILDEBRAND, German magician and champion

HINDU TRIAD, Brahma, Vishnu, and Siva

HIPPOCRENE (See Helicon)

HIPPODAMIA, wife of Pirithous, at whose wedding the Centaurs offered violence to the bride, causing a great battle

HIPPOGRIFF, winged horse, with eagle's head and claws

HIPPOLYTA, Queen of the Amazons

Hippolytus, son of Thesus

HIPPOMENES, who won Atalanta in foot race, beguiling her with golden apples thrown for her to

HISTION, son of Japhet

HODUR, blind man, who, fooled by Loki, threw a mistletoe twig at Baldur, killing him

HOEL, king of Brittany

HOMER, the blind poet of Greece, about 850 B C

HOPE (See PANDORA)

HORAE See HOURS

HORSA, with Hengist, invader of Britain

HORUS, Egyptian god of the sun

HOUDAIN, Tristram's dog

HRINGHAM, Baldur's ship

HROTHGAR, king of Denmark

HUGI, who beat Thialfi in foot races

HUGIN, one of Odin's two ravens

HUNDING, husband of Sieglinda

HUON, son of Duke Sevinus

HYACINTHUS, a youth beloved by Apollo, and accidentally killed by him, changed in death to the flower, hyacinth

HYADES, Nysaean nymphs, nurses of infant Bacchus, rewarded by being placed as cluster of stars in the heavens

HYALE, a nymph of Diana

HYDRA, nine headed monster slain by Hercules

HYGEIA, goddess of health, daughter of Aesculapius

HYLAS, a youth detained by nymphs of spring where he sought water

HYMEN, the god of marriage, imagined as a handsome youth and invoked in bridal songs

HYMETTUS, mountain in Attica, near Athens, celebrated for its marble and its honey

HYPERBOREANS, people of the far North

HYPERION, a Titan, son of Uranus and Ge, and father of Helios, Selene, and Eos, cattle of.

Hyrcania, Prince of, betrothed to Clarimunda

Hyrieus, king in Greece.

I

Iapetus, a Titan, son of Uranus and Ge, and father of Atlas, Prometheus, Epimetheus, and Menoetius.

Iasius, father of Atalanta

Ibycus, a poet, story of, and the cranes

Icaria, island of the Aegean Sea, one of the Sporades

Icarius, Spartan prince, father of Penelope

Icarus, son of Daedalus, he flew too near the sun with artificial wings, and, the wax melting, he fell into the sea

Icelos, attendant of Morpheus

Icolumkill SEE Iona

Ida, Mount, a Trojan hill

Idaeus, a Trojan herald

Idas, son of Aphareus and Arene, and brother of Lynceus Idu'na, wife of Bragi

Igerne, wife of Gorlois, and mother, by Uther, of Arthur

Iliad, epic poem of the Trojan War, by Homer

Ilioheus, a son of Niobe

Ilium SEE Troy

Illyria, Adriatic countries north of Greece

Imogen, daughter of Pandrasus, wife of Trojan Brutus

Inachus, son of Oceanus and Tethys, and father of Phoroneus and Io, also first king of Argos, and said to have given his name to the river Inachus

INCUBUS, an evil spirit, supposed to lie upon persons in their sleep

INDRA, Hindu god of heaven, thunder, lightning, storm and rain

INO, wife of Athamas, fleeing from whom with infant son she sprang into the sea and was changed to Leucothea

IO, changed to a heifer by Jupiter

IOBATES, King of Lycia

IOLAUS, servant of Hercules

IOLE, sister of Dryope

IONA, or Icolmkill, a small northern island near Scotland, where St Columba founded a missionary monastery (563 AD)

IONIA, coast of Asia Minor

IPHIGENIA, daughter of Agamemnon, offered as a sacrifice but carried away by Diana

IPHIS, died for love of Anaxarete, 78

IPHITAS, friend of Hercules, killed by him

IRIS, goddess of the rainbow, messenger of Juno and Zeus

IRONSIDE, Arthur's knight

ISABELLA, daughter of king of Galicia

ISIS, wife of Osiris, described as the giver of death

ISLES OF THE BLESSED

ISMARUS, first stop of Ulysses, returning from Trojan War
ISME'NOS, a son of Niobe, slain by Apollo

ISOLIER, friend of Rinaldo

ISOUDE THE FAIR, beloved of Tristram

ISOUDE OF THE WHITE HANDS, married to Tristram

ISTHMIAN GAMES, See GAMES

ITHACA, home of Ulysses and Penelope

IULUS, son of Aeneas

IVO, Saracen king, befriending Rinaldo

IXION, once a sovereign of Thessaly, sentenced in Tartarus to be lashed with serpents to a wheel which a strong wind drove continually around

J

JANICULUM, Roman fortress on the Janiculus, a hill on the other side of the Tiber

JANUS, a deity from the earliest times held in high estimation by the Romans, temple of

JAPHET (Iapetus)

JASON, leader of the Argonauts, seeking the Golden Fleece

JOSEPH OF ARIMATHEA, who bore the Holy Graal to Europe

JOTUNHEIM, home of the giants in Northern mythology

JOVE (Zeus), chief god of Roman and Grecian mythology, See JUPITER

JOYOUS GARDE, residence of Sir Launcelot of the Lake

JUGGERNAUT, Hindu deity

JUNO, the particular guardian spirit of each woman (See Genius)

JUNO, wife of Jupiter, queen of the gods

JUPITER, JOVIS PATER, FATHER JOVE, JUPITER and JOVE used interchangeably, at Dodona, statue of the Olympian

JUPITER AMMON (See Ammon)

JUPITER CAPITOLINUS, temple of, preserving the Sibylline books

JUSTICE, See THEMIS

K

KADYRIATH, advises King Arthur

KAI, son of Kyner

KALKI, tenth avatar of Vishnu

KAY, Arthur's steward and a knight

KEDALION, guide of Orion

KERMAN, desert of

KICVA, daughter of Gwynn Gloy

KILWICH, son of Kilydd

KILYDD, son of Prince Kelyddon, of Wales

KNEPH, spirit or breath

KNIGHTS, training and life of

KRIEMHILD, wife of Siegfried

KRISHNA, eighth avatar of Vishnu, Hindu deity of fertility in nature and mankind

KYNER, father of Kav

KYNON, son of Clydno

L

LABYRINTH, the enclosed maze of passageways where roamed the Minotaur of Crete, killed by Theseus with aid of Ariadne

LACHESIS, one of the Fates (which See)

LADY OF THE FOUNTAIN, tale told by Kynon

LAERTES, father of Ulysses

LAESTRYGONIANS, savages attacking Ulysses

LAIUS, King of Thebes

LAMA, holy man of Thibet

LAMPETIA, daughter of Hyperion LAOC'OON, a priest of Neptune, in Troy, who warned the Trojans against the Wooden Horse (which See), but when two serpents came out of the sea and strangled him and his two sons, the people listened to the Greek spy Sinon, and brought the fatal Horse into the town

LAODAMIA, daughter of Acastus and wife of Protesilaus

LAODEGAN, King of Carmalide, helped by Arthur and Merlin

LAOMEDON, King of Troy

LAPITHAE, Thessalonians, whose king had invited the Centaurs to his daughter's wedding but who attacked them for offering violence to the bride

LARES, household deities

LARKSPUR, flower from the blood of Ajax

LATINUS, ruler of Latium, where Aeneas landed in Italy

LATMOS, Mount, where Diana fell in love with Endymion

LATONA, mother of Apollo

LAUNCELOT, the most famous knight of the Round Table

LAUSUS, son of Mezentius, killed by Aeneas

LAVINIA, daughter of Latinus and wife of Aeneas

LAVINIUM, Italian city named for Lavinia

LAW, See THEMIS

LEANDER, a youth of Abydos, who, swimming the Hellespont to see Hero, his love, was drowned

LEBADEA, site of the oracle of Trophomus

LEBYNTHOS, Aegean island

LEDA, Queen of Sparta, wooed by Jupiter in the form of a swan

LEIR, mythical King of Britain, original of Shakespeare's Lear

LELAPS, dog of Cephalus

LEMNOS, large island in the Aegean Sea, sacred to Vulcan

LEMURES, the spectres or spirits of the dead

LEO, Roman emperor, Greek prince

LETHE, river of Hades, drinking whose water caused forgetfulness

LEUCADIA, a promontory, whence Sappho, disappointed in love, was said to have thrown herself into the sea

LEUCOTHEA, a sea goddess, invoked by sailors for protection (See Ino)

LEWIS, son of Charlemagne

LIBER, ancient god of fruitfulness

LIBETHRA, burial place of Orpheus

LIBYA, Greek name for continent of Africa in general

LIBYAN DESERT, in Africa

LIBYAN OASIS

LICHAS, who brought the shirt of Nessus to Hercules

LIMOURS, Earl of

LINUS, musical instructor of Hercules

LIONEL, knight of the Round Table

LLYR, King of Britain

LOCRINE, son of Brutus in Albion, king of Central England

LOEGRIA, kingdom of (England)

LOGESTILLA, a wise lady, who entertained Rogero and his friends

LOGI, who vanquished Loki in an eating contest

LOKI, the Satan of Norse mythology, son of the giant Farbanti

LOT, King, a rebel chief, subdued by King Arthur, then a loyal knight

LOTIS, a nymph, changed to a lotus-plant and in that form plucked by Dryope

LOTUS EATERS, soothed to indolence, companions of Ulysses landing among them lost all memory of home and had to be dragged away before they would continue their voyage

LOVE (Eros) issued from egg of Night, and with arrows and torch produced life and joy

LUCAN, one of Arthur's knights

Lucius Tiberius, Roman procurator in Britain demanding tribute from Arthur

LUD, British king, whose capital was called Lud's Town (London)

LUDGATE, city gate where Lud was buried, 387

LUNED, maiden who guided Owain to the Lady of the Fountain

LYCAHAS, a turbulent sailor

LYCAON, son of Priam

LYCIA, a district in Southern Asia Minor

LYCOMODES, king of the Dolopians, who treacherously slew Theseus

LYCUS, usurping King of Thebes

LYNCEUS, one of the sons of Aegyptus

M

MABINOGEON, plural of Mabinogi, fairy tales and romances of the Welsh

MABON, son of Modron

MACHAON, son of Aesculapius

MADAN, son of Guendolen

MADOC, a forester of King Arthur

MADOR, Scottish knight

MAELGAN, king who imprisoned Elphin

MAEONIA, ancient Lydia

MAGI, Persian priests

MAHADEVA, same as Siva

MAHOMET, great prophet of Arabia, born in Mecca, 571 AD, proclaimed worship of God instead of idols, spread his religion through disciples and then by force till it prevailed, with Arabian dominion, over vast regions in Asia, Africa, and Spain in Europe

MAIA, daughter of Atlas and Pleione, eldest and most beautiful of the Pleiades

MALAGIGI the Enchanter, one of Charlemagne's knights

MALEAGANS, false knight

MALVASIUS, King of Iceland

MAMBRINO, with invisible helmet

MANAWYD DAN, brother of King Vran, of London

MANDRICARDO, son of Agrican

MANTUA, in Italy, birthplace of Virgil

MANU, ancestor of mankind

MARATHON, where Theseus and Pirithous met

MARK, King of Cornwall, husband of Isoude the Fair

MARO See VIRGIL

MARPHISA, sister of Rogero

MARSILIUS, Spanish king, treacherous foe of Charlemagne

MARSYAS, inventor of the flute, who challenged Apollo to musical competition, and, defeated, was flayed alive

MATSYA, the Fish, first avatar of Vishnu

MEANDER, Grecian river

MEDE, A, princess and sorceress who aided Jason

MEDORO, a young Moor, who wins Angelica

MEDUSA, one of the Gorgons

MEGAERA, one of the Furies

MELAMPUS, a Spartan dog, the first mortal endowed with prophetic powers

MELANTHUS, steersman for Bacchus

MELEAGER, one of the Argonauts (See Althaea)

MELIADUS, King of Lionesse, near Cornwall

MELICERTES, infant son of Ino. changed to Palaemon (See Ino, Leucothea, and Palasmon)

MELISSA, priestess at Merlin's tomb

MELISSEUS, a Cretan king

MELPOMENE, one of the Muses

MEMNON, the beautiful son of Tithonus and Eos (Aurora), and king of the Ethiopians, slain in Trojan War

MEMPHIS, Egyptian city

MENELAUS, son of King of Sparta, husband of Helen

MENOECEUS, son of Creon, voluntary victim in war to gain success for his father

MENTOR, son of Alcimus and a faithful friend of Ulysses

MERCURY (See HERMES)

MERLIN, enchanter

MEROPE, daughter of King of Chios, beloved by Orion

MESMERISM, likened to curative oracle of Aesculapius at Epidaurus

METABUS, father of Camilla

METAMORPHOSES, Ovid's poetical legends of mythical transformations, a large source of our knowledge of classic mythology

METANIRA, a mother, kind to Ceres seeking Proserpine

METEMPSYCHOSIS, transmigration of souls--rebirth of dying men and women in forms of animals or human beings

METIS, Prudence, a spouse of Jupiter

MEZENTIUS, a brave but cruel soldier, opposing Aeneas in Italy

MIDAS

MIDGARD, the middle world of the Norsemen

MIDGARD SERPENT, a sea monster, child of Loki

MILKY WAY, starred path across the sky, believed to be road to palace of the gods

MILO, a great athlete

MLON, father of Orlando

MILTON, John, great English poet, whose History of England is here largely used

MIME, one of the chief dwarfs of ancient German mythology

MINERVA (Athene), daughter of Jupiter, patroness of health, learning, and wisdom

MINOS, King of Crete

MINO TAUR, monster killed by Theseus

MISTLETOE, fatal to Baldur

MNEMOSYNE, one of the Muses

MODESTY, statue to

MODRED, nephew of King Arthur

MOLY, plant, powerful against sorcery

MOMUS, a deity whose delight was to jeer bitterly at gods and men

MONAD, the "unit" of Pythagoras

MONSTERS, unnatural beings, evilly disposed to men

MONTALBAN, Rinaldo's castle

MONTH, the, attendant upon the Sun

MOON, goddess of, see DIANA

MORAUNT, knight, an Irish champion

MORGANA, enchantress, the Lady of the Lake in "Orlando Furioso," same as Morgane Le Fay in tales of Arthur

MORGANE LE FAY, Queen of Norway, King Arthur's sister, an enchantress

MORGAN TUD, Arthur's chief physician

MORPHEUS, son of Sleep and god of dreams

MORTE D'ARTHUr, romance, by Sir Thomas Mallory

MULCIBER, Latin name of Vulcan

MULL, Island of

MUNIN, one of Odin's two ravens

MUSAEUS, sacred poet, son of Orpheus

MUSES, The, nine goddesses presiding over poetry, etc-- Calliope, epic poetry, Clio, history, Erato, love poetry, Euterpe, lyric poetry; Melpomene, tragedy, Polyhymnia, oratory and sacred song Terpsichore, choral song and dance, Thalia, comedy and idyls, Urania, astronomy

MUSPELHEIM, the fire world of the Norsemen

MYCENAS, ancient Grecian city, of which Agamemnon was king

MYRDDIN (Merlin)

MYRMIDONS, bold soldiers of Achilles

MYSIA, Greek district on northwest coast of Asia Minor

MYTHOLOGY, origin of, collected myths, describing gods of early peoples

N

NAIADS, water nymphs

NAMO, Duke of Bavaria, one of Charlemagne's knights

NANNA, wife of Baldur

NANTERS, British king

NANTES, site of Caradoc's castle

NAPE, a dog of Diana

NARCISSUS, who died of unsatisfied love for his own image in the water

NAUSICAA, daughter of King Alcinous, who befriended Ulysses

NAUSITHOUS, king of Phaeacians

NAXOS, Island of

NEGUS, King of Abyssinia

NEMEA, forest devastated by a lion killed by Hercules

NEMEAN GAMES, held in honor of Jupiter and Hercules

NEMEAN LION, killed by Hercules

NEMESIS, goddess of vengeance

NENNIUS, British combatant of Caesar

NEOPTOLEMUS, son of Achilles

NEPENTHE, ancient drug to cause forgetfulness of pain or distress

NEPHELE, mother of Phryxus and Helle

NEPHTHYS, Egyptian goddess

NEPTUNE, identical with Poseidon, god of the sea

NEREIDS, sea nymphs, daughters of Nereus and Doris

NEREUS, a sea god

NESSUS, a centaur killed by Hercules, whose jealous wife sent him a robe or shirt steeped in the blood of Nessus, which poisoned him

NESTOR, king of Pylos, renowned for his wisdom, justice, and knowledge of war

NIBELUNGEN HOARD, treasure seized by Siegfried from the Nibelungs, buried in the Rhine by Hagan after killing Siegfried, and lost when Hagan was killed by Kriemhild, theme of Wagner's four music dramas, "The Ring of the Nibelungen,"

NIBELUNGEN LIED, German epic, giving the same nature myth as the Norse Volsunga Saga, concerning the Hoard

NIBELUNGEN RING, Wagner's music dramas

NIBELUNGS, the, a race of Northern dwarfs

NIDHOGGE, a serpent in the lower world that lives on the dead

NIFFLEHEIM, mist world of the Norsemen, the Hades of absent spirits

NILE, Egyptian river

NIOBE, daughter of Tantalus, proud Queen of Thebes, whose seven sons and seven daughters were killed by Apollo and Diana, at which Amphion, her husband, killed himself, and Niobe wept until she was turned to stone

NISUS, King of Megara

NOAH, as legendary ancestor of French, Roman, German, and British peoples

NOMAN, name assumed by Ulysses

NORNS, the three Scandinavian Fates, Urdur (the past), Verdandi (the present), and Skuld (the future)

NOTHUNG, magic sword

NOTUS, southwest wind

NOX, daughter of Chaos and sister of Erebus, personification of night

Numa, second king of Rome

NYMPHS, beautiful maidens, lesser divinities of nature Dryads and Hamadryads, tree nymphs, Naiads, spring, brook, and river nymphs, Nereids, sea nymphs Oreads, mountain nymphs or hill nymphs

O

OCEANUS, a Titan, ruling watery elements

OCYROE, a prophetess, daughter of Chiron

ODERIC

ODIN, chief of the Norse gods

ODYAR, famous Biscayan hero

ODYSSEUS See ULYSSES

ODYSSEY, Homer's poem, relating the wanderings of Odysseus (Ulysses) on returning from Trojan War

OEDIPUS, Theban hero, who guessed the riddle of the Sphinx (which See), becoming King of Thebes

OENEUS, King of Calydon

OENONE, nymph, married by Paris in his youth, and abandoned for Helen

OENOPION, King of Chios

OETA, Mount, scene of Hercules' death

OGIER, the Dane, one of the paladins of Charlemagne

OLIVER, companion of Orlando

OLWEN, wife of Kilwich

OLYMPIA, a small plain in Elis, where the Olympic games were celebrated

OLYMPIADS, periods between Olympic games (four years)

OLYMPIAN GAMES, See GAMES

OLYMPUS, dwelling place of the dynasty of gods of which Zeus was the head

OMPHALE, queen of Lydia, daughter of Iardanus and wife of Tmolus

OPHION, king of the Titans, who ruled Olympus till dethroned by the gods Saturn and Rhea

OPS See RHEA

ORACLES, answers from the gods to questions from seekers for knowledge or advice for the future, usually in equivocal form, so as to fit any event, also places where such answers were given forth usually by a priest or priestess

ORC, a sea monster, foiled by Rogero when about to devour Angelica

OREADS, nymphs of mountains and hills

ORESTES, son of Agamemnon and Clytemnestra, because of his crime in killing his mother, he was pursued by the Furies until purified by Minerva

ORION, youthful giant, loved by Diana, Constellation

ORITHYIA, a nymph, seized by Boreas

ORLANDO, a famous knight and nephew of Charlemagne

ORMUZD (Greek, Oromasdes), son of Supreme Being, source of good as his brother Ahriman (Arimanes) was of evil, in Persian or Zoroastrian religion

ORPHEUS, musician, son of Apollo and Calliope, See EURYDICE

OSIRIS, the most beneficent of the Egyptian gods

OSSA, mountain of Thessaly

OSSIAN, Celtic poet of the second or third century

OVID, Latin poet (See Metamorphoses)

OWAIN, knight at King Arthur's court

OZANNA, a knight of Arthur

P

PACTOLUS, river whose sands were changed to gold by Midas

PAEON, a name for both Apollo and Aesculapius, gods of medicine.

PAGANS, heathen

PALADINS or peers, knights errant

PALAEMON, son of Athamas and Ino

PALAMEDES, messenger sent to call Ulysses to the Trojan War

PALAMEDES, Saracen prince at Arthur's court

PALATINE, one of Rome's Seven Hills

PALES, goddess presiding over cattle and pastures

PALINURUS, faithful steersman of Aeeas

PALLADIUM, properly any image of Pallas Athene, but specially applied to an image at Troy, which was stolen by Ulysses and Diomedes

PALLAS, son of Evander

PALLAS A THE'NE (Minerva)

PAMPHA GUS, a dog of Diana

PAN, god of nature and the universe

PANATHENAEA, festival in honor of Pallas Athene (Minerva)

PANDEAN PIPES, musical instrument of reeds, made by Pan in memory of Syrinx

PANDORA (all gifted), first woman, dowered with gifts by every god, yet entrusted with a box she was cautioned not to open, but, curious, she opened it, and out flew all the ills of humanity, leaving behind only Hope, which remained

PANDRASUS, a king in Greece, who persecuted Trojan exiles under Brutus, great grandson of Aeneas, until they fought, captured him, and, with his daughter Imogen as Brutus' wife, emigrated to Albion (later called Britain)

PANOPE, plain of

PANTHUS, alleged earlier incarnation of Pythagoras

PAPHLAGNIA, ancient country in Asia Minor, south of Black Sea

PAPHOS, daughter of Pygmalion and Galatea (both of which, See)

PARCAE See FATES

PARIAHS, lowest caste of Hindus

PARIS, son of Priam and Hecuba, who eloped with Helen (which. See)

PARNASSIAN LAUREl, wreath from Parnassus, crown awarded to successful poets

PARNASSUS, mountain near Delphi, sacred to Apollo and the Muses

PARSEES, Persian fire worshippers (Zoroastrians), of whom there are still thousands in Persia and India

PARTHENON, the temple of Athene Parthenos ("the Virgin") on the Acropolis of Athens

PASSEBREUL, Tristram's horse

PATROCLUS, friend of Achilles, killed by Hector

PECHEUR, King, uncle of Perceval

PEERS, the

PEGASUS, winged horse, born from the sea foam and the blood of Medusa

PELEUS, king of the Myrmidons, father of Achilles by Thetis

PELIAS, usurping uncle of Jason

PELION, mountain

PELLEAS, knight of Arthur

PENATES, protective household deities of the Romans

PENDRAGON, King of Britain, elder brother of Uther Pendragon, who succeeded him

PENELOPE, wife of Ulysses, who, waiting twenty years for his return from the Trojan War, put off the suitors for her hand by promising to choose one when her weaving was done, but unravelled at night what she had woven by day

PENEUS, river god, river

PENTHESILEA, queen of Amazons

PENTHEUS, king of Thebes, having resisted the introduction of the worship of Bacchus into his kingdom, was driven mad by the god

PENUS, Roman house pantry, giving name to the Penates

PEPIN, father of Charlemagne

PEPLUS, sacred robe of Minerva

PERCEVAL, a great knight of Arthur

PERDIX, inventor of saw and compasses

PERIANDER, King of Corinuh, friend of Arion

PERIPHETES, son of Vulcan, killed by Theseus

PERSEPHONE, goddess of vegetation, 8 See Pioserpine

PERSEUS, son of Jupiter and Danae, slayer of the Gorgon Medusa, deliverer of Andromeda from a sea monster, 116 122, 124, 202

PHAEACIANS, people who entertained Ulysses

PHAEDRA, faithless and cruel wife of Theseus

PHAETHUSA, sister of Phaeton, 244

PHAETON, son of Phoebus, who dared attempt to drive his father's sun chariot

PHANTASOS, a son of Somnus, bringing strange images to sleeping men

PHAON, beloved by Sappho

PHELOT, knight of Wales

PHEREDIN, friend of Tristram, unhappy lover of Isoude

PHIDIAS, famous Greek sculptor

PHILEMON, husband of Baucis

PHILOCTETES, warrior who lighted the fatal pyre of Hercules

PHILOE, burial place of Osiris

PHINEUS, betrothed to Andromeda

PHLEGETHON, fiery river of Hades

PHOCIS

PHOEBE, one of the sisters of Phaeton

PHOEBUS (Apollo), god of music, prophecy, and archery, the sun god

PHOENIX, a messenger to Achilles, also, a miraculous bird dying in fire by its own act and springing up alive from its own ashes

PHORBAS, a companion of Aeneas, whose form was assumed by Neptune in luring Palinuras the helmsman from his roost

PHRYXUS, brother of Helle

PINABEL, knight

PILLARS OF HERCULES, two mountains--Calpe, now the Rock of Gibraltar, southwest corner of Spain in Europe, and Abyla, facing it in Africa across the strait

PINDAR, famous Greek poet

PINDUS, Grecian mountain

PIRENE, celebrated fountain at Corinth

PIRITHOUS, king of the Lapithae in Thessaly, and friend of Theseus, husband of Hippodamia

PLEASURE, daughter of Cupid and Psyche

PLEIADES, seven of Diana's nymphs, changed into stars, one being lost

PLENTY, the Horn of

PLEXIPPUS, brother of Althea

PLINY, Roman naturalist

PLUTO, the same as Hades, Dis, etc. god of the Infernal Regions

PLUTUS, god of wealth

PO, Italian river

POLE STAR

POLITES, youngest son of Priam of Troy

POLLUX, Castor and (Dioscuri, the Twins) (See Castor)

POLYDECTES, king of Seriphus

POLYDORE, slain kinsman of Aeneas, whose blood nourished a bush that bled when broken

POLYHYMNIA, Muse of oratory and sacred song

POLYIDUS, soothsayer

POLYNICES, King of Thebes

POLYPHEMUS, giant son of Neptune

POLYXENA, daughter of King Priam of Troy

POMONA, goddess of fruit trees (See VERTUMNUS)

PORREX and FER'REX, sons of Leir, King of Britain

PORTUNUS, Roman name for Palaemon

POSEIDON (Neptune), ruler of the ocean

PRECIPICE, threshold of Helas hall

PRESTER JOHN, a rumored priest or presbyter, a Christian pontiff in Upper Asia, believed in but never found

PRIAM, king of Troy

PRIWEN, Arthur's shield

PROCRIS, beloved but jealous wife of Cephalus

PROCRUSTES, who seized travellers and bound them on his iron bed, stretching the short ones and cutting short the tall, thus also himself served by Theseus

PROETUS, jealous of Bellerophon

PROMETHEUS, creator of man, who stole fire from heaven for man's use

PROSERPINE, the same as Persephone, goddess of all growing things, daughter of Ceres, carried off by Pluto

PROTESILAUS, slain by Hector the Trojan, allowed by the gods to return for three hours' talk with his widow Laodomia

PROTEUS, the old man of the sea

PRUDENCE (Metis), spouse of Jupiter

PRYDERI, son of Pwyll

PSYCHE, a beautiful maiden, personification of the human soul, sought by Cupid (Love), to whom she responded, lost him by curiosity to see him (as he came to her only by night), but finally through his prayers was made immortal and restored to him, a symbol of immortality

PURANAS, Hindu Scriptures

PWYLL, Prince of Dyved

PYGMALION, sculptor in love with a statue he had made, brought to life by Venus, brother of Queen Dido

PYGMIES, nation of dwarfs, at war with the Cranes

PYLADES, son of Straphius, friend of Orestes

PYRAMUS, who loved Thisbe, next door neighbor, and, their parents opposing, they talked through cracks in the house wall, agreeing to meet in the near by woods, where Pyramus, finding a bloody veil and thinking Thisbe slain, killed himself, and she, seeing his body, killed herself (Burlesqued in Shakespeare's "Midsummer Night's Dream")

PYRRHA, wife of Deucalion

PYRRHUS (Neoptolemus), son of Achilles

PYTHAGORAS, Greek philosopher (540 BC), who thought numbers to be the essence and principle of all things, and taught transmigration of souls of the dead into new life as human or animal beings

PYTHIA, priestess of Apollo at Delphi

PYTHIAN GAMES

PYTHIAN ORACLE

PYTHON, serpent springing from Deluge slum, destroyed by Apollo

Q

QUIRINUS (from quiris, a lance or spear), a war god, said to be Romulus, founder of Rome

R

RABICAN, noted horse

RAGNAROK, the twilight (or ending) of the gods

RAJPUTS, minor Hindu caste

REGAN, daughter of Leir

REGILLUS, lake in Latium, noted for battle fought near by between the Romans and the Latins

REGGIO, family from which Rogero sprang

REMUS, brother of Romulus, founder of Rome

RHADAMANTHUS, son of Jupiter and Europa after his death one of the judges in the lower world

RHAPSODIST, professional reciter of poems among the Greeks

RHEA, female Titan, wife of Saturn (Cronos), mother of the chief gods, worshipped in Greece and Rome

RHINE, river

RHINE MAIDENS, OR DAUGHTERS, three water nymphs, Flosshilda, Woglinda, and Wellgunda, set to guard the Nibelungen Hoard, buried in the Rhine

RHODES, one of the seven cities claiming to be Homer's birthplace

RHODOPE, mountain in Thrace

RHONGOMYANT, Arthur's lance

RHOECUS, a youth, beloved by a Dryad, but who brushed away a bee sent by her to call him to her, and she punished him with blindness

RHIANNON, wife of Pwyll

RINALDO, one of the bravest knights of Charlemagne

RIVER OCEAN, flowing around the earth

ROBERT DE BEAUVAIS', Norman poet (1257)

ROBIN HOOD, famous outlaw in English legend, about time of Richard Coeur de Lion

ROCKINGHAM, forest of

RODOMONT, king of Algiers

ROGERO, noted Saracen knight

ROLAND (Orlando), See Orlando

ROMANCES

ROMANUS, legendary great grandson of Noah

ROME

ROMULUS, founder of Rome

RON, Arthur's lance

RONCES VALLES', battle of

ROUND TABLE King Arthur's instituted by Merlin the Sage for Pendragon, Arthur's father, as a knightly order, continued and made famous by Arthur and his knights

RUNIC CHARACTERS, or runes, alphabetic signs used by early Teutonic peoples, written or graved on metal or stone

RUTULIANS, an ancient people in Italy, subdued at an early period by the Romans

RYENCE, king in Ireland

S

SABRA, maiden for whom Severn River was named, daughter of Locrine and Estrildis thrown into river Severn by Locrine's wife, transformed to a river nymph, poetically named Sabrina

SACRIPANT, king of Circassia

SAFFIRE, Sir, knight of Arthur

SAGAS, Norse tales of heroism, composed by the Skalds

SAGRAMOUR, knight of Arthur

St. MICHAEL'S MOUNT, precipitous pointed rock hill on the coast of Brittany, opposite Cornwall

SAKYASINHA, the Lion, epithet applied to Buddha

SALAMANDER, a lizard like animal, fabled to be able to live in fire

SALAMIS, Grecian city

SALMONEUS, son of Aeolus and Enarete and brother of Sisyphus

SALOMON, king of Brittany, at Charlemagne's court

SAMHIN, or "fire of peace," a Druidical festival

SAMIAN SAGE (Pythagoras)

SAMOS, island in the Aegean Sea

SAMOTHRACIAN GODS, a group of agricultural divinities, worshipped in Samothrace

SAMSON, Hebrew hero, thought by some to be original of Hercules

SAN GREAL (See Graal, the Holy)

SAPPHO, Greek poetess, who leaped into the sea from promontory of Leucadia in disappointed love for Phaon

SARACENS, followers of Mahomet

SARPEDON, son of Jupiter and Europa, killed by Patroclus

SATURN (Cronos)

SATURNALIA, a annual festival held by Romans in honor of Saturn

SATURNIA, an ancient name of Italy

SATYRS, male divinities of the forest, half man, half goat

SCALIGER, famous German scholar of 16th century

SCANDINAVIA, mythology of, giving account of Northern gods, heroes, etc

SCHERIA, mythical island, abode of the Phaeacians

SCHRIMNIR, the boar, cooked nightly for the heroes of Valhalla becoming whole every morning

SCIO, one of the island cities claiming to be Homer's birthplace

SCOPAS, King of Thessaly

SCORPION, constellation

SCYLLA, sea nymph beloved by Glaucus, but changed by jealous Circe to a monster and finally to a dangerous rock on the Sicilian coast, facing the whirlpool Charybdis, many mariners being wrecked between the two, also, daughter of King Nisus of Megara, who loved Minos, besieging her father's city, but he disliked her disloyalty and drowned her, also, a fair virgin of Sicily, friend of sea nymph Galatea

SCYROS, where Theseus was slain

SCYTHIA, country lying north of Euxine Sea

SEMELE, daughter of Cadmus and, by Jupiter, mother of Bacchus

SEMIRAMIS, with Ninus the mythical founder of the Assyrian empire of Nineveh

SENAPUS, King of Abyssinia, who entertained Astolpho

SERAPIS, or Hermes, Egyptian divinity of Tartarus and of medicine

SERFS, slaves of the land

SERIPHUS, island in the Aegean Sea, one of the Cyclades

SERPENT (Northern constellation)

SESTOS, dwelling of Hero (which See also Leander)

"SEVEN AGAINST THEBES," famous Greek expedition

SEVERN RIVER, in England

SEVINUS, Duke of Guienne

SHALOTT, THE LADY OF

SHATRIYA, Hindu warrior caste

SHERASMIN, French chevalier

SIBYL, prophetess of Cumae

SICHAEUS, husband of Dido

SEIGE PERILOUS, the chair of purity at Arthur's Round Table, fatal to any but him who was destined to achieve the quest of the Sangreal (See Galahad)

SIEGFRIED, young King of the Netherlands, husband of Kriemhild, she boasted to Brunhild that Siegfried had aided Gunther to beat her in athletic contests, thus winning her as wife, and Brunhild, in anger, employed Hagan to murder Siegfried. As hero of Wagner's "Valkyrie," he wins the Nibelungen treasure ring, loves and deserts Brunhild, and is slain by Hagan

SIEGLINDA, wife of Hunding, mother of Siegfried by Siegmund

SIEGMUND, father of Siegfried

SIGTRYG, Prince, betrothed of King Alef's daughter, aided by Hereward

SIGUNA, wife of Loki

SILENUS, a Satyr, school master of Bacchus

SILURES (South Wales)

SILVIA, daughter of Latin shepherd

SILVIUS, grandson of Aeneas, accidentally killed in the chase by his son Brutus

SIMONIDES, an early poet of Greece

SINON, a Greek spy, who persuaded the Trojans to take the Wooden Horse into their city

SIRENS, sea nymphs, whose singing charmed mariners to leap into the sea, passing their island, Ulysses stopped the ears of his sailors with wax, and had himself bound to the mast so that he could hear but not yield to their music

SIRIUS, the dog of Orion, changed to the Dog star

SISYPHUS, condemned in Tartarus to perpetually roll up hill a big rock which, when the top was reached, rolled down again

SIVA, the Destroyer, third person of the Hindu triad of gods

SKALDS, Norse bards and poets

SKIDBLADNIR, Freyr's ship

SKIRNIR, Frey's messenger, who won the god's magic sword by getting him Gerda for his wife

SKRYMIR, a giant, Utgard Loki in disguise, who fooled Thor in athletic feats

SKULD, the Norn of the Future

SLEEP, twin brother of Death

SLEIPNIR, Odin's horse

SOBRINO, councillor to Agramant

SOMNUS, child of Nox, twin brother of Mors, god of sleep

SOPHOCLES, Greek tragic dramatist

SOUTH WIND See Notus

SPAR'TA, capital of Lacedaemon

SPHINX, a monster, waylaying the road to Thebes and propounding riddles to all passers, on pain of death, for wrong guessing, who killed herself in rage when Aedipus guessed aright

SPRING

STONEHENGE, circle of huge upright stones, fabled to be sepulchre of Pendragon

STROPHIUS, father of Pylades

STYGIAN REALM, Hades

STYGIAN SLEEP, escaped from the beauty box sent from Hades to Venus by hand of Psyche, who curiously opened the box and was plunged into unconsciousness

STYX, river, bordering Hades, to be crossed by all the dead

SUDRAS, Hindu laboring caste

SURTUR, leader of giants against the gods in the day of their destruction (Norse mythology)

SURYA, Hindu god of the sun, corresponding to the Greek Helios

SUTRI, Orlando's birthplace

SVADILFARI, giant's horse

SWAN, LEDA AND

SYBARIS, Greek city in Southern Italy, famed for luxury

SYLVANUS, Latin divinity identified with Pan

SYMPLEGADES, floating rocks passed by the Argonauts

SYRINX, nymph, pursued by Pan, but escaping by being changed to a bunch of reeds (See Pandean pipes)

T

TACITUS, Roman historian

TAENARUS, Greek entrance to lower regions

TAGUS, river in Spain and Portugal

TALIESIN, Welsh bard

TANAIS, ancient name of river Don

TANTALUS, wicked king, punished in Hades by standing in water that retired when he would drink, under fruit trees that withdrew when he would eat

TARCHON, Etruscan chief

TARENTUM, Italian city

TARPEIAN ROCK, in Rome, from which condemned criminals were hurled

TARQUINS, a ruling family in early Roman legend

TAURIS, Grecian city, site of temple of Diana (See Iphigenia)

TAURUS, a mountain

TARTARUS, place of confinement of Titans, etc, originally a black abyss below Hades later, represented as place where the wicked were punished, and sometimes the name used as synonymous with Hades

TEIRTU, the harp of

TELAMON, Greek hero and adventurer, father of Ajax

TELEMACHUS, son of Ulysses and Penelope

TELLUS, another name for Rhea

TENEDOS, an island in Aegean Sea

TERMINUS, Roman divinity presiding over boundaries and frontiers

TERPSICHORE, Muse of dancing

TERRA, goddess of the earth

TETHYS, goddess of the sea

TEUCER, ancient king of the Trojans

THALIA, one of the three Graces

THAMYRIS, Thracian bard, who challenged the Muses to competition in singing, and, defeated, was blinded

THAUKT, Loki disguised as a hag

THEBES, city founded by Cadmus and capital of Boeotia

THEMIS, female Titan, law counsellor of Jove

THEODORA, sister of Prince Leo

THERON, one of Diana's dogs

THERSITES, a brawler, killed by Achilles

THESCELUS, foe of Perseus, turned to stone by sight of Gorgon's head

THESEUM, Athenian temple in honor of Theseus

THESEUS, son of Aegeus and Aethra, King of Athens, a great hero of many adventures

THESSALY

THESTIUS, father of Althea

THETIS, mother of Achilles

THIALFI, Thor's servant

THIS'BE, Babylonian maiden beloved by Pyramus

THOR, the thunderer, of Norse mythology, most popular of the gods

THRACE

THRINA'KIA, island pasturing Hyperion's cattle, where Ulysses landed, but, his men killing some cattle for food, their ship was wrecked by lightning

THRYM, giant, who buried Thor's hammer

THUCYDIDES, Greek historian

TIBER, river flowing through Rome

TIBER, FATHER, god of the river

TIGRIS, river

TINTADEL, castle of, residence of King Mark of Cornwall

TIRESIAS, a Greek soothsayer

TISIPHONE, one of the Furies

TITANS, the sons and daughters of Uranus (Heaven) and Gaea (Earth), enemies of the gods and overcome by them

TITHONUS, Trojan prince

TITYUS, giant in Tartarus

TMOLUS, a mountain god

TORTOISE, second avatar of Vishnu

TOURS, battle of (See Abdalrahman and Charles Martel)

TOXEUS, brother of Melauger's mother, who snatched from Atalanta her hunting trophy, and was slain by Melauger, who had awarded it to her

TRIAD, the Hindu

TRIADS, Welsh poems

TRIMURTI, Hindu Triad

TRIPTOL'EMUS, son of Celeus , and who, made great by Ceres, founded her worship in Eleusis

TRISTRAM, one of Arthur's knights, husband of Isoude of the White Hands, lover of Isoude the Fair.

TRITON, a demi god of the sea, son of Poseidon (Neptune) and Amphitrite

TROEZEN, Greek city of Argolis

TROJAN WAR

TROJANOVA, New Troy, City founded in Britain (See Brutus, and Lud)

TROPHONIUS, oracle of, in Boeotia

TROUBADOURS, poets and minstrels of Provence, in Southern France

TROUVERS', poets and minstrels of Northern France

TROY, city in Asia Minor, ruled by King Priam, whose son, Paris, stole away Helen, wife of Menelaus the Greek, resulting in the Trojan War and the destruction of Troy

TROY, fall of

TURNUS, chief of the Rutulianes in Italy, unsuccessful rival of Aeneas for Lavinia

TURPIN, Archbishop of Rheims

TURQUINE, Sir, a great knight, foe of Arthur, slain by Sir Launcelot

TYPHON, one of the giants who attacked the gods, were defeated, and imprisoned under Mt. Aetna

TYR, Norse god of battles

TYRE, Phoenician city governed by Dido

TYRIANS

TYRRHEUS, herdsman of King Turnus in Italy, the slaying of whose daughter's stag aroused war upon Aeneas and his companions

U

UBERTO, son of Galafron

ULYSSES (Greek, Odysseus), hero of the Odyssey

UNICORN, fabled animal with a single horn

URANIA, one of the Muses, a daughter of Zeus by Mnemosyne

URDUR, one of the Norns or Fates of Scandinavia, representing the Past

USK, British river

UTGARD, abode of the giant Utgard Loki

UTGARD LO'KI, King of the Giants (See Skrymir)

UTHER (Uther Pendragon), king of Britain and father of Arthur.

UWAINE, knight of Arthur's court

V

VAISSYAS, Hindu caste of agriculturists and traders

VALHALLA, hall of Odin, heavenly residence of slain heroes

VALKYRIE, armed and mounted warlike virgins, daughters of the gods (Norse), Odin's messengers, who select slain heroes for Valhalla and serve them at their feasts

VE, brother of Odin

VEDAS, Hindu sacred Scriptures

VENEDOTIA, ancient name for North Wales

VENUS (Aphrodite), goddess of beauty

VENUS DE MEDICI, famous antique statue in Uffizi Gallery, Florence, Italy

VERDANDI, the Present, one of the Norns

VERTUMNUS, god of the changing seasons, whose varied appearances won the love of Pomona

VESTA, daughter of Cronos and Rhea, goddess of the homefire, or hearth

VESTALS, virgin priestesses in temple of Vesta

VESUVIUS, Mount, volcano near Naples

VILLAINS, peasants in the feudal scheme

VIGRID, final battle-field, with destruction of the gods ind their enemies, the sun, the earth, and time itself

VILI, brother of Odin and Ve

VIRGIL, celebrated Latin poet (See Aeneid)

VIRGO, constellation of the Virgin, representing Astraea, goddess of innocence and purity

VISHNU, the Preserver, second of the three chief Hindu gods

VIVIANE, lady of magical powers, who allured the sage Merlin and imprisoned him in an enchanted wood

VOLSCENS, Rutulian troop leader who killed Nisus and Euryalus

VOLSUNG, A SAGA, an Icelandic poem, giving about the same legends as the Nibelungen Lied

VORTIGERN, usurping King of Britain, defeated by Pendragon 390, 397

VULCAN (Greek, Haephestus), god of fire and metal working, with forges under Aetna, husband of Venus

VYA'SA, Hindu sage

W

WAIN, the, constellation

WELLGUNDA, one of the Rhine-daughters.

WELSH LANGUAGE

WESTERN OCEAN

WINDS, THE

WINTER

WODEN, chief god in the Norse mythology, Anglo Saxon for Odin.

WOGLINDA, one of the Rhine-daughters.

WOMAN, creation of.

WOODEN HORSE, the, filled with armed men, but left outside of Troy as a pretended offering to Minerva when the Greeks feigned to sail away, accepted by the Trojans (See Sinon, and Laocoon), brought into the city, and at night emptied of the hidden Greek soldiers, who destroyed the town.

WOOD NYMPHS

WOTAN, Old High German form of Odin.

X

XANTHUS, river of Asia Minor.

Y

YAMA, Hindu god of the Infernal Regions.

YEAR, THE

YGDRASIL, great ash-tree, supposed by Norse mythology to support the universe.

YMIR, giant, slain by Odin.

YNYWL, Earl, host of Geraint, father of Enid.

YORK, Britain.

YSERONE, niece of Arthur, mother of Caradoc.

YSPA DA DEN PEN'KAWR, father of Olwen.

Z

ZENDAVESTA, Persian sacred Scriptures.

ZEPHYRUS, god of the South wind.

ZERBINO, a knight, son of the king of Scotland.

ZETES, winged warrior, companion of Theseus.

ZETHUS, son of Jupiter and Antiope, brother of Amphion. See Dirce.

ZEUS, See JUPITER.

ZOROASTER, founder of the Persian religion, which was dominant in Western Asia from about 550 BC to about 650 AD, and is still held by many thousands in Persia and in India

www.ingramcontent.com/pod-product-compliance
Lightning Source LLC
Chambersburg PA
CBHW071236160426
43196CB00009B/1089